D1554711

COLLEGE OF MARIN

3 2555 00095544 8

MEDIEVAL HISTORY
IN THE TUDOR AGE

DA
1
M3

Date Due

INDIAN VALLEY COLLEGES

BRO DART Printed in U.S.A.

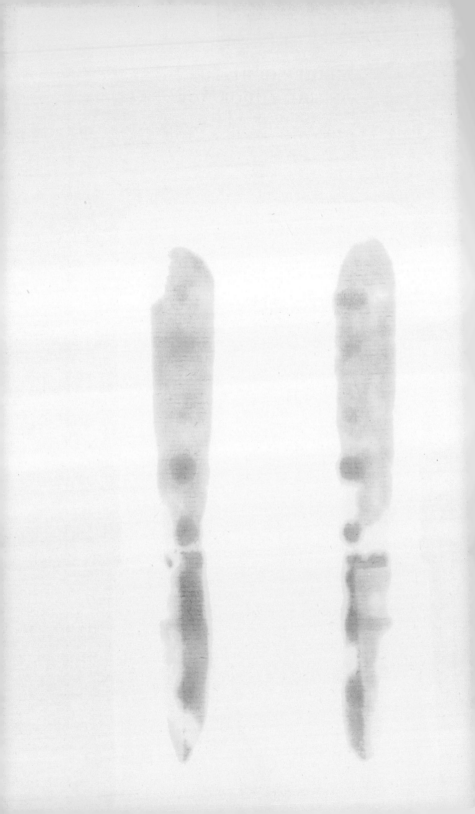

MEDIEVAL HISTORY IN THE TUDOR AGE

BY

MAY McKISACK

CLARENDON PRESS · OXFORD

1971

Oxford University Press, Ely House, London W. 1

GLASGOW NEW YORK TORONTO MELBOURNE WELLINGTON
CAPE TOWN SALISBURY IBADAN NAIROBI DAR ES SALAAM LUSAKA ADDIS ABABA
BOMBAY CALCUTTA MADRAS KARACHI LAHORE DACCA
KUALA LUMPUR SINGAPORE HONG KONG TOKYO

© OXFORD UNIVERSITY PRESS 1971

76 - 24496

Printed in Great Britain
by Alden & Mowbray Ltd
at the Alden Press, Oxford

CONTENTS

INTRODUCTION

TUDOR England offered many incitements to searchers into the nation's past. As Sir Thomas Kendrick has shown in his enthralling study of *British Antiquity* (1950), the accession of a prince of Welsh descent stimulated interest in the Brutus myth, first elaborated by Geoffrey of Monmouth early in the twelfth century, and in the legend of Arthur, hero of the Britons, after whom Henry VII named his first-born son. A system of case-law had long forced some awareness of the past on those trained in the Inns of Court. The dissolution of the monasteries under Henry VIII and the subsequent dispersal of many of their libraries meant that a mass of little-known historical material became accessible to those with antiquarian tastes. The breach with Rome enhanced national self-consciousness and the desire to demonstrate the scriptural (as distinct from Romish) foundations of the land's ecclesiastical traditions. The expansion of the trades of printing, bookbinding, and bookselling facilitated communication of knowledge. And an age of victories abroad, rising prosperity for many, and pride in a great Queen tended to arouse new interest in family trees, appreciation of ancient monuments, curiosity about the lay-out of towns, woods and fields, about how Britain and British institutions came to be as they were.

This book attempts a general survey of some of these phenomena, beginning with the pioneer antiquary, John Leland, active in the reign of Henry VIII, considering other well-known and less-known collectors of books, manuscripts and records, their patrons and supporters, writers of history, both national and local, and the appropriate culmination of all these activities in the foundation of the Elizabethan Society of Antiquaries. When my work was almost completed, the Huntington Library in California published F. J. Levy's valuable study of *Tudor Historical Thought*. Inevitably, there is some overlap between the two books. But the subject is a vast one, and I hope I am right in supposing that there is room for more than one approach to the historical and antiquarian activities of the Tudor age.

M.McK.

I

LELAND AND BALE

JOHN LELAND, that singular light and ornament of Great Britain', wrote Anthony Wood, '. . . At the time of the dissolution of monasteries . . . saw with very great pity what havock was made of ancient monuments of learning, and if no remedy should be taken, they would all perish.'[1] Wood exaggerated somewhat, after his fashion. None the less, it is with Leland and Bale that enquiry into medieval historical studies in the Tudor period must inevitably and properly begin. For the dispersal of great and famous libraries on a scale altogether without precedent in this country afforded a unique stimulus to historical research and was of crucial importance to the two friends who came to be regarded as the founding fathers of English antiquarian studies in the sixteenth century.

The story of Leland's life has been often and expertly told.[2] Born, probably, about 1503 and orphaned at an early age, he was befriended by one Thomas Myles who sent him to school at St. Paul's, under the great William Lyly, and subsequently to Christ's College, Cambridge, where he graduated B.A. in 1522. A couple of years as tutor in the household of the second Duke of Norfolk was followed by a further period of study at Oxford, possibly at All Souls, where he made the acquaintance of another future antiquary, Thomas Caius (or Key). Later, Leland removed to the University of Paris, aided, it seems, by a royal endowment.[3] In Paris, he found a learned society wholly to his taste, one that included Budé, the numismatist and restorer of Greek learning, and the Italian, Paolo Emilio who, nearly forty years earlier, had been appointed 'King's Orator and Chronicler' by Charles VIII. Thus, when he returned to

---

[1] *Athenae Oxonienses*, ed. Bliss, I. 197.
[2] e.g. by William Huddesford (1772), by Sir Sidney Lee in the *Dictionary of National Biography* (1903), by Miss L. Toulmin Smith in the Introduction to her edition of the *Itinerary* (1907), and by Sir Thomas Kendrick in *British Antiquity* (1950).
[3] Corollarium vitae J. Lelandi per me Willielmum Burton', *Collectanea*, ed. Hearne (2nd edn., 1774), I, sig. p. 2.

England about 1529 he had made a place for himself in the
world of Renaissance scholarship, abroad as well as at home.
He was highly praised for his Latin poems, an interesting group
of which is addressed to his friends in Paris;[1] and he was pro-
ficient in Greek as well as in several modern languages. His
elegant panegyrics on the King and his ministers had won him
favour at court and, having taken orders, he was presented by
Henry VIII to the living of Pepeling, in the marches of Calais,
which he held as an absentee. Other preferments, sufficient
to relieve him from financial anxiety, followed in due course.[2]
In 1533, the King gave him authority by commission to search
the libraries of monasteries and colleges for the monuments
of ancient writers: and although the precise dates of his numerous itineraries cannot be determined, it is clear that much of the
ensuing decade must have been spent in travel. About 1542 or
1543, he is believed to have settled near St. Paul's, in the parish
of St. Michael at Corne, hoping, no doubt, to carry out some of
his vast literary projects, and many of the written memorials
that we have must date from this period. But in 1547 he lost
his reason. Custody of his person was granted to his elder
brother and on 18 April 1552, he died in London.

   The Dictionary of National Biography and other standard lives of
Leland assert, further, that by 1530 he was Keeper of the King's
Libraries[3] and that in 1533 he was appointed King's Antiquary,
'an office in which he had neither predecessor nor successor.'
Both statements are puzzling. The succession of royal librarians
is known to us and Leland's name does not appear among them:
it seems likely that he was merely one of several sub-librarians
appointed to serve the libraries which Henry had established
at Westminster, Greenwich, and Hampton Court.[4] As for the
tradition—which does not seem to be traceable further back
than T. Smith's *Vita Camdeni* (1691)—that Leland was appointed King's Antiquary, this is almost certainly baseless;

   [1] L. Bradner, 'Some Unpublished Poems by John Leland', *PMLA* LXXI (1956),
829. On Leland's taste for poetry see F. J. Levy, *Tudor Historical Thought* (1967),
p. 129.
   [2] e.g. papal dispensation to hold four benefices to the total value of 1,000 ducats
(1533); the rectory of Haseley (Oxon.) (1542); a prebend at King's College (later
Christ Church), Oxford (1543).
   [3] *J. Weever, Ancient Funerall Monuments* (1631), p. 688, gives Leland this title.
   [4] B.M. *Catalogue of the Royal Manuscripts* I (1921), XIV–XVI.

but it is easy to understand how it could have arisen. On the one hand, we know that it was about this time that Leland began to style himself *Antiquarius*, probably in imitation of the term used in humanist circles abroad to describe those who were seeking to reconstruct Roman provincial antiquities from non-literary sources:[1] and, on the other, there is the royal commission authorizing him 'to peruse and diligently to serche al the libraries of monasteries and collegies of this yowre noble reaulme, to the intente that the monumentes of aunciant writers as welle of other nations, as of this yowr owne province mighte be brought owte of deadely darkenes to lyvely lighte.'[2]

From investigations of such a kind and on such a scale results might be expected, first, in the salvaging of books from the libraries of the dissolved houses and, secondly, in written memorials. But the question how many or which books Leland was able to save from the dissolved houses is beset with difficulty. What, we must first ask, lay behind the royal commission of 1533? Are we to suppose that Henry VIII (or Cromwell), being alive to the value of the great monastic collections, was at pains to appoint a scholar of repute to classify their contents and to preserve what he could, selecting the best for the royal libraries? A monarch of Henry's liberal education might well be presumed to have been concerned for the fate of the books: yet it remains hard to credit him with much forethought in the matter. The Visitation Articles issued to the Commissioners of 1536 and 1538 do not contain a single reference to books, libraries, or learning: and the tasks of inspection and classification, with a view to selective preservation, must have been far beyond the capacity of a single man, even a man of Leland's untiring zeal. Anthony Wood's allusion to a letter written by Leland to Cromwell in July 1536, 'wherein he intreats him to give him aid and assistance in bringing to light many ancient authors, and in sending them to the King's library', strongly suggests, despite Leland's polite assurance that he knew well that the King 'had no little esteem' for the books, that the initiative in the whole business came from Leland

---

[1] See A. Momigliano, 'Ancient History and the Antiquarian', *Journal of the Warburg and Courtauld Institutes* XIII (1950), App. I, pp. 313–14.

[2] *Itinerary*, ed. Toulmin Smith, I. xxxvii–xxxviii. Anthony Wood declared that the commission was under the 'broad seal', but no trace of it has been found among the State Papers.

himself.[1] Had the King or his minister been genuinely interested in the fate of the libraries, they must surely have made arrangements for their safety before, or at the time of, the Dissolution: but it is clear that many of Leland's visits were made after the ejection of the monks, when much damage had already been done.[2] Henry, no doubt, was willing to accept for his own libraries a selection from the books which Leland had been able to save. In a list (now in the collection of Royal manuscripts in the British Museum[3] and likely to have been the work of Leland) of books of history and divinity seen in Lincolnshire houses, thirty-five titles are marked with a cross and of these, twenty-four are known to have come into the King's possession.[4] The list may be compared with certain others preserved in Leland's *Collectanea*:[5] but, as it stands, it does not cover even all Lincolnshire, and it is most unlikely that any such method can have been systematically pursued throughout the country.

The question of which or how many of the monastic books found their way through Leland's agency into the Royal Library remains unanswerable. His literary remains give some idea of which books he had *seen* in the course of his journeyings through England and Wales: they do not tell us which books he had *removed*. It is clear that the Royal Library expanded considerably in the last years of Henry's reign, for an inventory made in the Augmentations Office in 1542 shows 910 books, many of them monastic in origin, and shortly afterwards the number had risen to 1,450. Some credit for these literary spoils may reasonably be allowed to Leland who, in his 'New Year's Gift' to Henry VIII (1546), claimed that, thanks to the King's commission, he had 'conserved many good autors, the which other wise had beene like to have perischid in no smaul incommodite of good letters, of the whiche parte remayne yn the moste magnificent libraries of yowr royal Palacis. Parte also remayne yn my custodye.'[6] But precise information is wanting, and the

---

[1] *Athenae Oxonienses*, ed. Bliss, I. 198.

[2] A. L. Clarke, 'John Leland and King Henry VIII', *The Library*, 3rd ser. II (1911), 132–49.

[3] MS. Royal. App. 69.

[4] J. R. Liddell, '"Leland's" Lists of MSS. in Lincolnshire Monasteries', *EHR* LIV (1939), 88–95; N. R. Ker, *Medieval Libraries of Great Britain* (1941), p. xii. None of the unmarked books is now to be found in the Royal Library.

[5] e.g. IV. 6–69.   [6] *Itinerary*, ed. Toulmin Smith, I. xxxviii.

enquirer finds himself confronted with some curious anomalies. Thus, Leland's *Collectanea* show that he had observed books in the libraries of at least 137 foundations in England and Wales, that is, in just under a quarter of the total number (584) listed by Mr. Ker in his survey of the medieval libraries.[1] A surprising omission is any description of the books in the cathedral library at Rochester:[2] for 99 Rochester books—more than from any other single religious community—remain in the Royal Library today, and we know that Leland had visited the town. On the other hand, neither the copy of Giraldus Cambrensis deriving from St. Augustine's Canterbury (now MS. Royal 13 B VIII) nor the Geoffrey of Monmouth from St. Albans (MS. Royal 13 DV) is noted by Leland among the books seen by him in these libraries, though he does seem to have been responsible for the copy of Ailred's Life of David King of Scots from Coggeshall (MS. Royal B. IX).[3] All that can be said with certainty is that the number of monastic books which can be proved to owe their place in the Royal Library to Leland is very small, and of the historical works, which are our chief concern, the number is negligible.

To turn to Leland's written memorials for evidence of his literary and bibliographical activities is to be confronted with problems of a different kind. He left a mass of papers behind him, but publication of most of these was long delayed. Apart from the *Assertio inclytissimi Arturii Regis* (1544) written to defend the British history against the impertinent questionings of Polydore Vergil,[4] the only work of historical or antiquarian interest published in the author's lifetime was the 'New Year's Gift' of 1546, printed by Bale in 1549 with comments of his own.[5] Here, Leland set forth his literary plans. He has already, he tells his royal patron, 'digestid in to foure bookes' the names of British authors from the time of the Druids, 'with theire lyves

[1] The libraries of Cambridge University, the Oxford and Cambridge colleges, Eton, Winchester, and St. George's Chapel, Windsor, are excluded from this survey.

[2] Apart from some brief notes on early monastic foundations, said to be taken *Ex veteri codice Rofensis monaster.* (*Collectanea* (1774), IV. 69). It may be of some significance that Leland left two pages of his manuscript blank when he came to Rochester. *Itinerary* IV. 45.

[3] *Collectanea* IV. 162.

[4] See Kendrick, *British Antiquity*, pp. 86 ff.; Levy, op. cit., p. 67.

[5] For the most recent edition, see *Itinerary*, ed. Toulmin Smith, I. xxxvii–xliii.

and monumentes of lerning', and to them added this title, 'De viris illustribus'. The list includes over one hundred historians who have 'perscribed the actes of your moste noble praedecessours, and the fortunes of thys your realme'. It was reading them that sent him on his travels:

I was totally enflammid with a love to see thoroughly al those partes of this your opulente and ample reaulme, that I had redde of yn the aforesaid writers; yn so muche that all my other occupations intermitted I have so travelid yn yowr dominions booth by these costes and the midle partes; that there is almoste nother cape, nor bay, haven, creke or peere, river or confluence of rivers, breches, waschis, lakes, meres, fenny waters, montaynes, valleis, mores, hethes, forestes, wooddes, cities, burges, castelles, principale manor placis, monasteries and colleges, but I have seene them; and notid yn so doing a hole worlde of thinges very memorable.

Thus instructed, he hoped, within the next twelve months, to write a 'Description of Britain', in which particular attention would be paid to place-names. Next, having 'matier at plenty al ready preparid to this purpose', he intended to write a history, to be entitled 'either *De Antiquitate Britannica*, or else *Civilis Historia*', to be divided 'yn to so many bookes as there be shires yn England, and sheres and great dominions yn Wales', fifty in all. A further six books would cover 'the isles adjacent to your noble reaulme and under your subjection'. Finally, 'as an ornament and a right comely garlande to the enterprises afore saide', he had collected stuff to be distributed into three books, to be entitled 'De Nobilitate Britannica'.

Four substantial works—a Dictionary of British writers (said to be already completed); a Description of Britain; a History of Britain; and a study of British noble families. Leland was not much above forty and might fairly expect to carry out his plan (or part of it) in some fashion. But possibly, as Gough suggests, 'intense application, joined perhaps to an apprehension of wanting abilities or encouragement to complete it, turned his head.'[1] He lost his reason: and on his death in 1552 his books and papers, by an order in Council, were entrusted to Edward VI's tutor, Sir John Cheke, himself a scholar of distinction. When Cheke went abroad after the accession of Mary the papers were dispersed, the most important of them

[1] R. Gough, *British Topography* (1780), I. 23.

eventually finding their way into the Bodleian Library at Oxford.[1] It was from this collection that Antony Hall, a Fellow of Queen's College, published, in 1709, an uncritical edition of the *Commentarii de Scriptoribus Britannicis*, this being the final volume of a series of four in Leland's autograph.[2] The 593 authors (actual and suppositious) are chronologically arranged, from the Druids to the early sixteenth century, with brief notes on their works: and the inclusion of a fair selection of the principal medieval historians, from Gildas, Nennius, and Bede to Capgrave and William Thorne, accords well with Leland's own account, in the 'New Year's Gift', of his *De Viris Illustribus*. The remaining three volumes of the series were edited by Hearne (with considerable critical apparatus) in 1715, under the title *Collectanea*.[3] The title is apt, for what we have in these volumes are raw materials: they are source-books, not treatises. The same is true of the celebrated *Itinerary*, first published by Hearne in 1710–12.[4] It is a work of reference, not of literature, consisting of a series of notes arranged on no coherent plan—a mine of information to the topographer, the genealogist, the local historian, but (unlike the *Collectanea*) containing relatively little about books.

Bale, who included Leland in his own Catalogue of Illustrious Writers (1557), credited him with a number of works, among them the three projects set out in the 'New Year's Gift', most of which are clearly schemes and source-books, rather than finished products. Two of these have lately been identified— the 'Antiquitates Britanniae' with a manuscript of Leland's autograph, comprising excerpts relating to Britain from various authors, chiefly classical: and the 'Descriptio Angliae' with a series of notes from the 1535 edition of Ptolemy's Geography, found in the same manuscript.[5] The *Syllabus Antiquarum Dictionum* and the *Elenchus Antiquorum Nominum* consist of brief explana-

[1] Some went to Lord William Paget, some to Cheke's brother-in-law, William Cecil. Cheke had already given four volumes to Humfrey Purefoy whose son, Thomas, bequeathed them, in 1612, to the Leicestershire antiquary, William Burton. Burton had been collecting Leland's papers and continued to do so after he had received the Purefoy bequest. It was through him that they came to the Bodleian.

[2] Now Bodl. MS. Top. Gen. c. 4.

[3] 2nd edn., 1774.   [4] Later editions, 1744–5; 1770.

[5] B.M., MS. Cott., Julius C. VI. See T. C. Skeat, 'Two "Lost" Works by John Leland', *EHR* LXV (1950), 505–8.

tory notes printed as appendixes, the one to Leland's poem,
Genethliacon (1543), the other to his *Assertio Arturii* (1544): and
there seems to be no reason to suppose that other titles in Bale's
list, such as the *De Academiis Brytannicis*, represent anything
more substantial.

His written memorials show Leland to have been well read
in the history of his own country and to have shared the preference of his age for the earlier centuries. With Bede and Gildas
he was inevitably familiar, for both had already appeared in
print before he began his searches, the *Historia Ecclesiastica*
at Strasburg in 1475, the *Liber Querulus*, edited by Polydore
Vergil, in 1525.[1] He had seen a manuscript of Nennius at
Jervaulx, and from Bale we learn that he was at one time in
possession of a manuscript of Asser:[2] though whether this
was the famous text destroyed in the fire at the Cottonian
Library in 1731 cannot now be determined. In his allusion to
'Asser historicus veraxque relator gestorum regis Alfredi',
Leland most unfortunately omits to record where he saw
the manuscript, and his notes offer no help in the solution of
problems relating to this much-debated work.[3] More remarkable is the evidence that he had access to a manuscript of the
Anglo-Saxon Chronicle (a work less highly esteemed than Asser
at the time)—'an old Saxon Booke caullid of summe the old
Englisch Historie'—which he uses to supply evidence of place-
names[4] and which he had borrowed from Robert Talbot, a
Norfolk rector who was the possessor of a considerable library.
Talbot had also lent Leland a manuscript of Alfred's translation
of Orosius: and since the 'C', or Abingdon, MS. of the Chronicle
is bound up with Orosius, it seems almost certain that this was
the copy which Leland saw, though how Talbot acquired it is
not known.[5] Further evidence of Leland's interest in Old
English history may be found in his notes on the lives of saints,

---

[1] In his comments on Fabian, Leland refers to this edition, 'wher in by open
wordes ys no mention of Arthure.' *Collectanea* III. 427.

[2] A manuscript of Asser is described as 'Ex bibliotheca Ioannis Lelandi'. Bale,
Index Britanniae Scriptorum, ed. R. L. Poole and M. Bateson (1902), p. 35.

[3] *Collectanea* I. 210; Asser, *De Rebus Gestis Alfredi*, ed. W. H. Stevenson (1904),
pp. xxxiii ff.

[4] *Collectanea* IV. 122.

[5] See Earle and Plummer, *Two of the Saxon Chronicles Parallel* II. xxx–xxxi.
Talbot is the subject of one of Leland's *Encomia Illustrium Virorum. Collectanea* V.
137–8. For Talbot see below, p. 24.

like Alphege and Swithun, and on some early charters; in his list of pre-Conquest religious foundations; and in his awareness that Aethelweard was writing Saxon history before the Conquest—as well as in his more celebrated championship of the Brut.[1]

With many of the standard histories of the eleventh, twelfth and following centuries he was likewise familiar. At Haughmond Abbey, near Shrewsbury, he had seen and partly read a copy of Eadmer's 'Historia Novorum':[2] he saw copies of William of Malmesbury's 'De Gestis Regum Anglorum' in five different libraries—at Faversham, Kirkham, Glastonbury, St. Paul's and in the house of the Austin friars in London—and made copious notes, both from this and from the 'De Gestis Pontificum' and the 'Historia Novella'.[3] A note of his is found on f. 137 of a copy of Giraldus Cambrensis, now in the National Library of Wales.[4] Reasonably enough, he looked for William of Newburgh's 'Historia Rerum Anglicarum' at Newburgh Abbey in the North Riding, but he notes, 'nusquam comparet: extat tamen in Wellensi bibliotheca',[5] and at Wells, or elsewhere, he took careful notes from the manuscript. He quotes freely from Henry of Huntingdon and tells us that he borrowed the manuscript from the canons of Southwick in Hampshire.[6] Numerous extracts from Howden covering the period 740–1201 are transcribed, and Leland, while admitting Howden's indebtedness to Simeon of Durham, is at pains to refute the suggestion that the last section of the book (1135–1201) is the work of another hand—'Nam phrasis & dictio arguit esse Hoveduni opus.'[7] His one real discovery in the field of medieval historical literature was, however, Walter of Coventry. On a leaf of a large manuscript, 'aliquot locis mancus', of historical collections he found the words 'Memoriale fratris Walteri de Coventria'. Perhaps because he readily perceived that much of the text was derived from Geoffrey of Monmouth, Henry of Huntingdon, Marianus Scotus, and Howden, he was not unduly elated by the discovery of an unknown author: but he proceeds to evolve a

---

[1] Ibid. I. 19, 21, 7 25–6; *Commentarii*, p. 171. See *The Chronicle of Aethelweard*, ed. A. Campbell (1962), p. ix.
[2] *Commentarii*, p. 180.   [3] *Collectanea* I. 136–48, 150–1; III. 234.
[4] MS. 3024 (Mostyn 83). See R. Flower, 'Richard Davies, William Cecil and Giraldus Cambrensis', *Journal of the National Library of Wales* III (1943–4), 11.
[5] *Collectanea* IV. 37.   [6] Ibid. IV. 148.   [7] Ibid. III. 212.

B

history and character for him, and Walter of Coventry is included in his Dictionary of British writers. Though he tended to antedate him and was ignorant of some of the sources, notably of 'Benedict of Peterborough' on which we now know Walter to have relied, Leland had analysed the work carefully and recognized the provenance of a great part of it.[1]

In 1535 Leland visited St. Albans with the express purpose of inspecting its famous library: but apart from the titles of some dozen volumes and a note that a fine copy of Matthew Paris had been stolen, he tells us little, and it was not without reason that Sir Frederic Madden reproached him for his 'most meagre and unsatisfactory notice' of what he saw.[2] His own transcripts from the 'Chronica Majora' of Matthew Paris may well have been made elsewhere, perhaps from a borrowed copy, though Madden's argument that it is incomprehensible that if he had found this great book in one of the religious houses, he should not have ordered its transfer to the Royal Library, is not altogether convincing in view of the obscurity surrounding the whole question of such removals. Talbot certainly had a copy of Volume II of the Greater Chronicle (now British Museum, Cottonian MS. Nero D.1) and it may have been to him that Leland was indebted for a sight of it.[3] In the St. Albans cell at Tynemouth he found what was apparently a copy of Rishanger and the 'Chronicon Angliae' bound together, but, though he recognized the author (or authors) as a monk of St. Albans he could not name him.[4] Strangely enough, he seems to have known little else of Walsingham. But he had seen a copy of Walter of Guisborough at Wells: he noted three copies of Higden's 'Polychronicon' in Oxford alone, at Exeter, Queen's, and Magdalen: and he found the 'Eulogium Historiarum' in the public library there. Adam Murimuth had been copied for him by Sir Brian Tuke; and he ingeniously deduced the authorship of the 'Scalacronica'. 'I gesse, that one of the Greys of Northumbreland was Autor of it by the Imagination of the Dreame that he showith of a Ladder yn the Prologe.'[5]

[1] *Collectanea* I. 284; III, 315; *Commentarii*, p. 250; Walter of Coventry, *Memoriale*, ed. Stubbs, R.S. (1872), I. ix–xvi.

[2] *Collectanea* IV. 163. See Matthew Paris, *Historia Anglorum*, ed. F. Madden, R.S. (1866–9), I. xv.

[3] Ibid. I. lvii, n. 2.   [4] *Collectanea* IV. 42.

[5] Ibid. IV. 41; III. 377, 379, 380; IV. 58; III. 403; II. 509.

Though by modern standards vastly credulous, Leland was
not lacking in critical capacity, particularly on points of detail.
Thus, of Nennius he complains 'scribit confuse & sine judicio';[1]
of Giraldus Cambrensis 'He plainly declares that he was
archdeacon of Brecon. This I can well believe, so much impressed was I when I was there by his description and praise of
the place. If he had devoted the same industry and care to
describing other Welsh districts, he would have written a great
and immortal work.'[2] Some suggestions of Harding's are given
short shrift: that Alcluith was the old name for York—'This
hath no shadow of trewth'; that Bladud, when he had studied
at Athens, brought philosophers with him to Britain who taught
in Stamford, as in a university—'This is like a dreme'; that
William Rufus built the new castle upon Tyne and caused the
town to be walled—'This is clene false as concerning the towne
waulle'. Fabyan, too, comes in for his share of criticism: that
Gloucester was once called Caerleon—'this ys manifestly false';
'Fabian errith sumwhat in the site of the castel', and so on.[3]

As has long been recognized, Leland's distinction as an antiquary derives, first and foremost, from the fact that he was a
pioneer in the method of direct enquiry and first-hand observation, the forerunner of Camden. The originality of his approach,
as revealed in the *Itinerary*, was not, however, obvious to his
contemporaries who tended to set more store by his Dictionary
of British writers, his poems, and his defence of the British
history. The reputation of the first, in which Leland was seeking
to do for Britain what had already been done for Germany by
Tritheim in his *Catalogue illustrium virorum Germaniae* (1491), was
deservedly high. But any consideration of its merits inevitably
brings the enquirer up against the question of the interdepend-
ence of Leland and Bale who, in 1548, soon after Leland had
lost his reason, published at Wesel and at Ipswich his *Illustrium
Maioris Britanniae Scriptorum . . . Summarium*, with a dedication
to Edward VI.

We seem to know more of John Bale than of John Leland,
largely because Bale left behind him an unusual amount of
autobiographical material—in the prefaces to his learned
works, in such of his letters as survive, in the formal autobio-
graphy which is included in his Catalogue of British Writers,

[1] Ibid. IV. 44.   [2] Ibid. III. 89.   [3] Ibid. III. 425–6, 427.

and in his lively account of his adventures as Bishop of Ossory, published in 1553.[1] He was a Suffolk man, the child of poor parents who sent him to be educated by the Carmelites at Norwich, in 1507 when he was twelve years old. From Norwich he proceeded to Cambridge where he was a student in the faculty of philosophy, living, probably, since he had now taken the habit, at the Carmelite house there:[2] it was at Norwich and Cambridge that he began making his collections on the history of the Carmelite order, especially in England. These enquiries were pursued during a short visit to France, c. 1525–7,[3] and after his return when, having proceeded B.D. in 1529, he served as prior of three Carmelite houses, at Maldon, Doncaster, and Ipswich.[4] But his religious opinions were changing and with them the slant of his historical interests. It seems to have been early in the 1530s that he made the acquaintance of Leland on whose advice he continued to work among the Carmelites and Augustinians, the Franciscans and Dominicans having refused to allow him access to their libraries.[5] His concern now was less to collect material for the history of a particular order than to preserve the names and works of monastic authors generally before the deluge threatening the religious houses overwhelmed them.

By about 1533, Bale, who had already earned some notoriety as a disseminator of unorthodox opinions, was ready for an open breach with Rome. He ascribes his conversion to the influence of Lord Wentworth, but makes no secret of the fact that it coincided with his desire to marry. Of his wife we know

[1] *The Vocacyon of Johan Bale to the bishoprick of Ossorie in Irelande.* Two studies oi Bale have been published in the U.S.A., J. W. Harris, *John Bale, A study in the Minor Literature of the Reformation* (1940), and Honor McCusker, *John Bale, Dramatist and Antiquary* (1942). See also W. T. Davies, 'A Bibliography of John Bale', *Oxford Bibliographical Society, Proceedings and Papers* V (1940), 203–79.

[2] The commonly held belief that Bale was at Jesus College is not supported by any discoverable contemporary evidence. I am indebted to Mrs. Freda Jones for valuable information on this subject. See J. Crompton, 'Fasciculi Zizaniorum I and II', *Journal of Ecclesiastical History* XII. i (1961), 40.

[3] Bale's *Collectiones Gallicae* (B.M., MS. Harl. 1819) has the sub-title 'De Religione Carmelitana et Scriptoribus ejusdem'. See McCusker, op. cit., pp. 97–8.

[4] The exact order of these promotions is not clear but it seems that he went to Doncaster c. 1530. Most of his collections on the Carmelites remain in manuscript, notable examples being MS. Bodley 73 and Selden Sup. 41: Cambridge University Library, MS. Ff. 6. 28; and B.M. MS. Harl. 3838.

[5] *Summarium*, p. 246 v.

nothing save that her name was Dorothy and that she accompanied him through all the vicissitudes of his strange career. Now a secular priest, Bale became curate of the parish of Thorndon in his native county; but in 1536 the Bishop of London summoned him on a charge of heresy and he found himself in gaol.[1] Leland, however, intervened with Cromwell on his behalf, commending him as a man of 'lerning, jugement, modesty',[2] and he was released without much delay. His experiments in a new form of morality play had evidently found favour with Cromwell, or so their author believed, for he states that on this, as on an earlier occasion when he had been in trouble with Archbishop Lee of York, his release was procured *ob editas comoedias*.[3] Between 1538 and 1540 the ex-Carmelite seems to have been in charge of a company of strolling players: but on the fall of Cromwell, he found it prudent to leave the country. Little is known of his movements during this, his first, period of exile, except that he seems to have spent part of the time in Switzerland, part in Holland and part in the neighbourhood of Frankfurt. From these strongholds of Protestantism he could denounce the Roman Church with impunity; and the year 1546 saw the publication, at Wesel, of the first part of his *chronique scandaleuse* of English monasticism, *The Actes of Englysh votaryes*. The accession of Edward VI made it safe for him to return to England and, for a time, he and his friend John Foxe the martyrologist enjoyed the hospitality of the Duchess of Richmond in London. In 1551 Bale was given the rectory of Bishopstoke in Hampshire.[4] But he must have been an embarrassing ally, even for Northumberland's party, and towards the end of 1552 he was offered the conveniently distant see of Ossory. Within a few months his attempts to purge and protestantize the Irish Church had made him the best-hated man in the country. The death of the King had put an end to any hope of success for such a policy: and, less than a year after his arrival, the new bishop was forced to abandon his see

---

[1] Bale's answer to this indictment, now in the Public Record Office, is printed by Miss McCusker, op. cit., pp. 6–11.

[2] H. Ellis, *Original Letters illustrative of English History*, 3rd ser. III (1846), 155.

[3] *Catalogus*, p. 702.

[4] W. T. Davies (op. cit., p. 220, n. 3) points out that Tanner's assertion (*Bibliotheca Britannica*, p. 69) that Bale was also presented to the vicarage of Swaffham lacks confirmation in the diocesan records.

and his library and to take refuge in a ship bound for Zeeland. The vessel was attacked by pirates and Bale tells us that he narrowly escaped being sold as a slave; but at length he reached the Low Countries and succeeded in making his way to Germany and Switzerland. After brief sojourns at Frankfurt and Zurich he moved on to Basel where again he joined Foxe, this time as the guest of the celebrated printer, John Oporinus. But 'the byrdes that flye abroade, do loue their owne nestes,'[1] and when Elizabeth succeeded her sister Bale joined the throng of returning exiles. The see of Ossory had been filled and he was offered a prebend in Canterbury cathedral, an appointment which brought him into contact with Matthew Parker, the most enthusiastic and successful bibliophile in England. His remaining years were passed in obscurity and, probably, poverty as well—'how I have bene rewarded of my contraye hytherto for my paynes, the Lord wele knoweth'[2]—and he died at Canterbury in November 1563.

Bale's working life was longer than Leland's, and the contribution made by his publications to medieval historical scholarship was substantially greater. In 1548, there was published at Wesel the *Illustrium Maioris Britanniae Scriptorum Summarium*, the work which appears to parallel Leland's *Commentarii de Scriptoribus Britannicis*. It is divided, chronologically, into five 'Centuries', or groups of one hundred writers, with an 'Additio'. Bale tells us that his motives in undertaking the work were 'literum cupiditas' and 'naturalis . . . erga patriam amor' and that he had begun to collect his materials in 1533 when he first understood the dangers threatening the religious houses. But he explains that he regards his book as merely a makeshift interim report, pending the appearance of Leland's much more important collections. A greatly enlarged version, consisting of nine 'Centuries' and entitled the *Catalogus*, to distinguish it from the earlier *Summarium*, appeared in 1557, bound together with a highly tendentious History of the Popes. Two years later (February, 1559) came the *Posterior Pars*, comprising five more 'Centuries'. The value of all these collections is vastly enhanced by the fortunate survival of an autograph notebook,

---

[1] *Laboryouse Journeye* (ed. W. A. Copinger), p. 29.

[2] H. R. Luard, 'A Letter from Bishop Bale to Archbishop Parker', *Camb. Ant. Soc. Comm.* III, 157–8.

not intended for publication, which (though it was known to scholars) remained in manuscript until the beginning of the present century. This *Index Britanniae Scriptorum*[1] is arranged alphabetically, not chronologically. Its unique importance derives from the fact that here, and here only, Bale refers to his sources, noting where the manuscript of a particular history is now to be found and giving his reasons for ascriptions of authorship.

Some critics have not hesitated to charge Bale with deliberate dishonesty in his use of Leland's materials. Anthony Wood declared that in the *Catalogus* Bale made use of Leland's collections, 'but not in the same words that Leland wrote. For as he delivered things impartially and in smooth language, so Bale quite contrary, and full of scurrilities.'[2] Antony Hall, in his preface to Leland's *Commentarii*, proclaimed himself Leland's first vindicator from the plagiarism of Bale and Pits: until he undertook the work no one had been found 'qui Lelandum Lelando restitueret'.[3] Tanner, however, gave a much more reasonable judgement. From the *Summarium* it would appear that Bale had not then seen the work of Leland: but in the *Catalogus*, he borrowed freely from him 'ut ipse millies fatetur', as he himself repeatedly admits.[4] Hearne, too, defended Bale whom he saw as blameworthy only in the acerbity of his language and his violent Protestant prejudice: apart from this, he esteems his work as 'a most valuable and judicious performance, and far preferable to the less perfect one that was left by Leland who, however in this ought to have the pre-eminence, that he laid the foundation of it.'[5]

This would appear to be very fair comment. In so far as Bale was a plagiarist, he was an open one. His admiration for Leland was profound, if not wholly uncritical. He loses no opportunity of paying tribute to his achievement and the excellence of his scholarship, commends his plan for a series of literary biographies and avers that, though he himself has put forth a book of much the same argument and has since collected much more material, 'yet wolde I haue no man to iudge my

[1] Eds. Poole and Bateson (1902). [2] *Athenae Oxonienses* I. 202.
[3] *Commentarii* (1709); no page-number.
[4] *Bibliotheca Britannica* (1748), p. xiii.
[5] *Athenae Oxonienses* I. 202, n. 4; *Collectanea* I. xli.

rude labours to Leylandes fyne workemanshyp in any poynt equal but at all tymes to geue place vnto it.'[1] It must have been shortly after the publication of his own first venture that Bale came on a version of Leland's collection of British writers and he describes the transports of joy into which the discovery threw him.[2] Foxe notes that he saw Leland's book in Bale's hands about this time, and it seems likely that he had succeeded in borrowing it from Leland's literary executor, Sir John Cheke.[3] Part of his excitement was doubtless due to the fact that it contained what purported to be a certificate written by Leland, authorizing Bale to use his work. An epitome of the work, including the certificate, in Bale's autograph, is now in the library of Trinity College, Cambridge. In this manuscript Bale's additions are carefully distinguished from Leland's original text, each of his addenda bearing the heading 'Johannes Balyeus'. Leland had been one of the first to encourage Bale to embark on his researches: the two were, in a sense, collaborators, and Bale did his friend no disservice when he incorporated the bulk of his materials in the volumes which he published after Leland's death.

As has long been recognized, it was the joint work of Leland and Bale which laid the foundation of medieval historical studies in sixteenth-century England. Bale's printed collections represented by far the most comprehensive conspectus of British authors which had yet been attempted. Judged by modern standards, it is somewhat too comprehensive, for among his Illustrious Writers Bale includes William the Conqueror as author of Domesday Book and King John as author of Magna Carta, as well as Merlin, author of various prophecies. But when the chaff has been sifted out, we are left with a remarkable series of biographies which include virtually all the medieval historians, with most of the works we know them to have written, as well as others which never were written, or have since disappeared. William of Malmesbury, for instance, is credited with a number of homiletical and other treatises which his modern editors have been unable to trace and which may have

---

[1] *Laboryouse Journey*, p. 55.

[2] 'Dici non potest quanta animi voluptate gestiuerim, quod tamdiu desyderatus regni nostri thesaurus . . . ex vastatricibus obliuionem cauernis emerserit tandem.' Trin. Coll. Camb. MS. R. 7. 15, f. 2.

[3] *Acts and Monuments* (1877), III. 705.

failed to survive because they were thought less worthy of preservation than his historical works. In the *Laboryouse Journey* (1549) Bale explains that, after his return from Germany, he had 'for the full correccyon and further augmentacyon' of his *Summarium* visited many libraries, in Oxford, Cambridge and elsewhere. Among stationers and bookbinders he had found 'many notable Antiquitees'; and he had been once more to Norwich where the contents of the libraries had been 'turned to the vse of their grossers, candelmakers sope sellers, and other worldly occupyers.' His zest in seeking out authors and their histories is well illustrated by his handling of the St. Albans chroniclers. In the *Summarium* of 1548 he notes only Matthew Paris and the supposed 'Matthew of Westminster'; but by the time he came to publish the *Catalogus* of 1558, he had discovered Rishanger, Thomas Walsingham, and the relatively obscure Amundesham. He had tracked down the various works which he ascribed to Rishanger in a manuscript in the Royal Library which subsequently became divided.[1] He also discovered several manuscripts of Walsingham's history.[2] One, covering the period 1066–1420, he had obtained from the Vice-Provost of Eton, William Horman; others, containing parts of Walsingham, had come to light, one at University College, Oxford, one in Leland's collection, a third in the library of 'Master Yaxleye', probably the Francis Yaxley who was hunting out books for Cecil in Paris at the end of Edward VI's reign.[3] The manuscript of Amundesham had been discovered at Ramsey Abbey.[4]

Bale himself was a great book-collector; and he was outraged by his fellow-countrymen's indifference to the fate of the monastic libraries. 'Avaryce . . . hath made an ende both of our lybraryes and bokes.' Men have tried to conserve antiquities since the beginning of the world. 'Their labour was to holde thynges in remembrance, whych otherwyse had most wretchedly peryshed. Our practyses now are, to do so muche as in us lyeth, to destroye their frutefull foundacyons . . . A fewe of us there be that woulde gladly saue the most necessary monumentes of their dyspersed remnaunt. But wretched pouerte wyll not permyt vs to shewe to our contrey suche a naturall and necessary

[1] *Index Brit. Script.*, pp. 145–6. [2] Ibid., p. 459.
[3] *Cecil MSS.* I. 118. [4] *Index Brit. Script.*, p. 176.

benefyte.'[1] None the less, by the time he was appointed to the see of Ossory, he had acquired a considerable number of medieval manuscripts. In a letter written to Parker in 1560, he explains how some of the collection had been amassed:

And as concernynge bokes of antiquite, not printed: whan I was in Irelande I had great plenty of them, whom I obtayned in tyme of the lamentable spoyle of the lybraryes of Englande, through much fryndeshypp, labour, and expenses. Some I found in stacyoners. . . . and other occupyers shoppes, some in shyppes ready to be carryed over the sea into Flaunders to be solde—for in those uncircumspect and carelesse dayes, there was no quyckar merchaundyce than lybrary bokes, and all to destructyon of learnynge. . . . only conscyence, with a fervent love to my contray moved me to save that myghte be saved.[2]

This great collection Bale took with him to Ireland where, no doubt, he expected to spend the remainder of his days; but on his precipitate flight he was forced to leave all behind. His residence, Holmes Court, was sacked by the angry mob soon after his departure; it seems certain however, that, though some were destroyed, many, if not most, of the books were saved. Their ultimate fate is one of the unsolved mysteries of bibliography. Bale himself declares that the majority of the books came into the hands of the Lord Deputy, Anthony St. Leger, who had, so he says, 'a great drye vessell full of those bokes' and that, after his death, they passed to St. Leger's brother, Robert, and his son, Warham. (All the St. Legers were suspect with Bale because of the Lord Deputy's conciliatory attitude towards the Irish Catholics.) In the summer of 1559 the Queen addressed a letter to Robert and Warham St. Leger, ordering them to send over 'the books and writings' of the late Bishop of Ossory, 'a man that hath byn studious in the serche for the history and antiquities of this our realme' and which he left behind 'in the tyme of our late sister Quene Mary, when he was occasioned to departe out of Ireland' and are now required 'for the illustration and setting forth of the storye of this our realme, by him, the said Bale.'[3] To this letter, the St. Legers, according to Bale, replied that they had never seen the books, 'their

---

[1] *Laboryouse Journey*, pp. 83–4; 95.
[2] *Camb. Ant. Soc. Comm.* III. 157.
[3] *Cal. State Papers for Ireland* I. 158.

mockynge excuse is, that they never had them, neyther yet
knowe where they ar become.' Bale was convinced that they
were lying and he told Parker that he knew for certain that 'they
have disparsed and distributed them amonge the most obstynate
papystes of all the whole contraye, to brynge them to naughte.'
Some of the books, he suggests, had found their way back to
England, for a certain Hugh Glazier, who was a prebendary
of Canterbury in Mary's reign 'had a great nombre of them,
and disparsed them among hys companyons, the Popes sworne
soldyours.' Many more, however, remained in Ireland, some,
so Bale averred, in the keeping of one Master Nicholas Hearne,
some in Dublin, some with the prebendaries of Kilkenny
cathedral, 'for I had in Ireland more than ii great wayne
loades of them.' He asks Parker to finance somebody, preferably
Robert Cage, vicar of Yalding, near Maidstone, to go to Ireland
and investigate the whole situation, 'for whye, he knoweth the
persones, places, bokes and all.'[1]

It seems impossible to discover what lies behind all this.[2]
The St. Legers may well have been speaking the truth when
they said they knew nothing of the books. Another possibility
is suggested by a note now among the Twyne papers in the
possession of Corpus Christi College, Oxford, which states that
the writer had been told by William Whitlock, the historian
of Lichfield, that 'Syr Henry Sidney had all Bales bokes in
Ireland.'[3] Sidney was in Ireland in the latter part of Mary's
reign, some years before his appointment as Lord Deputy
in 1565; he is known to have been a keen student of antiquities; and it is possible that he made a successful bid for some
of the Bale books. Yet if Sidney had the bulk of the collection,
it seems strange that Parker should not have known of it,
for he and Sidney were on friendly terms and in the habit of
corresponding with one another on antiquarian topics. Sidney
may have had the books for a time only, while he was in Ireland.
But, through whatever hands they passed, there can be little
doubt that their ultimate fate was dispersal. A few came back
to Bale and these he offered to Parker for inspection; but the

[1] *Camb. Ant. Soc. Comm.* III. 158–9.
[2] For a discussion of the whole question see McCusker, op. cit., Chap. II.
[3] C.C.C. Oxon. MS. 255, f. 136. (This collection is deposited in the Bodleian
Library.)

great majority went elsewhere. Thanks to the labours of Miss McCusker, a number of these have been traced. Among the historical manuscripts, Bale's copies of Bede, William of Malmesbury, Geoffrey of Monmouth, Gervase of Tilbury, Ralph Niger, Coggeshall, Trivet, Capgrave, Richard of Devizes, and the letters of Anselm are all in Corpus Christi College, Cambridge. They form part of the great Parker collection there and must have been acquired by the Archbishop after Bale's death. In the Bodleian Library is the unique manuscript of the Fasciculi Zizaniorum (MS. E. Mus. 86), which has an interesting history, for it was probably lent by Bale to Foxe, for his Book of Martyrs, passed later to Ussher and later again to Gerard Langbaine who bequeathed it to the Bodleian in 1658.[1] In Trinity College, Dublin, among books once the property of Bale, are two copies of Ralph of Diceto, a London chronicle and an anonymous history of Edward III: these had probably been in the hands of Archbishop Ussher. A copy of the 'Polychronicon', which Bale had obtained from Queen's College, Oxford, is in the Harleian collection at the British Museum:[2] and in the library of Lambeth Palace is the copy of 'Matthew of Westminster' which Bale had acquired from Nicholas Brigham. This had passed, on Bale's death, to the collection of William Darrell, his successor in the prebendal stall at Canterbury, and was ultimately acquired for Lambeth by Archbishop Secker in 1763.[3]

These, with the other non-historical works which Miss McCusker has been able to trace, amount to only a fraction of the original library claimed as Bale's, to some 40 out of a collection of between 150 and 200 volumes. It is not possible to say what happened to the others. Some may still be unidentified in college, or public, libraries; for Bale did not always leave his traces on his books. We know that Parker was keenly interested in Bale's library, not only by the query to which Bale's long letter is a reply, but also from the Archbishop's later correspondence. Shortly after Bale's death in 1563, he was

---

[1] See J. Crompton, 'Fasciculi Zizaniorum I and II', *Journal of Ecclesiastical History* XII ii (1961), 35–41; 155–66.

[2] See N. R. Ker, 'Oxford College Libraries in the Sixteenth Century', *Bodleian Library Record* VI (1959), 491.

[3] James and Jenkins, *Catalogue of the Manuscripts in the Library of Lambeth Palace*, pp. 819–20.

writing to William Cecil, 'Concerning the old antiquities of
Mr. Bale, I have bespoken them, and am promised to have them
for money if I be not deceived.'[1] But about three years later, he
informed the German Protestant theologian, Matthias Flacius,
who had been acquainted with Bale and was interested in his
library, that, after sending messengers here, there and every-
where in search of Bale's books, which he was in hope of
acquiring, he had learned into whose hands they had fallen
after Bale's flight from Ireland. Exasperatingly, he does not
tell his correspondent who this person was. When the books
reached him, the letter continues, none of them seemed to be
worth Flacius's attention; but since his agent desired to have
them he has lent them to him for a year.[2]

This extraordinary statement has puzzled all the biblio-
graphers. Bale's collection, as Miss McCusker rightly observes,
was not of a kind to be dismissed as unworthy of consideration.
Dr. M. R. James concluded that Parker had seen only a few of
the Bale books; but even so, the fact that he bequeathed about
seventeen of them to the library of his old college shows that he
did not really think those he saw worthless. It very much looks
as though the books which the Germans were invited to inspect
and borrow were those which remained after the Archbishop
had taken his pick. Dr. James hastened to the Grand Ducal
Library at Wolfenbuttel, where the bulk of Flacius's library is
preserved; but he was unable to identify any of the manuscripts
there as Bale's.[3] Whatever the truth of the matter, it seems clear
that neither Parker nor Flacius ever saw the whole, or anything
like the whole, of the Bale collection.

In the *cri du cœur* which he sent to Parker, Bale had tried to
give some idea of the magnitude of his loss. Of letters of popes,
bishops, emperors and kings, 'I have had a great nombre,
but they are disparsed by the Sellengers, God pardon their
frowarde hartes. . . . I had the 554 epistles of Thomas Becket. I
had the 127 epistles of Robert Grossetest, byshopp of Lincolne,
of whome I sende you here a ragged remnaunt. . . . I had
Epistolas Gilberti Folioth, episcopi Londinensis, I had *Epistolas*

---

[1] Parker *Correspondence*, eds. J. Bruce and T. T. Perowne (1853), p. 199.
[2] Ibid., pp. 287–8.
[3] M. R. James, *A Descriptive Catalogue of the Manuscripts in the Library of Corpus
Christi College, Cambridge* (1912), I. xvii.

Joannis Carnotensis, our countreyman, and of *Petrus Blessensis* . . .
and of many other more . . . but now all are disparsed—a very
pytiefull case, that our countreymen are so uncircumspecte,
and, as it were, unnaturall to the olde monumentes of their
nacyon.' Of histories and chronicles he had had 'an excedynge
great nombre' which, he said, Oporinus had been minded to
print in fair volumes at Basel if he could have conveyed them
thither, 'but good fortune fayled, to the excedynge great losse
and blemysh of thys whole realme.' Bale tells Parker where he
may find other copies of some of these histories, 'But I in my
tyme have had more than they all, if they myght be agayne
recovered.'[1]

It was, indeed, a cruel fate which deprived Bale of his library:
for no single individual had done so much to preserve the
names and works of innumerable authors whose memory must
otherwise have perished. We need not lament overmuch
the loss of the History of England which he had planned to
write after he was settled in Canterbury. His was not the judicious temper of the historian, and religious fanaticism must have
hopelessly distorted his picture of the Middle Ages. The brief
reconstruction of the early history of the English Church which
he offered to the readers of his *Vocacyon* speaks for itself. In A.D.
63 Joseph of Arimathaea had been sent to Britain by the
Apostle Philip, who was then preaching in France, so that 'from
the schole of Christe hymsel haue we receyued the documentes
of oure fayth, from Jerusalem & not from Rome whom both
Peter & also Christe hath called Babylon.' Timothy, the disciple
of St. Paul, baptized Lucius, King of the Britons. 'Nurrished,
brought up & continued was this British churche in ye doctrine
of faithe, without mennes tradiciones by ye wurthie doctours of
ye age.' Later, in the days of Ninian and St. Patrick, 'there
folowed a certain kinde of monkery with an heape of ceremonies but yet without blasphemouse supersticions'; but,
after the Saxon invasions, 'Then entered in an other swarme of
monkes muche wurse than the other. . . . These lyke laysye
locustes sprange fourth of the pytt bottomlesse.'[2] It is difficult
not to be repelled by the coarse virulence of much of Bale's
language, 'beastly blockheades', 'blody bellygods', and the like,

---

[1] *Camb. Ant. Soc. Comm.* III. 161–7.
[2] *Vocacyon* (1553), pp. 12v–14.

and by the tale of his episcopal activities in Ireland. Even his contemporaries, who were not squeamish, knew him as 'bilious Bale'. Yet his services in the cause of learning must command respect. Poverty, disgrace, exile, shipwreck, the loss of a great library—none of these could quench his zeal or deaden that lively sense of the past, of history as *lux veritatis*,[1] which seems to match so ill with his religious fanaticism. As sequel and complement to the work of Leland and as prelude to the work of Parker and the Elizabethans, Bale's efforts went far to save the history of medieval England for the modern world.

Leland, and Bale after him, tend to dominate the antiquarian scene in the period between the Dissolution and the age of Elizabeth; but the age produced others worthy of remembrance, including some of the new owners of the religious houses. Outstanding was the Welsh lawyer, Sir John Prise of Brecon (1507–55), whose appointment as one of the monastic visitors followed hard on his marriage to Cromwell's niece in 1534.[2] Prise made a collection of the foundation charters to those houses which he visited in his official capacity, and by 1539, at latest, he had begun to collect manuscripts. Among these were a twelfth-century Florence of Worcester[3] and the second part of the Historia of John of Tynemouth,[4] from Bury St. Edmunds (the surrender of which he signed in November of that year), a manuscript including Bede, Nennius and other early authors,[5] from the cell of Battle Abbey at Brecon, which he had bought from the Crown, and the fourteenth-century cartulary of St. Guthlac's, Hereford,[6] which was granted to him in 1542 and where he spent much of the latter part of his life. Prise bequeathed his theological manuscripts to Hereford Cathedral; but his historical collections remained with his family and in his will he asked his son, Richard, to publish such texts as William of Malmesbury and Henry of Huntingdon, as well as his own 'Historiae Brytannicae Defensio', 'from the written books in my house'. Richard Prise was only eighteen at the time of his father's death, and the 'Defensio' was not published till 1573.[7]

---

1 *Catalogus*, Preface, p. 3.
2 See N. R. Ker, 'Sir John Prise', *The Library*, 5th ser. X (1955), 1–24.
3 MS. Bodley, 297.   4 MS. Bodley, 240.
5 Hereford Cathedral MS. P. V. 1; Bodleian MS. E. Mus. 93.
6 Oxford, Balliol Coll. MS. 27.
7 On this, see Kendrick, *British Antiquity*, p. 88.

What Mr. Ker calls the 'plea for a Rolls Series . . . to be printed at the royal expense', which it contained, evoked no response. The manuscripts were dispersed, many were lost, and most of the survivors can be identified only by notes in Prise's autography. We know, however, that, in addition to those manuscripts already cited, he owned two copies of Geoffrey of Monmouth, several of the works of Giraldus Cambrensis, the 'Policraticus' of John of Salisbury (an early thirteenth-century text from Cirencester), a chronicle of Gloucester Abbey to 1381 and a fifteenth-century copy of Higden's 'Polychronicon'. Almost certainly, Prise's collection could not compare with Bale's; but his care for the monastic books to which his official position gave him access must do something to redeem the reputation of Henry VIII's commissioners, of whom Archbishop Parker was later to complain that they had examined the manuscripts 'leviter et perfunctorie'.[1]

Pre-eminent among the early collectors must be reckoned the Revd. Robert Talbot to whom Leland had been indebted for the loan of manuscripts. Of Talbot's own work on the Antonine Itineraries, Sir Thomas Kendrick has written that a modern antiquary will rightly insist that his name 'should stand at the head of the sixteenth century students of Roman Britain.'[2] Ortelius, Lambarde, and Camden all made use of his work on Roman towns. Educated at Winchester and New College, Talbot was a prebendary of Norwich by 1547. Marginalia in his autograph occur in large numbers of manuscripts which certainly came from Norwich cathedral priory.[3] He transcribed some of the charters from Abingdon, which had been given Godstow Abbey and the site of Rewley.[4] Among the medieval texts in Talbot's possessions were Gervase of Tilbury and William of Malmesbury's 'De Gestis Pontificum',[5] as well as Volume II of the Greater Chronicle of Matthew Paris.[6]

A strange character, with some interest in manuscripts, was Ralph Radcliff (1519–59), a former Carmelite, who obtained possession of his Order's priory at Hitchin, turned it into a school, for which he built a stage, and wrote Latin tragedies and

---

[1] From the preface to *De Antiquitate Britannicae Ecclesiae*.
[2] Op. cit., p. 136.
[3] Wormald, F. and Wright, C. E. *The English Library before 1700* (1958), p. 159.
[4] M. R. James, op. cit., I. 243, 244 (MS. 111).
[5] Bale, *Index*, pp. 88, 136.   [6] C.C.C. Camb., MS. 16.

comedies for his pupils to act. Bale, who once visited him, was impressed by these juvenile performances and by the library, in which he found a miscellaneous collection. Radcliff's possession of Walter Map and Giraldus Cambrensis suggests that his taste was for the lighter side of history.[1] Thomas Soleman (d. 1541), educated at Oxford, who became French secretary to Henry VIII in 1532 and Clerk of the Parliament in 1540, received the nunnery of Canonleigh. He made a transcript of an 'exemplar non mutilum' of Nennius for Leland, who honoured him with an *Encomium*:[2] and Bale, who described him as 'antiquitatum studiosus historiographus', said that he collected many English antiquities and credited him with a life of Becket.[3] But neither this, nor the 'select Antiquities relating to Britain', referred to by Harrison in the preface to the 1586 edition of Holinshed,[4] has been preserved. Finally, we may remember Robert Recorde (*c.* 1510–58), a Welshman, Fellow of All Souls in 1531, M.D. at Cambridge in 1545. Though primarily a mathematician, Recorde had a large collection of historical manuscripts, including Howden, some of the works of Giraldus Cambrensis, and Fortescue's 'De Laudibus Legum Angliae'.[5] More remarkable still is the fact that he knew Anglo-Saxon, as is shown by his notes in the margin of a volume of Chronica Varia, now at Corpus Christi College, Cambridge (MS. 138). On the flyleaf of this volume, at the end of a table made for Parker, we read 'Robertus Recorde erat qui notauit hunc librum characteribus Saxonicis.' In Recorde, the age of Leland and Bale had produced a forerunner of Parker and Joscelyn.

[1] Bale, *Index*, pp. 107, 423.
[2] *Collectanea* III. 45; V. 103.
[3] Bale, *Index*, p. 455.
[4] p. 32.
[5] Bale, *Index*, pp. 72, 402, 425–6.

C

II

MATTHEW PARKER AND HIS CIRCLE

MATTHEW PARKER, born at Norwich in 1504, the son of a prosperous weaver, was a near-contemporary of both Leland and Bale.[1] Educated at Bene't Hall (later, Corpus Christi College), Cambridge, he was elected its Master at the age of forty, after he had proceeded B.D. and had held the posts of chaplain to Anne Boleyn and Dean of her college of Stoke-by-Clare. Twice Vice-Chancellor of the University (1545 and 1548), he was appointed Dean of Lincoln in 1552. But a married priest of Protestant sympathies could hope for nothing under Queen Mary whose accession forced Parker into a retirement by no means uncongenial to a man of his scholarly tastes. In his own words, he 'lived as a private individual, joyful before God in my conscience, neither ashamed nor dejected, so that the most sweet leisure for study to which the good providence of God recalled me yielded me much greater and more solid pleasures than my former busy and dangerous way of life had ever afforded me.'[2] Thus, while Bale, Foxe and many of their friends were in exile in Germany or Switzerland, Parker was reading and writing quietly in England, thereby escaping the heady influence of the more extreme forms of continental Protestantism. His learning, his well-known moderation and his services to her mother marked him out, in the eyes of Elizabeth, as a suitable candidate for the primacy: at the end of 1559, his passionate protests having been swept aside, he was consecrated the first Anglican Archbishop of Canterbury and ruled the Church of England till his death in 1575.

In more ways than one, it was a happy choice that placed an enlightened traditionalist at the head of the Engish Church

---

[1] Strype's Life (1711; 2nd edn., 1821) is still indispensable. The most recent study of Parker is that of V. J. K. Brook (1962).

[2] From Parker's autobiographical notes in C.C.C. Camb., MS. 583. See R. Vaughan and J. Fines, 'A Handlist of MSS. in the Library of C.C.C. Cambridge, not described by M. R. James', Trans. Camb. Bibliographical Soc. III (1960), 120. The Latin text is printed by Strype, Life of Parker (1821), III. 19–24.

during these fifteen critical years. For the future of medieval historical studies it was a piece of supreme good fortune. Parker was much better placed than was Bale to secure the preservation of large numbers of monastic manuscripts. He was a fairly rich man; and, when it became known that the new Archbishop was 'a mighty collector of books',[1] loans and gifts flowed naturally to him. Nor, though it came belatedly, was official support lacking. Among Parker's papers is a draft (evidently his own handiwork) of a letter from the Privy Council (4 July 1568) which refers to the dispersal of the monastic books among private persons, authorizes the Archbishop to make enquiries as to their whereabouts, and exhorts all owners of such ancient records and monuments to allow him access to their collections.[2] These external advantages, coupled with his own tireless enthusiasm, enabled him to acquire by far the most important collection of historical manuscripts yet made in sixteenth-century England.

At the opening of Elizabeth's reign, the position in regard to the monastic books was still far from satisfactory. Following on the dispersals of Henry VIII's time, so vividly described by Bale, had come the destruction, under Edward VI, of many medieval books believed to be tainted with popery; and the possibility of a recurrence of this kind of fanaticism was a danger not to be ignored in 1558. Dr. Dee's bold supplication in 1556 for a royal commission to investigate the whole problem of the dispersed monastic manuscripts had evoked no response from Queen Mary.[3] Many of these were still at the mercy of the greed or ignorance of their new owners or of the sharp practices of foreign and native collectors. In a letter written to Cecil in January 1566, Parker echoed the laments made by Leland and Bale a generation earlier. Books, he says, are being sent overseas 'by couetouse statyoners, or spoyled in the poticarye shopis.'[4] A long note written by the Archbishop's secretary, John Joscelyn, in the magnificent folio of Homer, now in the Parker collection at Corpus Christi College,[5] affords a good illustration of the hazards attending such books. The Homer

---

[1] Strype, II. 497.   [2] *Parker Correspondence*, pp. 327–8.   [3] Below, p. 73.
[4] C. E. Wright, 'The Dispersal of the Monastic Libraries and the Beginning of Anglo-Saxon Studies', *Trans. Camb. Bibliographical Society* I (1951), 212.
[5] MS. 81.

had been found by the Dean of Canterbury in the possession of a local baker who had rescued it from among some waste papers remaining, it was thought, from St. Augustine's.[1] What was to be the remedy for such scandals? It was with good reason that Parker had urged upon his friend, William Cecil, that time was short: 'if this opportunity be not taken in our time, it will not so well be done hereafter.'[2]

His own methods of acquisition were various. According to his eighteenth-century biographer, Strype, 'he did employ divers men proper for such an end, to search all England over and Wales (and perhaps Scotland and Ireland too,) for books of all sorts, more modern, as well as ancient; and to buy them up for his use: giving them commission and authority under his own hand for doing the same.'[3] One such agent was Stephen Batman who, in *The Doome Warning all men to the Judgemente* (1581), wrote:

Thys reuerende Father by vertue of commission from oure soueraigne Queene hyr Maiestie, didde cause to be diligently gathered many bookes of Antiquitie . . . of Diuinite, Astronomie, Historie, Phisicke, and others of sundrye Artes and Sciences. . . . sixe thousand seauen hundred Bookes, by my onelye trauaile. . . . I was not the onlye man in this businesse.[4]

With one or two exceptions, most of Batman's acquisitions seem, however, to have been printed books.[5] For the collection of manuscripts, the Dean of Canterbury, Nicholas Wotton, and John Twyne, master of the grammar-school and sometime mayor of the city, were doubtless more useful; for some 75 of those in the Parker collection at Corpus Christi College derive either from Christ Church or St. Augustine's. The most valuable of the historical manuscripts is probably the 'A', or Parker, text of the Anglo-Saxon Chronicle (MS. 173), a Christ Church book, often referred to by Parker or his secretaries as 'Liber quem habet doctor Wutton decanus eccl. Christi Cant.', or as being 'in manibus Doctoris Wotton Decani Cant.'[6] The earlier

---

[1] M. R. James pointed out that the baker was almost certainly wrong and that the Homer is much more likely to have been a Christ Church book. *A Descriptive Catalogue of the Manuscripts in the Library of Corpus Christi College, Cambridge* I. (1912), 166.

[2] *Parker Correspondence*, p. 328.   [3] Strype, II. 497.

[4] pp. 399–400.   [5] M. R. James, op. cit., I. xvi.

[6] Earle and Plummer, *Two of the Saxon Chronicles Parallel* II. xxvii; *Roberti de Avesbury, Historia de Mirabilibus Gestis Edwardi III*, ed. Hearne (1720), p. 268.

part of this, the most important, manuscript of the Chronicle was written at Winchester in the tenth century, the latter part at Christ Church, where the whole remained until the Dissolution. Another remarkable Christ Church book which Parker acquired through Dr. Wotton was the volume (MS. 46) containing the 'Policraticus' and the *Metalogicon* presented by John of Salisbury to Becket. Yet another, which may have reached Parker in the same way, is the copy of Ralph of Diceto which had once belonged to Stephen Langton. Moreover, Nicholas Wotton had been Dean of York before he came to Canterbury and he was responsible for one of the very few manuscripts in the collection deriving from a northern house. This was the volume (MS. 139) containing the chronicles of Simeon of Durham and John of Hexham which was probably in the library of Hexham priory before the Dissolution. John Twyne succeeded in accumulating a fair number of manuscripts, mainly from St. Augustine's: the copy of the 'Itinerarium Regis Ricardi' (MS. 129) has a note on the fly-leaf, 'Sent from Mr Twyne'. Strype adds that Parker also obtained Anglo-Saxon books from Leland's friend, Robert Talbot, who died in the year of Elizabeth's accession, and that some of these had come to Talbot through Dr. George Owen.[1]

It appears that Parker also sent questionnaires to dignitaries of the English and Welsh cathedrals about manuscripts surviving in their libraries. Replies from some of these have been preserved. '. . . for all suche olde monuments as we had', wrote Richard Davies, Bishop of St. David's, in March 1565, 'Mr Secretary [Cecil] hathe them ij yeares ago . . . but in the library of St. D ther is none at all. he had of me Geraldus Cambrensis, a Cronicle of England, the author unknowne and Galfredus Monemutensis.'[2] 'There is not in this cuntrey any monumentes of antiquitie lefte', wrote Nicholas Robinson, Bishop of Bangor, a former member of Parker's household, in October, 1567,

but certaine fabulose histories and yt [that] lately written, as ye rude labors of one Howell Daa, and ye Life of a troublesome prince or two, which were subdued since ye Conquest: yet the peeple here will talke of many thinges which appeere in no where. Mr Darell had an

[1] Strype, II. 499.
[2] C.C.C. Camb., MS. 114. Printed in *Parker Correspondence*, no. cciv, p. 493.

aunceant booke out of my howse here, which I wold be glad your grace cold gett of him, or if he haue pledged it here I wold gladly quite it out and send it your grace, whatsoeuer the charge there of shalbe. I am promysed dayly from other parties of Wales the sight of some Welshe histories, but as yet I see nothing, neither can heare certainely of any doynges of ye olde Brittans so yt [that] I suspecte that there there remayneth nothing in writing. . . .

The Bishop did, however, promise to send part of a transcript of Eadmer's history which he hoped to have completed in the course of the winter.[1] From the other side of the country, John Aylmer, Archdeacon of Lincoln, wrote about the same time, 'Yt pleased you to require me by Mr Hewitt to send your grace the names and tytles of suche old wrytten ecclesiasticall hystoryes as I haue: yt may please your grace to understand that I have made ye best searche I can bothe in my own study and elles wheare and Indeed I can find none, the most parte are old fellowes that I have . . . schole men, as Alexander de Hales . . . but for hystoryes I have none.'[2] Early in 1569 Bishop John Jewel wrote,

I haue ransacked our poore Libraries of Sarisburie, and haue founde nothinge worthye the findinge, sauinge onely one booke written in the Saxon tonge, which I minde to sende to yor Grace by the next conveniente Messenger. . . . it may be Alfricus for al my cunninge. But yor grace wil soone finde what he is. Other certaine bookes there are of Rabanus and Anselmus, but as common so also litle woorthe. If I had any leasure, I would sende yor grace the titles of al. But as nowe I am entringe into the visitation of my diocese. By the waye if I maie learne of any antiquities, I wil do yor grace to understande. . . .

Some two weeks later, Jewel wrote again,

. . . I haue made enquirie for suche antiquities, as I haue passed through my Cleregie in this uisitation, but as yet I can finde nothinge. If there by any thinge founde, I shal haue understandinge of it.[3]

To his friend, Sir Henry Sidney, Parker proposed a bargain:

Whereas I purposed to your Lordship one of my poore Bookes of *Thomas Walsinghams* Storie, etc. latelie sett owte: the rather, for that

---

[1] Ibid., p. 503.   [2] Ibid., p. 897.
[3] C.U.L. MS. I. i. 2. 4, ff. 149*, 149**, quoted by Wright, op. cit., p. 223.

I knowe your Lordship to loue Antiquities: soe I sende you, by this Bearer, one; and if you will lett mee haue the Sight of sum Bookes, that you haue, peradventure, I maie enlarge them, or, by sum Comparison, amende those that I haue in Hande, by Diuersitie of Copies; and soe maie the Worlde enioye sum Comoditie by vs, in such rare Bookes. And if that your Lordship will effectuouslie sende to mee the Bookes, which you haue at Home in your Howse; I maie further vnto you sum other Booke, that I haue of late caused to be printed, meate for your Knowledge. And thus I bid you hartely well to fare as my self. From my Howse at *Lamhith*, this First of *December*, 1574.[1]

Such letters give a lively impression of co-operative (if not notably fruitful) effort in the search for antiquities; others reflect discussion of the problems relating to the early history of the Church in Britain which were Parker's first concern. 'It may please your grace to be advertised', wrote the Bishop of St. David's from Abergele, in February, 1567,

I am not able at this tyme fully and precysly to answere to yor graces question what tyme Sulgenus was Byschop of St. M.[2] and whether I shall learne any further when I go to St. M. whych by Goddes helpe wylbe within this iij wekes I doubt. But presently thus moche I can say. Bernardus was made Bischope of St. D, in the tyme of Henry Beuclerk that is H the fyrst after he had subdued Walles. next after [sic] that Bernard was Wilfredus b of St. M and next before hym was Abraham and next before that Abraham was the same Sulgenus. ... And forasmoche as there were no more yeres betwene the conquest and H the fyrst but xxxiiij and that there were but ij bischopes betwene the aforesayd Bernard and Sulgenus it is very like that he was about the tyme of the conquest either next before or next after or both. ... .[3]

Another letter indicates that Parker had asked the Bishop to enlist the help of the Welsh scholar, Dr. William Salisbury, in deciphering what is described as a 'quire of strange charects'. 'Mr Salisbury', Davies replied, 'doth declare unto your grace how little we could do in it.'[4] By a fortunate chance, the

---

[1] A. Collins, *Letters and Memorials of State* (1746), I. 67.
[2] i.e. Menevia, the original name of St. David's.
[3] C.C.C. Camb., MS. 114, p. 391. That the bishop was puzzled is hardly surprising. The most recent authorities judge it impossible to name with certainty any of the predecessors of Bernard in the see of St. David's (1115–48). See *Handbook of British Chronology* (1961), pp. 273, 279.
[4] *Parker Correspondence*, p. 266.

Bishop transcribed a single word written in these 'strange charects' with sufficient accuracy to enable Dr. M. R. James, some three and a half centuries later, to identify the manuscript as C.C.C. Camb., MS. 478, an Armenian psalter.[1] Later on, the bishop had evidently put a problem of his own to Parker who replied, 'As for those charects wherein some of your records of donations be written, whereof he [Mr Salisbury] sent a whole line written, it is the speech of the old Saxon, whereof I have divers books and works, and have in my house of them which do well understand them.'[2]

The most important of these widespread and sustained endeavours to gather in manuscripts and news of manuscripts was the Archbishop's famous collection, the bulk of which, apart from 25 vellum manuscripts presented to the University Library in Cambridge during his lifetime, came by bequest to Corpus Christi College.[3] Parker was not the only scholar to believe that, failing a great royal or national storehouse, the best way to secure the preservation of valuable books and manuscripts was to house them in university or college libraries. Writing to Cecil in 1568 about a collection of Greek manuscripts, Bishop Jewel had urged that 'if they should be divided amongst the bishops . . . upon their departures, and dissolution of their libraries, they would soon be lost. Therefore if you shall think it good to have the said books kept within this realm, in my judgement it shall be best they be brought into certain of the colleges of Oxford or Cambridge, whereas they may be safely kept for ever.'[4] The dangers of the time and the uncertainty of the future may fairly be pleaded in extenuation of what has sometimes been seen as shameless pillaging of the cathedral libraries by the bishops themselves. When Parker, and Whitgift after him, caused Canterbury books to be removed to their respective Cambridge colleges, Corpus Christi and Trinity, or to the University Library, one, at least, of their

---

[1] M. R. James, op. cit. II. 419. W. W. Greg, 'Books and Bookmen in the Correspondence of Archbishop Parker', *The Library* XVI (1961), 273, 279.

[2] *Parker Correspondence*, p. 271.

[3] Parker's original bequest comprised 457 volumes but some 24 (or perhaps 28) of these never came to the college. Some found their way into the Cottonian collection, others to the library of Trinity College Cambridge. See M. R. James, op. cit. I. xiv–xv, xliii.

[4] *The Works of John Jewel*, ed. R. W. Jelf (1848), VIII. 196.

objects was to put the books in the safest places they knew. To leave them in Canterbury or Lambeth would be to expose them to the caprices of prelates who might be ignorant, or bigoted, or both; to house them in a college was to put them in the care of a learned corporation where some interest in them might be hoped for and—most important—where the donor could impose his own conditions. Parker himself clearly was determined to take no chances. His deed of gift laid down a series of shrewdly calculated rules for the custody of his bequest. The manuscripts and books were to be kept under three locks, the keys being in the hands of the Master of the College and the two keepers of one of the college funds. Every year, on the donor's birthday, 6 August, the Master of Caius College and the Master of Trinity Hall (or their deputies), assisted by two scholars of these colleges, were to begin an inspection of the manuscripts, leaf by leaf. While thus engaged, they were to dine at the charge of Corpus Christi, the inspectors to receive payment at the rate of 3s. 4d. a day, the scholars 1s. For every leaf of a manuscript found missing (and Parker and his secretaries had numbered the leaves of many of them) the Masters of the other two colleges were to impose a fine of 4d. on Corpus Christi; for a missing volume, the fine was at the discretion of the inspectors. In the event of 'supine negligence', involving the loss of a large number of books, the whole collection, together with the plate which Parker had also bequeathed, was to pass to Caius; should Caius also prove negligent, both were to go to Trinity Hall.[1] Few college authorities could contemplate with equanimity the prospect of fines being imposed on them by other colleges for negligence in the care of their own property, still less the horrifying possibility of its confiscation to a rival foundation. Parker had not been Head of a House for nothing, and time was to prove the efficacy of his system, which was maintained until early in the present century. No single loss was suffered between 1575 and the Second World War, when it was judged wise to send the books out of Cambridge.

Some examples of the wealth of historical material included in the Parker collections at Cambridge have already been cited.[2] Thirty-eight of his manuscripts at Corpus Christi are written in Old English, among them being the translation of Bede's

---

[1] M. R. James, op. cit. I. xii–xiii.   [2] Above, p. 20.

'Historia Ecclesiastica' which Bishop Leofric had given to his cathedral church of Exeter in the eleventh century (MS. 41), and the Alfredian translation of Pope Gregory's 'Cura Pastoralis' which derived from Worcester (MS. 12). Parker books in the University Library include the only surviving ancient copy of the 'Historia Brittonum' ascribed to Nennius, written in the twelfth century; a transcript, from about the same period, of Gildas, 'Liber Querulus de Excidio Britanniae' (MS. Ff. i. 27) and an Anglo-Saxon Bede from Worcester (MS. Kk. 3. 18). There are twelfth-century copies of Florence of Worcester, Henry of Huntingdon and Geoffrey of Monmouth at Corpus Christi (MSS. 92, 280, 281) deriving respectively from Peterborough, St. Augustine's, and St. Andrew's, Northampton, and a thirteenth-century collection of Becket's letters from Christ Church (MS. 295). William of Malmesbury's 'Gesta Regum' (MS. Ii. 2. 3) and 'Gesta Pontificum' (MS. Ff. 1. 25), the former a fine twelfth-century folio, are both in the University Library, as are also the manuscript of Gervase of Canterbury (Ff. i. 29), thought by Stubbs to derive from a better original (possibly in an autograph) than the Cottonian MS. Vesp. B. 19 which had hitherto been used as authoritative for the text,[1] and the copy of the 'Polychronicon' (MS. Ii. 2. 24) which the Rolls Series editor placed first in importance among many surviving manuscripts.[2] At Corpus Christi is to be found the best text of Matthew Paris's 'Chronica Majora' in two volumes, the first of which (MS. 26) had belonged to Edward Aglionby of the Middle Temple, the second (MS. 16) to Sir Henry Sidney; and two texts of Walsingham's 'Historia Anglicana' (MSS. 7 and 195).

The value of these great benefactions is beyond question: but Parker's treatment of his manuscripts is quite another matter. There can be no doubt that he took what any modern scholar would regard as unpardonable liberties with them. Strype, who saw nothing to criticize in his methods, describes them thus:

And he kept such in his family as could imitate any of the old characters admirably well. One of these was Lyly, an excellent writer,

---

[1] Gervase of Canterbury *Opera Historica*, ed. W. Stubbs, R.S. 2 vols. (1879), I. l–liv.

[2] *Polychronicon*, ed. C. Babington, R.S. 9 vols. (1865–86), I. xlvi–xlviii.

and that could counterfeit any antique writing. Him the Archbishop customarily used to make old books complete, that wanted some pages; that the character might seem to be the same throughout.[1]

and again,

But beside the books he writ or published, and the antiquities he collected, he commonly made improvements to MSS by additions of his own, and so particularly he did in the Black Book, belonging to the Archdeacon of Canterbury: . . . That which our Archbishop added in this said book were two charters: one whereof was a charter of Archbishop Richard, to Archdeacon Herbert; whereby the archidiaconal jurisdictions were said to be enlarged. And in the margin was writ by our Archbishop's own hand this note, *Concessio personalis circa annum Domini* 1230. . . .[2]

Confirmation comes from Parker himself. Writing to Cecil in 1565, he thanks him for the loan of an Old English manuscript and continues thus:

I had thought to have made up the want of the beginning of the Psalter, for it wanteth the first psalm, and three verses in the second psalm, and methought the leaf going before the xxvith psalm would have a meet beginning before the whole Psalter, having David sitting with his harp, or psaltrery . . . and then the first psalm written on the back side: which I was in mind to have caused Lylye to have counterfeited in antiquity, etc, but that I called to remembrance that ye have a singular artificer to adorn the same, which your honour shall do well to have the monument finished, or else I will cause it to be done and remitted to your library. . . .[3]

The manuscripts themselves afford further evidence for the prosecution. Volume II of Matthew Paris (C.C.C. Camb., MS. 16) has been drastically 'improved'. On the verso of f. 3, at the bottom, we find a note in a sixteenth-century hand— 'hic plura desunt', followed by (in a different ink) 'sed sequuntur'. The eight missing folios, in a counterfeit hand, are there inserted into this thirteenth-century manuscript. Again, on the verso of f. 38, where there is a large dark stain on the vellum, Parker's scribe has pasted a piece of paper on to the margin (leaving one side loose so that the original is accessible) and on this has re-written nineteen lines of the text, in a counterfeit

---

[1] Strype, II. 500.   [2] Ibid. II. 456.
[3] *Parker Correspondence*, pp. 253–4.

medieval hand. In many other places, where the writing has become obliterated, it has been supplied by words written on the manuscript itself. Into the manuscript of Ralph of Diceto (MS. 76) two leaves have been inserted after f. 18 and a list of the names of pre-Conquest Archbishops has been added to f. 23. In the C.U.L. manuscript of Malmesbury's 'Gesta Pontificum' (Ff. 1. 25), certain contractions have been extended and somewhat illegible words written more clearly in the margins. A large incision in the outer margin of f. 54 has been neatly repaired by the pasting in of a piece of paper on which the missing words are supplied. A flyleaf in the fourteenth-century manuscript of Gervase of Tilbury's 'Otia Imperialia' shows the heading 'In gratiam eorum qui huiusmodi abbreviationes antiquorum non sunt exercitati', followed by a transcript of the opening lines of the text, with the contractions extended.[1] As for the manuscript of Walsingham which Parker is thought to have used for his edition of 1574 (C.C.C. Camb., MS. 195), this, as Professor Galbraith has said, was treated by him like a copy for a printer. He defaced it 'by writing over the margins, crossing out words in ink, inserting headings, enclosing passages in brackets, interlining passages for insertion, keying up the manuscript to the pages of the printed version.'[2] Virtually all the historical manuscripts in the collection contain addenda in the hands of Parker or his scribes—tables of contents, sometimes a sketchy index, marginalia innumerable.

Deplorable methods no doubt; but they were the methods of an age which did not regard the Latin text as sacred and approved the restoration, physically as well as conjecturally, not only of what the author was believed to have written, but of what he might have written had he been in possession of other sources of information. Much more remarkable than the mishandling of the manuscripts is the evidence afforded by the texts of the close attention with which they were read by Parker or his secretaries. The various autographs are by no means always easy to identify, but Parker himself has been thought to be traceable by his habit of using red chalk for page-numberings, underlinings and many notes. This tradition has a long history; for it was in 1600 that Thomas James, the first Bodley's

---

[1] C.C.C. Camb., MS. 414.
[2] V. H. Galbraith, *The St. Albans Chronicle, 1406-20* (1937), p. xi.

Librarian, writing to Thomas Allen about a manuscript of
Asser which he had seen in Lord Lumley's library, observed
'. . . That this booke did belong unto the Archbyshop sometimes, it was told me by the keeper of his librarie, and I fownd
it by the Archbyshop's notes of redd oker in diuerse places of
the booke, which was usually by him used in all his bookes
which he read, as I had seene at Cambridg amonge his bookes
there.'[1] The tradition was accepted by Strype,—'he often
made use of a red lead pen'—[2] it has been generally accepted
at Cambridge; and there is, indeed, no good reason to question
it. What remains impossible to prove is that Parker was the
only one in his circle to use red chalk. Dr. C. E. Wright has
suggested that it is unlikely that the Archbishop would have
had time to spare for such tedious work as pagination and ruling
and has drawn attention to evidence pointing to the use of red
chalk by his son, John Parker.[3] The matter is not, perhaps,
of fundamental importance; for the master and his friends and
servants worked as a team, and whichever the hand or hands that
wielded the red pen, the guiding spirit was Parker's. Almost all
the historical manuscripts in his collection bear the marks of
careful reading from cover to cover by one or other of them.
Underlinings and marginal notes show meticulous care for
detail. Attention is drawn, not only to proper names and dates,
but also to passages which may throw light on authorship
and sources. Examples are a note on the inside cover of C.U.L.
MS. Dd. 2. 5, 'Author huius operis monachus Abindoniae ut in
fol. 47a, 42a, 100a, 21b, 38b, 40a'; and a marginal note in the
chronicle of Sigibert of Gemblours with the continuation by
Robert de Monte, where, against the heading 'Chronicon
Roberti', we read 'Hic Robertus de Torrineio monacho Becci
ut Henricus Archdiaconus Huntingtonia testatur in epistola
sua ad Warinum britone. Hic Robertus monachus Beccensis, et
dictus Robertus de Torineio et prior illius monasterii ut in anno
sequenti 1153, Et postea Abbas S. Michaelis.' The subsequent
passage in which the author declares himself to have been a
monk at Bec is heavily underlined and 'oyer' written in the
left-hand margin, in red chalk.[4] Cross-references in Parkerian

[1] See W. H. Stevenson, *Asser's Life of King Alfred*, p. xxxviii, n. 1.
[2] Strype, II. 484.   [3] Op. cit., p. 228.
[4] C.U.L. MS. Ff. 1. 31, ff. 130, 169.

hands are numerous—from Richard of Chichester to Asser, 'vide ipsum Asserum, pag. 55'; 'non sic in Asser';[1] from Sigibert to William of Malmesbury on the origins of the Franks, 'Sic inde deriuatim fecit Willelmus de Malmesbiria, f. 22b, Historie sue li. j';[2] from Ralph of Diceto to Matthew Paris, 'Vide Mat. Paris in histor. maior fo. 163. Et in parua histor. A° 1170'; and[3] where William of Malmesbury records differences between Bede and other writers on the length of the reign of Ethelbert, a Parkerian hand has written 'Dissonancia' in the margin.[4] Points of special interest to the Church historian are often underlined, sometimes with marginal notes—in Gervase of Canterbury, against his allusion to the death of Lanfranc, 'Archiepiscopus Cant' dicitur patriarcha';[5] 'Hic nota quod Sanctus Thomas instituit festum principale Sancti Trinitatis';[6] 'Nota hic Baldewynys erat albus monachus.'[7] Allusions to the marriage of priests are noted in Henry of Huntingdon, where Bale's hand has written 'Sacerdotibus uxores primi prohibitae'[8] and in the 'Polychronicon' where 'Sacerdotes uxorati' or 'Sacerdotum uxores' appear in the margins: and it is normally to Bale that we owe such comments as 'Papa oppressor ecclesiae anglicanae' and 'Cupiditas Romana',[9] though 'papa fatetur posse se errare et ecclesiae subditum esse' in a collection of *Chronica Varia* is not traceable to him.[10] The copy of William of Malmesbury, now in the Cambridge University Library, reflects the reactions of an enthralled and somewhat naïve reader. 'Lector, vide mirabile', 'Hoc mirabilis [*sic*]', 'Horrendum factum'.[11] Occasionally, the glosses throw some light on the reader's own interests and prejudices, as in Guisborough (C.U.L. MS. Dd. 2. 5, f. 203), where he notes 'Hic multa desunt de Bruto et Arthuro'. Against the reference to King Alfred at Oxford in the 'Polychronicon' a hand of the fourteenth century had written in the margin 'Nota sub quo universitas Oxon incipit', below which a Parkerian hand has added 'Sed quantum hic scriptur errauit vide Jo. Caium de

[1] C.U.L. MS. Ff. 1. 28, ff. 134, 135v.   [2] C.U.L. MS. Ff. 1. 31, f. 58.
[3] C.C.C. Camb., MS. 76, f. 18.   [4] C.U.L. MS. Ii. 2. 3, f. 5v.
[5] C.U.L. MS. Ff. 1. 29, f. 15.   [6] Ibid., f. 88v.
[7] f. 128v.   [8] C.C.C. Camb., MS. 280, f. 127v.
[9] C.C.C. Camb., MS. 259, ff. 185v, 200.
[10] C.C.C. Camb., MS. 138, f. 159.   [11] C.U.L. MS. Ii. 2. 3, ff. 51, 42.

antiquitate Cantab.', the whole enclosed in an ornamental border with a pointing finger.[1]

While we need not deny him some disinterested curiosity about the past, there can be little doubt that the driving force behind all this antiquarian activity was Parker's desire to present the history of the Church of England in a way that would justify the Elizabethan settlement. Hence, the emphasis laid on the earlier periods, before the full development of papal claims, and the preference for authors like Matthew Paris who were critical of the papacy. That his editorial ventures were inspired by a similar motive seems clear from the words of his secretary, John Joscelyn:

Besides he was verie carefull and not without some charges to seeke out the monuments off foremer tymes to knowe the religion off thancient fatheres and those especiallye which were off the Englishe churche. Therfore in seekinge upp the cronicles off the Brittones and Inglishe Saxons which laye hidden euery wheare contemned and buried in forgetfullness and through the ignoraunce off the Languages not wel understanded, his owen especially and his mens diligence wanted not.

And to the ende that these antiquities might last longe and be carefullye kept he caused them being broughte into one place to be well bounde and trymly couered. And yet not so contented he indeuored to sett out in printe certaine off those aunciented monumentes whearoff he knew very fewe examples to be extante and which he thoughte woulde be most profitable for the posterytye to instructe them in the faythe and religion off the elders.[2]

It is interesting to contrast the attitude of Parker's contemporary, Thomas Stapleton who, in 1565, published at Antwerp his translation of Bede, with a dedication to the Queen and a plea for the return of England to the old religion. Stapleton had been among John Twyne's pupils at Canterbury, whence he proceeded to Winchester and Oxford, but soon after 1558 he left England and settled in France, where he established a reputation as one of the most learned Catholics of his age. Though his interests were primarily theological, he, like Parker, had a lively appreciation of the value of original sources, and in the preface to his Bede he asserts that Virtue 'properly commendeth

[1] C.U.L. MS. Ii. 2. 24, f. 113.
[2] *The Life off the 70.Archbishopp of Canterbury presentlye Sitting* (1574), C. 1.

an historiographer, and discharges him from all surmises and suspicions of false reporting or poeticall fayning . . .'.[1]

In the last decade of his life Parker edited and published four important medieval texts, beginning with the *Flores Historiarum*, ascribed to 'Matthew of Westminster'. The ascription derives from a Norwich manuscript of the early fifteenth century (B.M. MS. Cott., Claudius E. 8). Bale had accepted it and Parker followed him, thereby perpetuating the error until modern times. His first edition, printed by Thomas Marshe in October 1567, is taken from a manuscript written in Merton Priory, now in the possession of Eton College,[2] but, as the last leaf is missing, the history of the year 1307 was taken from Trivet. Inevitably, there are misreadings and other small errors but, on the whole, the manuscript is followed faithfully enough, without large-scale alterations or amendments. It would have been well for Parker's reputation as editor had he left it at that. Unfortunately, soon after he had published his edition of the Merton text, he came across other manuscripts of the Flores, one (now Bodley MS. Laud 572), which is probably the 'vetustissimum illius historiae exemplar' referred to by Parker in his preface, and others now in the Cottonian collection (Otho. C. 2, Nero D. 2 and Claudius E. 8). He began reading these; and at the same time he was preparing to edit Matthew Paris's Greater Chronicle. In 1570 there appeared his second edition of the *Flores* (also printed by Marshe), a substantial folio of over 900 pages, furnished with an Index and revealing itself as an extraordinary conflation of sources, for Parker introduced into the text, not only variant readings from the manuscripts he had discovered subsequently, but also passages from Matthew Paris, Malmesbury, Trivet, Rishanger and other chroniclers, no attempt being made to distinguish these for the benefit of the reader.

Matthew Paris's Greater History, printed by Reyne Wolfe, appeared in the following year (1571), another stout folio of over 1,300 pages, introduced by an elaborate *Prefatio ad Lectorem* in which Parker discusses the authorship of the chronicle and

---

[1] *The History of the Church of Englande. Compiled by Venerable Bede, Englishman. Translated out of Latin in to English by Thomas Stapleton Student in Diuinitie*, p. 2.

[2] MS. Merton (Eton Coll.). *Flores Historiarum*, ed. H. R. Luard, R.S., 3 vols. (1890), I. ix–xvi, xxxiii–xlv.

describes the manuscripts he has used. In addition to the two belonging respectively to Edward Aglionby and Sir Henry Sidney,[1] he had borrowed from Cecil a manuscript compiled in the fifteenth century from both the greater and the lesser histories of Matthew Paris.[2] A transcript (now C.C.C. Camb., MS. 56) of another, containing the lesser history, had been made for him by permission of its owner, the Earl of Arundel,[3] and from John Stow he had borrowed a manuscript of the Greater History (now B.M. MS. Cott., Nero D. 5). These were all the copies of Matthew Paris then known to exist—that they were so few was ascribed by Parker to the malevolence of the papists in suppressing them—and with these before him he prepared for the press the edition which has incurred such severe condemnation.[4] Like the second edition of the *Flores*, it was a 'mixed text', made up, it must be admitted, with unbounded licence and with interpolations which belie the editor's claim never to have added anything to or subtracted anything from the books he published.[5] H. R. Luard filled five pages of the Rolls Series edition with examples of Parker's mistakes, and Sir Frederick Madden held it to be 'a subject of congratulation' that he did not carry out his intention of editing the lesser history also.[6]

The Archbishop's third editorial venture was a volume containing the *Historia Anglorum* and *Ypodigma Neustriae* of Thomas Walsingham, printed, the first by Henry Binneman, the second by John Day, in 1574. In his preface to the *Historia Anglorum* Parker gives his readers no information about the manuscript, or manuscripts, to which he was indebted for the text of what, on his own authority, he named 'Historia Brevis'. H. T. Riley surmised that he relied mainly on a manuscript now in the College of Arms (Arundel MS. 7) or on a close copy of it; but Professor Galbraith is satisfied that he drew mainly from

---

[1] C.C.C. Camb., MSS. 26 and 16.   [2] B.M. MS. Nat. 6048 B.
[3] The original is B.M. MS. Royal, 14 C VII.
[4] See Matthew Paris, *Chronica Majora*, ed. H. R. Luard, R.S., 7 vols. (1872–83), II. xxiii–xxviii; and Matthew Paris, *Historia Anglorum*, ed. Sir F. Madden, R.S., 3 vols. (1866–9), I. xxxvii.
[5] In the preface to his Asser (1574) '. . . . hoc te scire volo . . . in omnibus iis libris quos diuulgaui, nihil vt de meo adiecerim, aut diminuerim . . .'.
[6] In the preface to his Matthew Paris, Parker had suggested that he should do so, unless Arundel wished to undertake it himself.

D

one then in the possession of Lord William Howard (C.C.C. Camb., MS. 195), of which the Arundel manuscript is itself a copy, turning to the latter only to fill in gaps where the earlier manuscript was defective, or in order to discover variant readings.[1] In the preface to the Rolls Series edition, Riley added his voice to the chorus of condemnation; but Professor Galbraith is prepared to put in a good word for Parker whose edition, conflated from two or more manuscripts, is essentially sound, gives 'a good working copy' and even provides a letter of Edward III which is missing in the Rolls Series edition because Riley, having overlooked the very existence of the C.C.C. Camb., MS. 195, printed from the inferior Arundel MS. 7. The manuscript used for Walsingham's *Ypodigma* was among those presented to Corpus Christi College (MS. 240) and it too bears traces of red chalk.

Finally, in this same year, 1574, John Day printed for Parker an edition of Asser's life of King Alfred. In more ways than one, this was a strange production. The manuscript from which Day printed (almost certainly the lost Cottonian MS. Otho A XII, Parker's own property) was written in Caroline minuscule. But Parker states that 'out of veneration for the antiquity of the archetype' (a phrase which has been responsible for many a scholarly wild-goose chase), he had caused it to be printed in Old English characters, 'lingua Latina, sed literis Saxonicis'. An English scribe writing Latin in Alfred's time would undoubtedly have used Anglo-Saxon characters which, indeed, bear some resemblance to the Caroline minuscule introduced into England in the next century:[2] but Parker himself makes it clear that his own manuscript was written in the latter and admits that his motive was propagandist. His edition is prefaced by an impassioned plea for the study of the Old English language: the publication of the four Old English Gospels had been designed to the same end.[3] Since many ancient documents, both pre- and post-Conquest, survive in the Saxon tongue,

---

[1] Thomas Walsingham, *Historia Anglicana*, ed. H. T. Riley, R.S., 2 vols. (1863), I. I. xi–xii; V. H. Galbraith, *The St. Albans Chronicle, 1406–20* (1937), p. xi.

[2] See Asser, *De Rebus Gestis Alfredi*, ed. W. H. Stevenson, pp. xi–xxi; E. N. Adams, *Old English Scholarship in England from 1566–1800* (1917), p. 34.

[3] *The Gospels of the fower euangelistes tr. in the olde saxons tyme . . . into the vulgare toung* (1571).

'cohortabor, ut exiguo labore, seu pene nullo huius sibi linguae cognitionem acquirant.'[1] Except, perhaps, for the pronunciation, it will cause his readers little or no trouble. To encourage them the editor provided a key to the Saxon characters at the beginning of the book. Though it was eagerly awaited and enthusiastically received by his contemporaries,[2] the Asser has found no defenders among modern scholars. W. H. Stevenson mitigated his strictures by a tribute to Parker's 'unparalleled services' in rescuing priceless manuscripts for posterity; but he comments adversely on the liberties he took with his text, on his corrections of style and spelling and on his interpolations from the Annals of St. Neot's and even from Matthew Paris.

By common consent, then, Parker was a poor hand at editing manuscripts. Yet he should surely be given some credit for even attempting the task of publication. He was the first Englishman to organize the printing of a series of important historical texts and by his efforts he stimulated others, like Lord William Howard and Sir Henry Savile, to follow his example. The publication of an impeccable text, even had such a thing been conceivable in that age, was much less important than the arousing of interest in the medieval chronicles and in medieval history generally. All too many of Parker's contemporaries were ready to share the suspicion of Archbishop Grindal's agent who regarded the possession of medieval texts as indicative of leanings towards popery. Parker himself, in the preface to his edition of Walsingham, is at pains to counter the argument that the medieval historians are not worth reading. Walsingham may write in a rough and heavy style—'crasso ac leuidensi stilo'—but it is the law of history that truth is to be preferred to elegance of oratory. The editor of this and similar histories may be charged with putting forth works in which will be found 'monastica quaedam fragmenta aut potius aniles fabulae'; but it is better to publish Matthew Paris and Matthew of Westminster, with all their fables and portents (which no one now believes), than to deprive good men and honest writers of the rest of their histories. Ancient histories are not to be

---

[1] From the preface to Asser, A iiij.
[2] 'Of this edition of Asserius there had been great expectation among the learned.' Strype, II. 381.

rejected merely because false miracles appear in them: for these are all the histories we have.

Parker himself made, or sponsored, one venture into historiography, the *De Antiquitate Britannicae Ecclesiae & Priuilegiis Ecclesiae Cantuariensis, cum Archiepiscopis eiusdem 70*, printed by Day in 1572, for private circulation. This was the first privately printed book in English and only about fifty copies are believed to have been struck off.[1] How many of its closely printed 449 pages are the Archbishop's own composition cannot now be determined. In writing to present Cecil with a copy of the work[2] Parker describes it as 'this my pore collection' and explains that his object was 'to note at what tyme Augustyne, my first predecessour, cam into this land, what religion be brought in with hym, and how it contynued, how it was fortified and increased . . . untyl the dayes of King Henry the VIIIth, when the religion began to grow better, and more agreable to the Gospel.' He describes the work as the solace of his leisure hours —'So spending my wasteful tyme within myn own wallys, tyl Almighti God shal cal me out of this tabernacle.'[3] Yet, as even Strype admits,[4] Joscelyn must have had a large share in the amassing of the materials, as his surviving collections in the Cottonian Library testify. The text of much of the manuscript in Vit. E. XIV is in his hand; and in the account of his father's disbursements which John Parker drew up after his death we find the entry 'To Sir Thomas Josselin's brother, an antiquary who wrote this history *De Antiquitate Britannicae Ecclesie*, a prebend worth £30 per annum and procured for him £300.' There is also reason to believe that the first section of the book, introducing the lives of the Archbishops, was the work of George Acworth.[5] The book opens with a preface, defending the writing and reading of history, pointing to such illustrious exemplars as Thucydides and Livy, commending, in particular, the study of Church history, and deploring the loss of valuable manuscripts at the Dissolution. The sentiments are reminiscent of Parker's other prefaces and this one is likely to have been his work. There follows a sketch of the early history

[1] *D.N.B.* article on John Day, by H. R. Tedder.
[2] Now in C.U.L. (Sel. 3. 229).   [3] Letter printed by Strype, III. 267–9.
[4] Ibid. II. 245–6, 251–2.
[5] L. G. H. Horton-Smith, *George Acworth* (1953), pp. 8, 35.

of the Church in Britain before the coming of St. Augustine, in which the familiar tale of Joseph of Arimathaea having been sent by St. Philip to evangelize Britain is reproduced. The origins and mutations of the English sees occupy fourteen pages, the privileges and prerogatives of the See of Canterbury another sixteen; then comes the lives of the Archbishops from Augustine to Reginald Pole (444 pp.). The work is well documented for the earliest period, in so far as full use is made of Bede and the letters of Pope Gregory; but the author does not hesitate to draw also on such writers as Geoffrey of Monmouth, Howden, and Capgrave. For the age of Stephen Langton and Boniface of Savoy he relies almost exclusively on Matthew Paris; though in the section on the See of Canterbury reference is made, not only to the literary authorities, but also to the registers of Peckham, Winchelsey, Courtenay, Arundel, Chichele and Morton, to the records of the Court of Wards and Liveries, to the Charter Rolls in the Tower, and to the records of the Court of Arches.

Though he remains a curiously elusive figure, pride of place among the learned members of the Archbishop's *familia* should almost certainly be given to John Joscelyn, the son of an Essex country gentleman and a former Fellow of Queens' College, Cambridge, whom Parker appointed as his secretary and chaplain soon after his elevation to the primacy. Joscelyn's services were rewarded with a prebend in Hereford Cathedral, and his written memorials suggest that his help must have been invaluable. He assisted Parker in the hunt for manuscripts and knew his way about the principal medieval chronicles. Among his papers there is preserved a list of English historians with notes on the present whereabouts of manuscripts of some of their works.[1] Although, as Dr. Wright has shown,[2] the list owes much to Bale, it affords interesting additional information about owners of manuscripts and supplied a good conspectus of the chronicle literature of medieval England from Gildas and Nennius to Capgrave and Rudborne.[3] Under Parker's direction,

---

[1] 'Nomina eorum, qui scripserunt historiam gentis Anglorum & ubi extant; per Joannem Joscelinum.' B.M. MS. Cott., Nero C. III, ff. 208b–212b. Printed by Hearne in *Roberti de Avesbury, Historia de Mirabilibus Gestis Edwardi III* (1720), pp. 269–98.

[2] Op. cit. pp. 215–16.

[3] The copy of William of Newburgh (now MS. Trin. Coll. Dublin E. 4. 21) was

Joscelyn wrote in Latin a short history of Corpus Christi College, Cambridge, not, it seems, intended for publication,[1] in the course of which he took opportunity to correct Stow's error in ascribing the foundation of the college to John of Gaunt and also to depict Parker, 'honesto zelo motus erga honorem collegii', as its supreme benefactor. But Joscelyn's main interest lay in Anglo-Saxon studies and it was here that he made his most significant contribution. In 1567, John Day printed an edition of Gildas (reissued in 1568), with a preface by Joscelyn in which he explains that Parker had allowed him access to two manuscripts unknown to Polydore Vergil, one deriving from St. Augustine's, Canterbury,[2] and the other from Glastonbury, but now in the possession of 'cuiusdam generosi iurisperiti Cantiani', who may well have been Lambarde.[3] These manuscripts have enabled him to improve on and supplement Polydore's edition. Though there are misreadings in the text, Joscelyn supplies some useful marginal notes, gives references for all the biblical quotations and illustrates Bede's use of Gildas. About the same time, Day printed an edition of Aelfric's 'Homily' in Anglo-Saxon type, under the title *A Testimonie of Antiquitie*, the preface to which is attributed to Joscelyn. In this, he tells his readers that many books of Old English sermons are yet to be seen, some in private hands and taken out of the monasteries at their dissolution, some yet reserved in the libraries of such cathedrals as Worcester, Hereford, and Exeter, 'From which places diuerse of these bookes haue bene deliuered into the handes of the moste reuerend father, Matthewe Archbyshop of Canterbury, by whose diligent search for such writings of historye, and other monumentes of antiquitie, as might reueale unto vs what hath ben the state of our church in England from tyme to tyme, these thynges that been here made knowen vnto thee, do come to lyght.' The Saxon writings, Joscelyn says, 'be set out in such forme of letters, and darke speech, as was vsed when they were written', and at the end of the book he provides a key to 'the Saxon Caracters or letters, that be moste straunge'.

once Joscelyn's property. See R. Howlett, *Chronicles of the Reigns of Stephen, Henry II and Richard I*, R.S. 4 vols. (1884–89), I. xliv–xlvi.

[1] It remained in manuscript until edited for the Cambridge Antiquarian Society by J. Willis Clark in 1880.

[2] C.U.L. Bd. 1. 17.   [3] Vit. A. VI destroyed in the fire of 1731.

Many Old English manuscripts with Joscelyn's notes, and transcripts, in his hand, of several others are now in the Cottonian collection at the British Museum. Most notable are the collections in Vit. E. XIV which include a transcript of Asser, extracts from chroniclers such as William Thorne and Thomas Sprott and from the registers of religious houses so far apart as Whitby, Lewes, and Tewkesbury. MS. Cal. A. VI consists of excerpts made by Joscelyn from the history of the monastery of Abingdon in the Saxon period; MS. Vesp. A. IX has some collections from Domesday Book and manorial documents. MS. Tib. B. IV contains Joscelyn's collations of different texts of the Anglo-Saxon Chronicle. His methods of handling his manuscripts were much the same as Parker's. He wrote notes on them for purposes of collation, supplemented and otherwise 'improved' the text, and into the 'D' MS. of the Chronicle he inserted paper leaves on which he wrote extracts from the other manuscripts in a fake Old English hand. But against these offences may be weighed his appreciation of the necessity of a philological basis for the study of Old English history. Two manuscripts in the Cottonian collection—Tit. A. XV and XVI—contain an Anglo-Saxon–Latin dictionary said to have been written by Joscelyn and the Archbishop's son, John Parker: Joscelyn is also credited with the authorship of an Anglo-Saxon grammar.

Clearly, Joscelyn was a man of great learning and a good servant to his master. If echoes of some ancient grudges reach us across the centuries, they need not be taken too seriously. Dr. John Caius evidently thought Joscelyn indiscreet. In the covering letter to Parker which accompanied a draft of his defence of the antiquity of Cambridge, he writes irritably, 'Your man, Mr Joscelyn, I fear wil shew it to every body, and give out copies *ante maturitatem*, and do little good in it himself. I beseech your Grace remember what I writ to you in that matter heretofore.'[1] Possibly, this dark allusion may be in some way linked with another, found on Joscelyn's tombstone in High Roding Church in Essex:

In Learning tryde, whereto he did his mind alwaies incline
But others took the Fame and Praise of his deserving Witt,
And his Inventions, as their owne, to printing did committ.[2]

[1] Strype, III. 162 (8 Apr. 1567).   [2] Cooper, *Athenae Cantabrigienses* II. 366.

The innuendo must have been directed against Parker, probably with reference to the *De Antiquitate Britannicae Ecclesiae*. Joscelyn's friends perhaps considered that his work had not received due recognition; and the absence of his name from the list of mourners at the Archbishop's funeral may possibly have some significance. Yet direct evidence is wanting; and the warmth of Joscelyn's own references to Parker lends support to Fuller's comment: 'But we will not set the memories of the Patrone and Chaplaine at variance (who loved so well in their lives time) nor needeth any *Writ of partition* to be sued out betwixt them, about the authorship of this book, though probably one brought the *matter*, the other *composure* thereof.'[1]

Also in Parker's household and assisting him in his researches were two other Cambridge men—Alexander Neville of St. John's and George Acworth of Peterhouse. Neville, who was brother to the Dean of Canterbury, Thomas Neville, had studied law before he entered the Archbishop's service and is described as a competent writer of Latin verse and prose. Under Parker's direction, he compiled a *Tabula Heptarchiae Saxonicae*;[2] and he was paid £100 by his master for writing the story of Ket's rebellion, printed by Binneman in 1575, with an appendix treating of the antiquities of Norwich. This last is interesting, if only because it is largely based on Bartholomew Cotton, a chronicler of whom we hear little in the sixteenth century. The manuscript which Neville used was probably that now in the Cottonian collection (Nero C. V), in which traces of red chalk foliation may still be seen.[3] Acworth, who had been Public Orator at Cambridge and Chancellor and Vicar-General to the Bishop of Winchester, joined the household (described by Strype as 'a kind of common receptacle for learned and ingenuous men')[4] about 1570, and it was Parker who, in addition to seeking his collaboration in researches into the early history of the British Church, entrusted him with the preparation of an answer to the Jesuit Nicholas Sanders's *De Visibili Monarchia Ecclesiae*.[5]

---

[1] *Church History of Britain* (1655), ed. J. Nichols (1861), book IX, p. 60.
[2] Tanner, *Bibliotheca Britannica*, p. 544.
[3] B. Cotton, *Historia Anglicana*, ed. H. R. Luard, R.S. (1859), pp. xviii–xix, lxvii.
[4] Strype, II. 182.
[5] L. G. H. Horton-Smith, *George Acworth* (1953). He is not to be confused with the George Acworth who was M.P. for Hinton in 1563–7.

We know less of the learned interests of some other members of the household. They included at least one Oxford man, Thomas Bickley, a former Fellow of Magdalen, who was one of Parker's domestic chaplains and subsequently became Warden of Merton and Bishop of Chichester. Bale had noted him as the possessor of a manuscript of Henry of Huntingdon.[1] There was Parker's steward, Thomas Doyley, who had been admitted to Gray's Inn in 1555 and towards the end of the century may have been reading papers to the Society of Antiquaries.[2] William Darell, prebendary of Canterbury, 1564–80, is mentioned by Wharton as one of Parker's band of scholars.[3] He had acquired Bale's copy of the 'Flores Historiarum'[4] and was himself the author of a Latin treatise on Kentish castles. There was Thomas Yale, Dean of the Arches, Parker's Vicar-General and one of the supervisors of his will, who possessed a copy of the 'Polychronicon' with a continuation to 1460 and made collections for the Archbishop out of the Canterbury registers.[5] There was Lyly, that 'excellent writer', and, no doubt, many more. Strype, in what appears to be a paraphrase of a Latin tribute composed by Alexander Neville, draws an attractive picture of the Archbishop's *familia*:

And for learning, his house was a kind of flourishing University of learned men: and his domestics, being provoked by the Archbishop's exhortations and precepts, often published to the world the fruits of their studies. For when he took any into his family, he would always exhort him to pursue learning and piety with an ardent desire. And his own example went before them for both. And though he was busied in the weighty offices and affairs of Christ's commonwealth, yet he was always of that mind towards learning, that no thoughts could ever wholly take him off from his studies, and from the embracement of the best sorts of learning. He read over all good books, especially the monuments of the ancients. . . . For he would admit none to live under him, but such as truly and sincerely feared God, and, beside their daily attendance, employed themselves at their leisure hours in some kind of laudable exercise; as in reading, making collections, transcribing, composing, painting, drawing, or some other application in learning or art.[6]

[1] *Index*, p. 165, 'ex camera Thome Bycley, Oxon.'   [2] Below, p. 158.
[3] *Anglia Sacra*, I. xviii.   [4] James and Jenkins, *Lambeth MSS.*, p. 819.
[5] Strype prints samples from the collections in B.M. MS. Cott., Cleopatra F. 1 (op. cit. III. 177–82).
[6] Op. cit. II. 441–2.

III

PATRONS AND COLLECTORS

As collector of antiquities and friend to struggling scholars, Matthew Parker did not stand alone. Among rich men with a taste for history there were several who followed his example in combining the accumulation of manuscripts and printed books with offering encouragement and, sometimes, employment to students. Conspicuous among such patrons was William Cecil, created Baron of Burghley in 1571, whose correspondence with Parker has already revealed him as a keen collector of 'old monuments', who kept artificers in his household for the purpose of 'improving' manuscripts. As early as 1553, Nicholas Wotton, from Paris, and Francis Yaxley, from Poissy, were offering to buy books for Cecil:[1] and, as has been seen, he anticipated Parker in the hunt for manuscripts at St. David's. Unfortunately, though he gave a few books to the University Library at Cambridge, Cecil's collection was not preserved with the same care as Parker's. On 21 November, 1687, there was an auction at the sign of the Bear in Ave-Mary Lane, near the west end of St. Paul's Cathedral. The Advertisement to the Reader which prefaces the catalogue of this sale (now preserved in the British Museum) claims that it comprises the main part of Burghley's library, and also that it contains 'a greater number of rare manuscripts than ever yet were offered together in this way, many of which are rendered the more valuable by being remark'd upon by the hand of the said great Man.' Since many of the printed books were published after Burghley's death, they cannot have been his; but there seems to be no reason to doubt that the bulk of the manuscripts came from his library.[2] These were scattered as a result of the sale and many of them cannot now be traced; but sufficient evidence remains to prove Burghley's interest in

[1] S. Haynes, *Burleigh State Papers*, p. 152; *Salisbury MSS.* (Hist. MSS. Com.), I. 118.

[2] W. W. Greg, 'Books and Bookmen in the Correspondence of Archbishop Parker', *The Library*, XVI (1936), 274–7; Sears Jayne, *English Libraries of the Renaissance* (1956), p. 132.

and possession of numerous medieval historical manuscripts. Among those listed in the sale catalogue is a copy of Matthew Paris, likely to have been that which Cecil lent to Parker for his edition of 1571;[1] two copies of the 'Gesta Regum' of William of Malmesbury, one of which may be the present All Souls MS. 33, the binding of which shows it to have been once the property of a Cecil;[2] and two copies of Geoffrey of Monmouth, one of which is bound together with Giraldus Cambrensis and John Mayor's Scottish history. The Giraldus has been identified as MS. 3024 in the National Library of Wales, a paper copy of the 'Itinerarium' and 'Descriptio Cambriae'. At the foot of the first page Cecil himself has written 'Gulielmi Cecilii ex dono Rich Daviss', and there are some other notes in his hand in the early pages of the book.[3] Dr. M. R. James identified the chronicle of Froissart listed in the catalogue 'folio grand avec des belles Figures' as MS. Mostyn 206: it bears Cecil's name and was given to him by another antiquary, Thomas Sackville, Lord Buckhurst.[4] The 'Vetus Chronicon Angliae & Hiberniae' is likely to have been the original chronicle of Henry de Marleburgh, a fifteenth-century vicar of Ballyshaddan, near Dublin, which now survives only in a series of extracts transcribed in the sixteenth century:[5] and the manuscript described as 'The Bible [sic] of English Politie, for keeping the narrow Seas, an old Poem in English' is now B.M. Add. MS. 40673. The description on the vellum cover, 'An exhortation to contynew ye strength of ye Navy of England in ye Narrow Sea, wrytten about H. ye 6 tyme', is in Burghley's hand.[6] Unidentified manuscripts relating to medieval British history include three copies of Higden's 'Polychronicon', one of which, described as 'vetus MS. . . . nunquam Latine impressum', fetched £11; a second copy of Geoffrey of Monmouth; three copies of Giraldus Cambrensis, 'Historia Hiberniae'; and a copy of 'Matthew of Westminster'.

[1] Above, p. 41.

[2] William of Malmesbury, *De Gestis Regum Angliae*, ed. Stubbs, R.S. 2 vols. (1887–9), I. lxxxv.

[3] R. Flower, 'Richard Davies, William Cecil and Giraldus Cambrensis', *National Library of Wales Journal* III (1943–44), 11–14.

[4] W. W. Greg, op. cit., p. 279. For Sackville, see below, p. 60.

[5] B.M. MS. Cott., Vit. E. V. See R. Flower, 'Laurence Nowell and the Discovery of England in Tudor Times', *PBA* XXI (1935), 66.

[6] *The Libelle of Englyshe Polycye*, ed. Sir G. Warner (1926), p. liv.

Other manuscripts, not listed in the sale catalogue, but known to have been in Cecil's possession, are the 'E' MS. of the Anglo-Saxon Chronicle[1] and the 'Gesta Henrici Secundi' of 'Benedict of Peterborough' (now B.M. MS. Cott., Julius A XI), which he had read carefully, noting the supposed authorship, before handing it on to Sir Robert Cotton.[2] The fifteenth-century copy of Howden, now preserved among the Hatfield MSS., was once his property and is said to contain a few notes in his hand.[3] Parker had sent him a transcript of the 'Dialogus de Scaccario' (then generally ascribed to Gervase of Tilbury), thinking it 'not onmete for your office',[4] and had allowed him to borrow a large volume containing several charters written in a fourteenth-century hand.[5] Nor was Cecil's interest in the past limited to its literary memorials. Writing to the Dutch geographer, Abraham Ortelius in 1577, the young William Camden paid tribute to the notable collection of coins and other rarities in the possession of this 'Antiquitatis perscrutator diligentissimus';[6] and it may not have been merely the knowledge that treasure-trove was a perquisite of the Crown that prompted Sir William Strickland to send to the Lord Treasurer a description of the finding of a number of Roman coins in the ruins of a house demolished by the sea on the coast near Holderness.[7]

His combination of a great public position with a well-known zest for antiquities induced scholars to look to Cecil, as they looked to Parker, for help and support. Dr. Dee, to whom he had already given a testimonial, sought Cecil's advocacy in his efforts to save the manuscripts of Wigmore Abbey;[8] Richard Prise dedicated his father's *Historiae Britannicae Defensio* (1573) to him, and when Lord William Howard produced his edition of Florence of Worcester in 1592, he claimed Burghley as his

[1] Bodleian MS. Laud Misc. 636. See C. E. Wright, op. cit., p. 219.

[2] Benedict of Peterborough, *Gesta Regis Henrici Secundi*, ed. Stubbs, 2 vols. R.S. (1867), I. xxxi.

[3] Roger Howden, *Chronica*, ed. Stubbs, 4 vols. R.S. (1868–71), I. lxxxiii.

[4] Strype, *Parker* III. 267; *Parker Correspondence*, p. 424.

[5] M. R. James and C. Jenkins, *Catalogue of MSS. in the Library of Lambeth Palace*, p. 176.

[6] *Ecclesiae Londino-Bataviae Archivum*, ed. J. H. Hessels (1887), I. no. 72.

[7] *Cal. State Papers Domestic, 1547–80*, p. 406.

[8] *Letters of Eminent Literary Men*, ed. Sir H. Ellis (Camden Society, 1843), p. 39; *Chetham Miscellanies* I. 10; below, p. 74.

patron. The Welsh antiquary, Dr. David Powel, acknowledged his indebtedness to the Lord Treasurer, not only for the loan of 'rare monuments of antiquitie', but also for letters directing him 'to all the offices where the Records of this realme are kept'.[1] A notable protégé was Lawrence Nowell, brother to Alexander Nowell, Dean of St. Paul's.[2] He was a Brasenose man and a good classicist who, after the fashion of the day, migrated to Cambridge and became a schoolmaster in 1546. On his return from exile under Queen Mary, he was given the Deanery of Lichfield; and from 1563 he lived in Cecil's house in the Strand while acting as tutor to his ward, the young Earl of Oxford. Nowell owned some valuable manuscripts, including the continuation of the 'Polychronicon' written at Westminster, the French Life of Edward the Confessor (now in the Cambridge University Library),[3] and several collections of Old English laws. Dr. Flower summed up his three principal objectives as the mapping of England, the discovery of sources for English topography, and the restoration of Old English language and literature. In Cecil's house he made numerous transcripts, among them that of the manuscript, afterwards MS. Cott., Otho B. XI, which was almost totally destroyed in the fire of 1731. Nowell's transcript has thus been the means of preserving knowledge of a text which includes the Alfredian translation of Bede, the Anglo-Saxon Chronicle, and a collection of Old English laws. He also helped to transcribe Matthew Paris for Parker; and, in copying the 'Vita et Mors Edwardi Secundi', he was the first to ascribe it (mistakenly) to Thomas de la More.[4] He was a pioneer in his attempt to construct a connected account of Irish history, to which Holinshed's 'Description of Ireland' is likely to have been indebted. Nowell corresponded with Ortelius about geography; and it was to Cecil, 'tibi cui tantum debeo', that he expounded his plans for making more accurate maps, both of individual counties and of the whole country.[5] The Lord Treasurer's range of intellectual sympathies

---

[1] *The Historie of Cambria* (1584); from the Advertisement to the Reader. In the dedication to Sir Philip Sidney which prefaces his edition of Giraldus Cambrensis (1585), Powel refers to manuscripts lent him by Cecil.

[2] See R. Flower, *PBA* XXI, 47–73.   [3] MS. Ee. 3. 59.

[4] *Chronicles of the Reigns of Edward I and Edward II*, ed. Stubbs, 2 vols. R.S. (1882–3), II. lvii–lix.

[5] *Letters of Eminent Literary Men*, pp. 22–3.

may have been limited. He had no great opinion of poets, and Spenser, for one, had little reason to be grateful to him.[1] But his sense of history—well illustrated by the sketch of the development of the medieval papacy which he included in his essay on *The Execution of Justice in England* (1583)—his care for antiquities, and his desire to further the study of the past must stand to his lasting credit.

Another centre of historical studies, where a remarkable library was built up, was the royal palace of Nonesuch in Surrey which Henry, the last Fitzalan Earl of Arundel, had undertaken to complete for Queen Mary. The nucleus of the library was Arundel's own collection of some fifty manuscripts which he had acquired at the time of the Dissolution, when he was Lord Chamberlain to Henry VIII, together with another 400 volumes bought, partly, it seems, from motives of show-manship.[2] To these was added, by favour of Queen Mary, a large part of the confiscated library of Thomas Cranmer; and in the 1570s there were some exchanges of books with Parker who, as has been seen, borrowed the copy of Matthew Paris's 'Historia Anglorum' which Arundel had obtained from a former Royal Librarian, Bartholomew Traheron, and presented the Earl with his own edition of Asser. Though described by his anonymous biographer as 'not unlearned',[3] Arundel's scholarship could not compare with that of John, Baron Lumley, who married the Earl's daughter Jane (herself a young woman of bookish tastes), and joined the household at Nonesuch in 1557, bringing his own library with him. Lumley's reputation as a scholar, as one who 'pursued recondite learning as much as any of his honourable rank in those times',[4] grew steadily throughout the reign of Elizabeth. Thomas James, the first Bodley's Librarian, resorted to 'the riche and well-furnisht librarie of the right Honourable and right courteous Lord Lumley' in his search for the manuscript of Asser,[5] and the Queen herself knew him as 'a lover of antiquities'.[6] Towards

---

[1] P. H. Sheavyn, op. cit., pp. 170–1.

[2] *The Lumley Library: the Catalogue of 1609*, ed. Sears Jayne and F. R. Johnson (1956), p. 4, n. 3.

[3] G. Goodwin in *D.N.B.*

[4] G. Goodwin in *D.N.B.*, quoting J. Hacket, *Scrinia Reserata*.

[5] *Asser*, ed. W. H. Stevenson, p. xxxviii, n. 1.

[6] J. Nichols, *Bibliotheca, Topographica Britannica* I. 526.

the end of Lumley's life, there was some dispersal of the books, 89 volumes (from among his duplicates) going to the University Library at Cambridge, 34 to the Bodleian and others to individual friends. After his death, on 11 April 1609, James I's son, Prince Henry, ordered that a catalogue be made of the whole remaining collection. The books were then removed to the Prince's private library in St. James's Palace, whence most of them passed to the Royal Library and so, ultimately, to the British Museum. Lumley, it seems, had either allowed them to revert to the Crown, together with the palace of Nonesuch where they were housed, or else had made a gift of them direct to Prince Henry. The commonly held belief that he sold them to James I lacks foundation.[1]

The Catalogue of 1609 shows that, in addition to works on theology, medicine, philosophy, and the liberal arts, the Lumley library contained some six hundred works labelled 'Historici', relating to many different ages and many different lands. The sources for British history range from Gildas and Nennius to Holinshed and include such recently printed books as Polydore Vergil's English History (1555), the Bede published at Louvain in 1566, Parker's editions of Asser and other historians, Stow's *Summarie of English Chronicles* (1566 or 1573), Camden's *Britannia* (1590 or 1596) and Sir Henry Savile's *Scriptores post Bedam* (1596). Manuscripts ran from Nennius (MS. Royal 13 B. XV), through Asser (probably MS. Cott., Otho A. XII), Ailred's life of Edward the Confessor (Gonville and Caius College MS. 153), Henry of Huntingdon (MS. Royal 13 C. II), Giraldus Cambrensis (MS. Royal 13 B. XII), Glanvill and Howden (MS. Royal 14 C. II), 'Matthew of Westminster' (MS. Royal 14 C. VI) and Froissart (MS. Royal 18 E. 11) to extracts from Thomas of Elmham's life of Henry V (MS. Royal 13 A. XVI) and an English translation of Polydore Vergil (MS. Royal 18 C. VIII, IX). The great majority of the historical manuscripts were once the property of Lumley. His name appears on many of them, and in the margin of the relevant folio of the manuscript of Howden he has made a note of his own descent from Liulf of Bamborough.[2]

The great library rightly bears Lumley's name; but it undoubtedly owed much to the enterprise of another notable

[1] *The Lumley Library*, pp. 14–17.   [2] Howden, *Chronica*, ed. Stubbs, I. lxxvii.

antiquary. A few years before Lumley went to live at Nonesuch, Arundel had brought a young Welshman, Humfrey Lhuyd of Denbigh, from Oxford to serve as physician in his household. Lumley outlived Lhuyd (who married Lumley's sister, Barbara)[1] by over forty years, but Lhuyd's name is found in at least seventy of the books. Such was his reputation that Parker's correspondent, the learned Dr. William Salisbury, went so far as to link the name of 'one H. Lloyd of Denbigh, a retainer to the Earl of Arundel', with those of Leland and Bale. The three of them, he said, 'of any of those parts, were the most universally seen in history, and most singularly skilled in rare subtilties.'[2] Lhuyd ('Geographistoricus') was a friend of Ortelius to whom he furnished a map of England and the map of Wales which Ortelius inserted in his *Theatrum Orbis Terrarum*, whence it passed to Camden.[3] The moving letter which accompanied the maps allows us a glimpse into the mind and spirit of a devoted scholar on his deathbed and is worth quoting in full:

> Dearly beloued *Ortelius*, that day wherein I was cōstayned to depart from *London*: I receyued your Description of ASIA and before I came home to my house: I fell into a very perillous Feuer, which hath so torne this poore body of mine, these x continuall dayes: that I was brought into despayre of my life. But my hope *Iesus Christe*, is layde vp in my bosome. Howbeit, neither the dayly shakynge of the continuall Feuer, with a double Tertian, neither the lookyng for present death, neither the vehement headache without intermission: coulde put the remembrance of my *Ortelius*, out of my troubled brayne. Wherefore, I send vnto you my *Wales*, not beutifully set forth in all poyntes, yet truly depeinted, so be that certyn notes be obserued, which I gathered euen when I was redy to die.
>
> You shall also receaue the description of *England*, set forth as well with the auntient names: as those which are now vsed, and an other *England*, also drawne forth perfectly enough. Besides certein fragmentes written with mine owne hande. Which, notwithstandynge that they be written foorth in a rude hande, and seeme to be inperfect: yet doubt not, they be well grounded by proofes, and authorities of auntient writers. Which,

---

[1] M. F. S. Hervey, *The Life, Correspondence and Collections of Thomas Howard, Earl of Arundel* (1921), p. 54.

[2] Strype, *Parker* I. 418.

[3] T. M. Chotzen, 'Some Sidelights on Cambro–Dutch Relations', *Trans. Hon. Soc. of Cymmrodorion* (1937), p. 140.

also (if God had spared me life) you should haue receaued in better order, and in all respects perfect. Take therfore, this last remembrance of thy *Humfrey*, and for euer *adieu*, my deare friend *Ortelius*. From *Denbigh*, in *Gwynedh* or *North Wales*, the xxx of August. 1568.
Yours both liuyng and diyng
Humfrey Lhuyd.[1]

Unlike many of his contemporaries, Lhuyd appreciated the importance of the Celtic element in the study of place-names, showing, in his *Breuiary of Britayne*, 'how imperfect all the Accounts of this Island are, which we have from the *Roman* writers, and how dark, for want of a little skill in the old *British* language.'[2] He himself made a useful contribution to the topographical picture of Britain and he had some influence on Camden.[3] Unfortunately, though no doubt inevitably, his critical sense deserted him when he came to consider Brutus, Arthur and the rest. His *Historiae Britannicae Defensio*, dedicated to Ortelius[4] and translated into English by Thomas Twyne under the title *The Breuiary of Britayne*, was, as its name suggests, a defence of the British history against the scepticism of Polydore Vergil. In one of the many eulogies which introduce the text of the English edition, Edward Grant, Headmaster of Westminster School, congratulated Lhuyd,

> By whose endeuour *Polidore*
> must now surcease to prate,
> To forge, to lie, and to defame,
> kynge BRUTUS worthy state.[5]

The same fervent patriotism had already inspired Lhuyd to undertake an English translation of 'Brut y Tywysogion', the History of the Princes, then ascribed to one Caradoc of Llancarfan,[6] prefacing it with a greatly enlarged version of Sir John Prise's *Descriptio Cambriae*. After Lhuyd's death, this manuscript[7] came into the hands of Sir Henry Sidney.

[1] Printed as preface to *The Breuiary of Britayne* (1573).
[2] W. Nicholson, *The English Historical Library* (1714), p. 4.
[3] Ibid.   [4] Published at Cologne, 1568.
[5] *The Breuiary of Britayne* f. lv. For a critical appreciation of Lhuyd's work, see Kendrick, *British Antiquity*, pp. 136–7.
[6] The ascription seems to derive from Lhuyd. See J. E. Lloyd, 'The Welsh Chronicles', *PBA* XIV (1928), 371.
[7] B.M. MS. Cott., Caligula A. VI (dated London, 17 July 1559).

E

Sidney's was another great house where medieval books were collected and read. It was from him that Parker had borrowed the second volume of Matthew Paris (C.C.C. Camb., MS. 16); and another manuscript in the Corpus collection (MS. 101) includes a transcript made by one of the Archbishop's secretaries of a description of the Church of Llandaff, 'ex antiquissimo quodam libro scripto D. Henrici Sidnei.' As Lord President of the Council of Wales for nearly thirty years (1559–86), with his official residence at Ludlow, Sidney, 'whose disposition is rather to seeke after the antiquities, and the weal publike of those countries which he governeth, than to obtaine lands and reuenewes within the same',[1] was naturally attracted to Welsh antiquities and disposed to help Welsh scholars. It was at his instigation that Dr. David Powel, Fellow of All Souls and Vicar of Ruabon, agreed to revise Lhuyd's translation of 'Brut y Tywysogion' and to prepare it for the press. Though he tells his readers that he undertook the task with some reluctance, Powel's methods were scholarly. He used records; and he collated Lhuyd's translation with two other manuscripts of the same chronicle, though it was not until the book was already in print that he received from Robert Glover, Somerset Herald, another and better-corrected copy of the translation. He consulted the published works of all the authors he could find who had written anything of Wales; and from John Stow, 'who deserueth commendation for getting together the ancient writers of the histories of this land', he had borrowed the manuscripts of several unpublished chronicles.[2] The result was *The Historie of Cambria*, printed in London in 1584, and embellished, we now know, by woodcuts lifted from the first edition of Holinshed and adapted to illustrate the history of Wales, so that Athirco masquerades as Llewellyn ap Iorwerth and Henry II as Howel Dha.[3] Sidney must have been well satisfied, for he appointed Powel as one of his domestic chaplains and encouraged him in the pioneer venture of printing Giraldus's 'Descriptio' and 'Itinerarium Cambriae', supplying him with an 'exemplar pervetustum' of the latter. In the

---

[1] *The Historie of Cambria*: from the Address to the Reader.

[2] See Strype's Life of Stow. *Survey of London* (1720), I. xi–xii.

[3] J. E. Lloyd and V. Scholderer, 'Powel's "Historie" 1584', *Nat. Lib. of Wales Journal* III (1941–4), 15–18.

dedication of this work (1585) to Sir Philip Sidney, Powel asserts that he had collated Sir Henry's copy with two others, one supplied by Burghley, the other by a judge, named William Awbrey.[1] He tells his readers that it had once been his plan to omit from his edition all the fables and absurd miracles related by Gerald, but that his friends had dissuaded him from this, so that what he now presents is an unexpurgated text. What he does not reveal is that he has omitted, not only much of the chapter on St. Thomas of Canterbury, which was doubtless offensive to his stout Protestantism, but also all the unflattering judgements on the Welsh contained in the second book, *De Illaudilibus*. It was not without some justification that the Rolls Series editor referred, in this context, to 'bad, inexcusable dishonesty'.[2] None the less, the edition was reprinted, as it stood, by Camden in 1602 and 1603.

Other members of the governing classes appear as collectors, or patrons, or both. Bale told Parker, in 1560, that Lord William Paget (1505–63), who had obtained some of Leland's papers from Sir John Cheke, was 'thought to have many notable monuments.'[3] Lord Henry Howard (1540–1614), who became Earl of Northampton in 1604, was a member of the Society of Antiquaries, described as 'nobilium doctissimus et doctorum nobilissimus'.[4] Sidney's son-in-law, Henry Herbert (*c.* 1534–1601), Earl of Pembroke; Thomas Sackville (1536–1608), first Earl of Dorset; and George Lord Carew (1555–1629), Earl of Totnes, were all members of the same Society. Herbert's collections included coins and ancient sculpture, as well as manuscripts.[5] Sackville, 'excellently bred in all learning', inspired and wrote some of *The Mirror for Magistrates*. He made bequests of nearly 200 volumes to the Bodleian Library and showed concern for the preservation of the public records.[6] George Carew made most of his historical collections in Ireland and took occasion to attempt an English translation (paraphrase might be an apter word) of that part of Creton's poem on the Deposition of Richard II which related to it.

---

[1] Presumably William Aubrey (1529–95), a master in Chancery and chancellor to Archbishop Whitgift.

[2] *Giraldi Cambrensis Opera*, ed. F. J. Dimock, 7 vols. R.S. (1861–77), VI. liii–lviii.

[3] *Camb. Ant. Soc. Comm.* III. 173.   [4] *Archaeologia* I. xvi.

[5] Kenrick, op. cit., p. 166.

[6] *Bodleian Benefactors' Register* I. 1–4; *Archaeologia* I. xix.

The manuscript on which Carew worked had been in the possession of Dr. Dee in 1575 and was later presented by Carew to the library of the Archbishop of Canterbury.[1] The Lord Keeper of the Great Seal, Sir Nicholas Bacon (1509–79), was friendly with both Parker and Cecil, and it is said to have been at Parker's suggestion that, in 1574, he gave 73 volumes to the University Library at Cambridge. Bacon had acquired some of the lands of the Abbey of Bury St. Edmunds and in Bale's time he was in possession of a copy of Gildas and of the Chronicle ascribed to the Bury monk, John of Eversden.[2] The antiquarian interests of Sir Robert Hare (1530–1611), who had been to Caius College, were concentrated mainly on the history and privileges of his own university[3], and much of his long life was spent in collecting and arranging relevant documents, now in the archives of the University of Cambridge, to which he also bequeathed, in 1594, the early fifteenth-century treatise of Thomas Marhaunt on the privileges of the University. Two volumes of his collections were given to Caius, and among his numerous gifts to Trinity Hall were a 'Polychronicon' and Thomas of Elmham's History of St. Augustine's. On the first folio of the latter is found a note which may serve to remind us how uncertain the future looked to the Elizabethan collector:

This book formerly belonged to the convent of the blessed Apostles, Peter and Paul, or Augustine, outside the walls of the city of Canterbury. This monastery having been suppressed in the reign of King Henry VIII, and all the goods of the monks despoiled and turned to the king's use, by chance this book came into the hands of master Robert Hare, who gave it to the college or hall of the Holy Trinity in Cambridge, there to be kept safe and secure. On this condition, however, that if hereafter (*favente deo*), the monastery should happen to be rebuilt, then the Master and Fellows of the College or Hall of Holy Trinity aforesaid should cause the said book

---

[1] 'The Story of King Richard the Second, His last being in Ireland', *Hibernica*, ed. W. Harris (1747), pp. 23–8; *Archaeologia* XX (1824), 4; Lambeth MS. 598. For Carew's Irish collections, now at Lambeth, see *Cal. of the Carew MSS.*, Book of Howth etc. (1867). 4 volumes are now in the Bodleian Library, MSS. Laud, Misc. 611–14. Carew gave Bodley (in 1603) £95 for the purchase of books (*Benefactors' Register* I. 59).

[2] Bale, *Index*, pp. 94, 200.

[3] He did, however, present two volumes of collections relating to its history to Oxford.

to be restored to the monks of that convent. Since of right it belongs to them.[1]

Hare was at pains to copy the inscriptions of the hangings at Westminster and he is likely to have been responsible for the note in a thirteenth-century manuscript of the 'Vita Sancti Edwardi' which reads:

This Booke was left by Islip (sometime Abbot of Westminster) as he was visiting the Lands of his owne monastery in Glocestershire, with Thomas Seabrooke, then Abbot of Glocester.

Soe John Suttell (aged fowerscore and sixteen yeares) sayd, that be heard his father report, whoe was some time Butler to the sayd Seabrooke.

All the stories which are in the hangings of the Church of Westminster are heer related, and are hence taken.[2]

In the north of England, Lord William Howard of Naworth, 'Belted Will' (1563–1640), not only formed a large library which included such medieval historical texts as Howden, a fifteenth-century folio of Bede, the 'Topographica Hibernica', and Walter of Guisborough, many of which are now in the College of Arms;[3] he was also a member of the Society of Antiquaries and copied inscriptions for Camden;[4] and marginalia in the copy of Florence of Worcester, now in the Library of Trinity College Dublin (MS. 502, ff. 2, 10, 23v.) show that he consulted Lambarde on points of detail and was at pains to identify place-names. This was the Chronicle which he chose to publish early in his life, in 1592, in small quarto, with a dedication to Burghley, claiming that it had never before seen the light of day, although, in fact, the Chronicle of Marianus, which forms the basis of that of Florence of Worcester, had been printed at Basel in 1559. The best manuscripts, deriving respectively from Worcester and Abingdon,[5] were unknown to him. There are the inevitable mistakes in transcription. But Lord William did not deliberately tinker with his text and, in his preface, he is at pains to explain the double system of dating

---

[1] M. R. James, *Catalogue of the MSS. of Trinity Hall*, p. 1.

[2] James and Jenkins, *Catalogue of the MSS. in the Library of Lambeth Palace*, p. 804.

[3] Howden, *Chronica*, ed. Stubbs, I. lxxxii; *Hist. Eccles*, ed. Plummer, I. ccxxvi; *Gir. Cambr. Opera*, ed. Dimmock, V. xix; *Walter of Guisborough*, ed. H. Rothwell, p. xii.

[4] *Britannia* (1607), p. 644.   [5] C.C.C. Oxon. MS. 157; MS. Lambeth, 42.

used by Florence and to commend the book, not for any stylistic distinction, but because it is original and pleasant to read.[1]

The collection of Henry Savile (1568–1617) of Banke, near Halifax, contained a large number of historical works. The 'long chain of medieval chroniclers' listed in the catalogue of his library[2] begins with Bede and Gildas, Marianus Scotus, and Ailred of Rievaulx and includes Henry of Huntingdon, Geoffrey of Monmouth, Walter of Guisborough, Nowell's transcript of the 'Vita Edwardi Secundi', Thomas Walsingham (4 copies), Elmham, and Polydore Vergil, as well as the ubiquitous Giraldus and 'Polychronicon'. The Henry of Huntingdon (which Lord William Howard borrowed from him) is the only one to bear Savile's book-plate, with its legend, 'Henry Savill cawled longe Henri Savell ownes this booke, He that fynddes yt let hem have yt.' The provenance of many of the manuscripts remains obscure but it seems that, as might be expected, Savile drew largely on the northern houses,[3] from Byland, Fountains and Rievaulx in particular, but also from York, Durham, and Mount Grace.

In contrast to the great laymen, ecclesiastical antiquaries were in a minority in the latter part of the century. Yet if Edmund Grindal, who succeeded Parker, was a man with little sense of the past, no such charge could be laid against the third of Elizabeth's Archbishops, John Whitgift, who ruled at Canterbury from 1583 to 1604. In dedicating his *Annales* to this Archbishop, John Stow referred to his 'great loue and entire affection to all good letters in generall, and to the Antiquities in particular.' Whitgift had been Master of two Cambridge colleges, Pembroke and Trinity, and his magnificent donations to the latter, which included sixteen books from Buildwas Abbey,[4] reveal him as the owner of copies of Gervase of Canterbury, Robert of Avesbury, William of Malmesbury's 'Gesta Regum' and 'Gesta Pontificum', the Abingdon Chronicle, the 'Polychronicon' and the 'Brut'.[5] Working closely with Whitgift was Thomas Neville (brother to Parker's secretary) who became Master of Trinity in 1593 and Dean of Canterbury in 1597. Like Whitgift, Neville was a generous benefactor to his

---

[1] Reprinted, Frankfurt, 1601.

[2] B.M. Add. MS. 35213. See J. P. Gilson, 'The Library of Henry Savile of Banke', *Trans. Bibliog. Soc.* IX (1906–8), 127–210.

[3] N. R. Ker, *Medieval Libraries*, p. xiii.   [4] Ibid.

[5] See M. R. James, *Catalogue of the MSS. in the Library of Trinity College, Cambridge*.

college to which he bequeathed a number of standard medieval chronicles,[1] some of them previously the property of Parker. His gifts included the treatise, 'De Antiquitate Academiae Oxoniensis' (R. 5. 21), and Francis Godwin's catalogue of the Bishops of Bath and Wells (R. 7. 12). Less well-known collectors also included some clergymen. The Revd. Christopher Watson (d. 1581) was responsible for important collections entitled 'History of Duresme' which later passed into the Cottonian library.[2] Several of the manuscripts of the Revd. John Pilkington (c. 1529–1603), Archdeacon of Durham from 1562, found their way into the library of Sidney Sussex College; they included the two-volume MS. 30, comprising late medieval transcripts of the 'Historia Tripartita' and Bede's 'Ecclesiastical History'.[3] The Revd. Thomas Allen (1542–1632), an Oxford mathematician, left historical as well as mathematical manuscripts behind him. His name may be seen in a fifteenth-century copy of Bede, now in the Bodleian Library;[4] he was acquainted with Aethelweard's Chronicle, and he corresponded with Thomas James about the missing manuscript of Asser.[5] The Revd. George Savage, described by Professor Galbraith as 'a sixteenth-century Vicar of Bray', owned the manuscript of the 'Polychronicon' which is now in the Huntington Library in California.[6] The Revd. William Whitlock (d. 1584), prebendary of Curborough in Lichfield, compiled his history of the Church of Lichfield 'e veteribus historiis et monumentis'.[7]

A few other students of the past were academics. Such was William Marshall, Fellow of Merton from 1541, who in 1583 bequeathed a large collection of books to his college. Marshall's name occurs in seven medieval manuscripts which later belonged to Thomas Allen, and he also possessed copies of Ailred's Life of Edward the Confessor and of Geoffrey of Monmouth's 'De Gestis Regum'.[8] But the outstanding academic

---

[1] e.g. John of Glastonbury (R. 5. 16), Polychronicon (R. 5. 24), Geoffrey of Monmouth and William of Malmesbury (R. 5. 34), and the latter's Gesta Pontificum (R. 7. 4) which has the Neville arms on its cover.

[2] Vit. CIX, ff. 61–125.

[3] M. R. James, *Catalogue of the MSS. of Sidney Sussex College Cambridge*, p. 14.

[4] Bodley, MS. 302, f. 7.   [5] *Asser*, ed. W. H. Stevenson, p. xxxviii.

[6] *Huntington Library Quarterly*, XXIII (1959–60), 6.

[7] Bodleian MS. Ashmole 770.

[8] N. R. Ker, 'Oxford College Libraries in the Sixteenth Century', *Bodleian Library Record* VI (1957), 505–6.

antiquarian was the Warden of Merton, Henry Savile (1549–1622), whose notes on religious foundations in the British Isles found their way into the Bodleian Library[1] and who found time to spare from his multifarious activities to undertake the editing of no fewer than seven important medieval historical texts. The substantial folio volume, published in 1596 (with a dedication to the Queen) under the title *Rerum Anglicarum Scriptores post Bedam*, comprised William of Malmesbury's *Gesta Regum*, *Historia Novella*, and *Gesta Pontificum*, Henry of Huntingdon, Howden and the chronicles of Aethelweard and Ingulph. Savile's avowed object was to present something like a comprehensive picture of medieval English history, since all that Polydore Vergil had left was 'historiam . . . mendosam'. Among his chosen authors William of Malmesbury takes first place: he is reliable and mature. Next to him stand Henry of Huntingdon and Howden, good and diligent writers. Aethelweard and Ingulph are included because of their antiquity. Stubbs was satisfied that this edition of Malmesbury's *Gesta Regum* 'was based on a collation of good manuscripts, but with only an indistinct recognition of their relation and bearing upon one another.' They included the oldest recension, written *c.* 1130 (MS. Arundel 35), the second, written *c.* 1170 (Trin. Coll. Camb. MS. R. 7. 10), upon which Savile came increasingly to rely, and the fourteenth-century manuscript (Bodley 712), which was once his own property.[2] Some variant readings are given in the margins. Either deliberately or inadvertently, Savile did not recognize that, in 1587, Commelin had published at Heidelberg a collection of chronicles which included most of the first three books of the *Gesta Regum*, ascribed by him to an anonymous author. The *Historia Novella* was written as a sequel to the *Gesta Regum*, and for this Savile's principal source seems to have been a thirteenth-century manuscript[3] with corrections in a sixteenth-century hand, derived from a text of the late twelfth century which came to Trinity College from Archbishop Whitgift.[4] For the *Gesta Pontificum* he probably used a variety of

---

[1] MS. Bodley, e. Mus. 55, ff. 50–9. Savile seems to have been planning to write a history of English monasteries. Nicholson, *English Historical Library*, p. 143.

[2] William of Malmesbury, *De Gestis Regum Anglorum* (R.S. 2 vols. 1887–9), I. xciv.

[3] Trin. Coll. Camb. R. 7. i (739).

[4] R. 7. 10 (748); see *Historia Novella*, ed. K. R. Potter (1955).

manuscripts to which he could have had easy access since they were, or had been, in the possession of Parker or Whitgift.[1] The result was a 'mixed' text described by the Rolls Series editor as 'full of errors amounting at times to downright unintelligibility.'[2] The *Historia Anglorum* of Henry of Huntingdon now appeared in print for the first time and, like the *Gesta Pontificum*, is largely a patchwork based on the numerous manuscripts in circulation by the last decade of the sixteenth century. Manuscripts of Howden were also very numerous, and it appears that Savile had access to some of the best of them, including MS. Arundel 150, the property of Lord William Howard. But, whichever texts he used, the editor followed his normal policy of omitting, abridging, and 'improving' at will. One peculiarly unfortunate emendation, which makes Pipin and Charles consult William the Conqueror on their right to take the title of King, derives from the Arundel MS.[3]

Curiously enough, it was his edition of the short Chronicle of Aethelweard (which occupies only 20 of the 1,000-odd pages of his massive volume) that was to prove Savile's most valuable legacy to posterity. For the only known manuscript of this work[4] was practically destroyed in the fire of 1731, and the modern critical edition has had to be based on Savile's text, supplemented by the charred fragments which survive. The coincidence between the two suggests that this was the manuscript which Savile used.[5] Ingulph's Chronicle of Croyland Abbey likewise survives in only one manuscript and that a sixteenth-century transcript,[6] but this does not coincide with Savile's printed text, the source of which remains unknown.[7]

Among schoolmaster medievalists, the best-known, after Camden himself, was probably John Twyne who, as has been seen, helped Parker with his collections. The most valuable of Twyne's own manuscripts, most of which went to Corpus Christi

[1] C.U.L. MSS. Ff. 1. 25, C.C.C. Camb. 43, Trin. Coll. Camb. R. 7. 13, and R. 7. 28, all bear the marks of Parker's secretaries. The arms of Whitgift are on the cover of MS. Trin. Coll. Camb. R. 5. 36.

[2] *De Gestis Pontificum*, ed. N. E. S. A. Hamilton (1870), p. x.

[3] *Scriptores post Bedam*, pp. 345, 471v. For a detailed account of Savile's edition see Howden, *Chronica*, ed. Stubbs, II. xv–xix.

[4] MS. Cott., Otho A. X.

[5] *The Chronicle of Aethelweard*, ed. A. Campbell (1962), pp. ix–xii.

[6] B.M. Arundel MS. 178.

[7] *Ingulph's Chronicle of Croyland Abbey*, ed. W. de G. Birch (1883).

College, Oxford, was probably the 'B' MS. of the Anglo-Saxon Chronicle.[1] Twyne was a remarkable character. He grew rich on the profits of his free grammar-school in Canterbury, bought property in Kent, represented the city in the parliament of 1555 and served as its mayor in the following year. Yet, during an ecclesiastical visitation in 1560, he was ordered, not only 'to abstayn from ryot and drunkeness', but also (probably because he was suspected of popery) 'not to intermeddle with any public office in the town.'[2] In his *De Rebus Albionicis*, dedicated to his son, Thomas, who published it in 1590, John Twyne expresses his earnest desire that Thomas, who was about to enter Corpus Christi College, Oxford, should combine knowledge of antiquity with the reading of philosophy, as he himself had done, ignorance of history and antiquity being only less deplorable than ignorance of divinity.[3] The theme of the book is a discussion of antiquarian topics which is said to have taken place at the summer lodgings of John Foche, last Abbot of St. Augustine's, between himself, Nicholas Wotton, who was then prior, and a number of young men, including the author. Sir Thomas Kendrick has emphasized the originality of Twyne's thinking about the British history, not all of it, however, happily inspired, for it was Twyne who first introduced the Phoenicians, 'eager for Cornish tin'.[4]

A small group whose profession forced them to be, in some sense, antiquaries was that of the heralds who, in the age of Elizabeth, were flourishing as never before. From the Queen downwards, the nobility, the gentry and all who aspired to their ranks were, in the words of J. H. Round, 'pedigree-mad'.[5] To establish their claims such evidence as ancient charters and seals was a necessity; and a happy hunting-ground lay open to the forger. Round has shown that men of the status of Sir William Dethick, Garter King of Arms from 1586 to 1605, Richard St. George, Norroy from 1603 to 1623 and Clarenceux

---

[1] MS. Cott., Tib. A. V. See R. Flower in *PBA* XXI (1935), 69.

[2] A. F. Pollard in *D.N.B.*

[3] *De Rebus Albionicis*, p. 3. 'Atque certe fuit mihi semper haec mens, quod secundum diuinorum oraculorum, in quibus aeternae salutis cuiusque spes continetur, ignorationem, nulla potuerit esse gravior, quam antiquitatis et historiarum imperitia . . .'.

[4] Kendrick, op. cit., pp. 105–8; cf. Stuart Piggott in *English Historical Scholarship in the Sixteenth and Seventeenth Centuries* (1956), p. 99.

[5] *Family Origins* (1930), p. 5.

from 1623 to 1635, and even the great Camden himself, Clarenceux from 1597, were taken in by these forgers.[1] That this should have been so was rather less reprehensible than Round suggested, for the age was nothing if not credulous and critical genealogy was as yet unborn.[2] And Camden was by no means the only genuine antiquarian among the heralds. 'That notorious herald, William Dethick, Garter' is thought to have bought many books that had been the property of one of his predecessors, Sir Thomas Wriothesley. He was a member of the Society of Antiquaries to which he read several papers. Richard St. George, Windsor Herald, 1602; Norroy, 1604; and Clarenceux, 1623, owned two manuscripts now in the Bodleian Library, 'Matthew of Westminster' (MS. Laud, 572) and the 'Polychronicon' (MS. Laud, 545). The high standard maintained by Robert Glover, Somerset Herald from 1571 to 1588 and described by Sir Anthony Wagner as a 'critical scholar of the first rank',[3] is admitted even by Round. MS. Ashmole 848 is a volume of his collections. In the books of his visitations, some of them undertaken as deputy to William Flower, Norroy, 1562–88, we find entered, for the first time, copies of charters, sketches of their seals, and extracts from the public records used as evidences of the arms and pedigrees entered.[4] And when Francis Thynne became Lancaster Herald in 1602, his scholarly reputation was already well established. He was a leading member of the Society of Antiquaries to which he delivered several discourses; he has been described as 'at least potentially, and for his day, a really great Chaucerian scholar';[5] he was one of the continuators of Holinshed and his numerous collections in the Cottonian Library testify to his zeal for transcribing medieval historical texts and monumental inscriptions. He copied passages from the lives of Patrick, Becket, and other saints, from Henry of Huntingdon and the 'Scalacronica' and from inscriptions in Kentish churches; and he transcribed and

[1] Ibid., pp. 5, 12, 69, 88.
[2] See A. Wagner, *The Records and Collections of the College of Arms* (1952), pp. 16–17.
[3] Wagner, op. cit., p. 17.
[4] e.g. the Visitation of Staffordshire in 1583, ed. H. S. Grazebrook, *William Salt Archaeological Society* III (1883). Lord Treasurer Winchester, in 1567, referred to 'Heraulds, that maketh their Books at Aduenture and not by the Records', Leland, *Collectanea* II. 655.
[5] H. R. Steeves, *Learned Societies and English Literary Scholarship* (1913), p. 16.

translated passages from Saxon chronicles and homilies.[1]
One of his commonplace books included notes on Knighton,
the account of the Rising of 1381 from the Anonimalle Chronicle
of St. Mary's York, and extracts from 'the grete-lieger booke
belonginge to the Abbey of Osney in Oxfordshyre borrowed
of Mr. Stone.'[2]

Thynne was a lawyer; and so were many of the Tudor
medievalists. One of the most enterprising was Nicholas
Brigham, 'Anglicarum antiquitatum amator maximus', who
died in London in 1558. He was an Oxford man, a teller of the
Exchequer, best known to posterity as the builder of Chaucer's
tomb in Westminster Abbey. Writing to Parker after Brigham's
death, Bale asserted that his executors had 'many noble anti-
quytees', and we know that among them were Gildas, the letters
of Eadmer and several medieval chronicles, including the Matthew Paris which was in Brigham's hands before it passed to
Cecil.[3] William Fleetwood (c. 1535–94), Recorder of London
and twice member of Parliament for the City, possessed manuscripts of the London 'Liber Custumarum'.[4] Dr. Henry Johns,
admitted a member of Doctors' Commons in 1552, was at one
time owner of the manuscript of the 'Historia Novorum', now
at Corpus Christi College, Cambridge.[5] George Gilpin (c. 1514–
1602), who had studied civil law at Mechlin and became a
trusted English agent in the Low Countries, was well acquainted
with the fine volume of 'Matthew of Westminster' which had
turned up in the house of an Antwerp merchant.[6] Francis Tate
(1560–1616) of Magdalen College, Oxford, and the Middle
Temple, was a man of considerable learning. A member of the
Society of Antiquaries, he kept a small journal of its proceedings
from 1590 to 1601.[7] From a manuscript in Tate's autograph,
Hearne listed twenty-eight subjects on which he wrote discourses, one being an essay on the antiquity of Parliament.[8]
In 1589 he made the first fairly full transcript of the 'Textus

[1] B.M. MS. Cott., Cleopatra C. III, ff. 49b, 50, 158, 210, 55–8, 97b, 155b.

[2] B.M. Stowe MS. 1047, ff. 22, 64b, 102.

[3] *Camb. Ant. Soc. Comm.* III. 167; Bale, *Index*, pp. 93, 64.

[4] N. R. Ker, 'Liber Custumarum and other MSS. formerly at the Guildhall',
The Guildhall Miscellany I (1952–9), p. 41.

[5] *Historia Novorum*, ed. M. Rule, R.S. (1884), p. xii.

[6] See article on Gilpin in *D.N.B.*; *Camb. Ant Soc Comm.* III. 166.

[7] *The English Library before 1700*, pp. 183–6.

[8] Hearne, *Curious Discourses*, p. xiii; ibid., ed. Ayloffe, I. 302.

Roffensis' that has survived;[1] and he gave Coke a volume containing abstracts of the Parliament Rolls.[2] His manuscripts of the London 'Liber Custumarum', some of which were afterwards acquired by Cotton, came to him from Fleetwood. Joseph Holland of the Inner Temple, who read half a dozen papers to the Society of Antiquaries, sometimes showed his collections of coins and charters there.[3] Notable, too, was the Scottish judge, Sir Thomas Craig, who had studied law in Paris from 1555 to 1561 and whose substantial Latin treatise, *Jus Feudale*, was published in 1603, with a dedication to James I. Craig, whose main objective was to show that the feudal law of England and Scotland had a common origin, argued forcefully that feudalism is post-1066, whereas payment of heriot was an ancient custom.[4]

Other collectors fit into none of these categories or remain little more than names. William Cary, who figures in Bale's *Index* as owner of a 'Descriptio Kambriae', and was lent a copy of Robert of Avesbury, possibly by Joscelyn, may be the same as the 'Wyllyam Carre at London' who, so Bale informed Parker, had Howden and some of the works of Giraldus Cambrensis.[5] The fly-leaf of a manuscript of the French 'Brut', which had belonged to John Parker, has a note of the foundation of Cambridge University, Anno Mundi 4321, 'hoc in libro quondam Mri [Magistri] Record iam in manibus W. Carye.'[6] John Ducket of Lynn owned some collections of Old English laws and a manuscript of 'Matthew of Westminster' which Bale believed to be still in the possession of his widow in 1560.[7] Reginald Mohun owned part of John Skewys's transcript of Matthew Paris:[8] and Richard Atkyns of Lincoln gave a volume of medieval tracts to Lambarde.[9]

In a class by themselves stand two notable eccentrics with antiquarian tastes, Dr. John Caius (1510–73) and Dr. John

[1] B.M. MS. Cott., Julius C. II; see P. Sawyer, *Textus Roffensis* I (1957), p. 20.

[2] F. S. Fussner, *The Historical Revolution* (1962), pp. 83–4.

[3] *The English Library before 1700*, p. 188.   [4] *Jus Feudale*, pp. 29–30.

[5] *Index*, p. 427; James and Jenkins, *Lambeth MSS.*, pp. 708–9; *Camb. Ant. Soc. Comm.* III. 166.

[6] James, *Trinity College Cambridge MSS.* II. 229–30 (MS. R. 7. 14). For Record see above p. 25.

[7] *Index*, pp. 52, 288, 473, *Camb. Ant. Soc. Comm.* III. 166.

[8] B.M. MS. Harl. 2258; *Index*, pp. 255–6.

[9] *Hist. MSS. Com., 4th Report*, App. 411.

Dee (1527–1608). A Fellow of Gonville Hall, Cambridge, under Henry VIII, Caius went to Italy to study Greek and medicine, graduating M.D. from Padua in 1541 and becoming physician, first to Edward VI and then to Mary. He refounded Gonville Hall as Gonville and Caius College and served as its Master from 1559 to 1573. Dr. M. R. James's analysis of the authorities listed by Caius at the end of his *De Antiquitate Cantabrigiensis Academiae* shows that he had access to a large number of books afterwards bought by Cotton, most of which, like the 'Eulogium Historiarum' (B.M. MS. Galba E. VII) which was owned by a Mr. Dickenson of Poplar who afterwards gave it to Dr. Dee, were probably in private hands in or near London when he saw them.[1] Caius had recourse to the libraries of other Cambridge colleges, Peterhouse, King's and, probably, Queens', and he made copious use of the Parker collection before it passed to Corpus Christi College. Writing from Herefordshire in April 1572, his old school-friend, Richard Willison, referred to Caius's antiquarian tastes: 'I have said often tymes that I have knowen you almost these fiftie yeares of good remembraunce, & besides the benefight of greate memorie you have been as errant a drudge in tumbling over of papers, that scase the like is anywhere to be had.'[2] The subjects on which Caius wrote ranged from Greek pronunciation to British dogs. Unhappily, much of his intellectual energy was dissipated on the fantastic controversy with his namesake, Thomas Caius, Registrar of the University of Oxford, over the relative antiquity of the two Universities. The dispute went back to the Middle Ages; but the Elizabethan controversy originated during the Queen's visit to Cambridge in August 1564, when the Cambridge orator stated briefly that Cambridge was much more ancient than Oxford. It was in answer to this that Thomas Caius obtained leave to present his 'Assertio Antiquitatis Oxoniensis Academiae' to Elizabeth, when she visited Oxford two years later. This, it seems, had not been intended for publication; but John Caius got hold of it and printed it as a postscript to his own much more elaborate *De Antiquitate*

---

[1] Note by Dr. James in *The Works of John Caius*, ed. E. S. Roberts (1912), pp. viii–x. The manuscript has a note 'Ioh Dee 1574 Sept 25 of the gift of Mr. Dickenson at Popular by London in 155.' M. R. James, 'Lists of Manuscripts formerly owned by Dr. John Dee, '*Trans. Bibliog. Soc. Suppt.* i (1921), p. 18.

[2] J. Venn, Memoir of John Caius, ibid., p. 43.

Cantabrigiensis Academiae, in the first edition of which (1568) he concealed his identity, being barefaced enough to pose as a disinterested observer from London. The Cambridge claim was to foundation by the Spanish prince, Cantaber, Anno Mundi 4317, or 4321, and that Paris, Oxford and Cologne were all her daughters. The Oxford claim was that King Alfred founded University College and restored the University which had its origin in the migration thither of some Greek philosophers who had come with Brutus to England and settled at Cricklade (Greeklade). One of the most remarkable features of the whole controversy, it has been justly said, is the vast number of authors quoted and the worthlessness of most of them.[1] Well might Richard Willison wonder how his friend was 'hable to gather suche a fardell of straunge Antiquities together.'[2] Caius bequeathed to his own College 'all my books newe and olde wherein thes words be written, Johannes Caius Collegio suo dono dedit'. None of these works was historical. As his literary executor he selected his friend Matthew Parker, to whom he gave 'all my books which I have made not yet printed, and all those that I have made that be printed and augmented, upon condicion that it maie plaise his grace to cause them to be printed, as my trust is wholie in him that he will so doe in a faire letter and forme all togeather in one volume.'[3] Parker fulfilled these instructions by arranging for John Day to print a second edition (1574) of the *De Antiquitate Cantabrigiensis Academiae*, in which the author's name appears for the first time. At the end of it there was printed another treatise found among Caius' papers and entitled *Historia Cantabrigiensis Academiae* which purported to be a judicious summing-up of the whole question from a historical standpoint.

Dr. Dee, at once mathematician, astrologer, physician, and —many believed—sorcerer, was also a zealous collector of antiquities.[4] A Fellow of St. John's College, Cambridge, and one of the original Fellows of Trinity, Dee became rector of Upton-upon-Severn in 1553. It was early in January 1556 that he presented to Queen Mary his remarkable petition 'for the

[1] J. Parker, *The Early History of Oxford* (1885), p. 38; see also Kendrick, op. cit. pp. 76–7.
[2] *Works of Caius*, p. 42.   [3] Ibid., pp. 73, 75.
[4] The most recent study of John Dee is by Richard Deacon (1968).

recovery and preservation of ancient writers and monuments.'[1] In this he refers to 'the spoile and destruction of so many and so notable libraries, wherein lay the treasure of all Antiquity.' '. . . . Yet if, in time, great and speedy diligence be shewed, the remnants of such incredible store . . . might be saved and recovered.' In the articles which accompanied the petition Dee made what presumably he judged to be a number of practical suggestions. (1) The Queen's commission should be granted 'for the seeing and perusing of all places within this her Graces realm, where any notable or excellent monument may be found, or is known to be.' Such monuments as the owner wishes to retain should be borrowed by the Royal Commissioner and transcribed in the Royal Library. (2) An order should be made for payment of all necessary charges. (3) The Commission should be despatched with all possible speed, lest rumours of it 'might cause many to hide and convey their good and ancient writers'. (4) A suitable repository for the books should be selected and (5) Dr. Dee himself will procure for the Royal Library 'all the famous and worthy monuments, that are in the notablest Librarys beyond the sea (as in Vaticana at Rome, S. Marci at Venice, and the like at Bononia, Florence, Vienna etc.) . . . the charges thereof (beside the journeying) to stand in the copying of them out, and the carryage into this realm only.' A laudable project, no doubt; but hardly one to commend itself to a Government struggling for survival; and the petition fell on deaf ears.

That the subject of the monastic books was still in Dee's mind some twenty years later is evident from the letter he addressed to Burghley, in October 1574, asking, *inter alia*, for an introduction to the Keeper of the Records of Wigmore Castle:

For that at my late being there, I espied an heap of old papers and parchments, obligations, acquittances, accounts, &c. (in tyme past belonging to the abbey of Wigmor) and there to lye rotting spoyled and tossed, in an old decayed chappel, not committed to any mans speciall charge: but thre quarters of them, I understand, to have byn taken away, by diuerse (eyther taylors or other) in tymes past. Now my fantasie is, that in some of them will be some mention made of Noble men and Jentlemen of those dayes. Whereby (eyther for chronicle, or pedigree) som good matter may be collected out of them by me (at my leysor) by the way of a recreation.[1]

We do not know the results of this appeal, but we do know that Dee had a very valuable library. Two almost identical catalogues of his books survive in his autograph (B.M. MS. Harl. 1879, ff. 20–108, and Trin. Coll. Camb. MS. O. 4. 20) each bearing the heading 'Catalogus Librorum Bibliothecae Externae Mortlacensis D.John Dee Ao.1583, 6 Sept.'[2] From his private diary, we learn that Dee left his house at Mortlake (for Poland) on 21 September of that year.[3] After his departure, some of his neighbours—doubtless, those who were suspicious of his occult activities—destroyed many of the books.[4] Other books were acquired later, so that the Mortlake list as it stands does not constitute a full record of the manuscripts Dee possessed at his death. Also extant are two lists of manuscripts earlier than 1583 (C.C.C. Oxonford, MS. 191 and B.M. Add. MS. 35213, ff. 1–4b). Dee was always in financial difficulties: litigation probably relating to his debts prevented the dispersal of his library until 1626, eighteen years after his death. When it was finally sold, the considerable purchases made by Archbishop Ussher, Sir Robert Cotton and, above all, by Brian Twyne—for a number of John Twyne's manuscripts from St. Augustine's had come into Dee's hands—resulted in many of the books finding their way ultimately to Trinity College Dublin, the British Museum, and Corpus Christi College, Oxford. The great majority relate, of course, to natural science, but history is well represented. Dr. M. R. James was successful in identifying a considerable proportion of the books listed in the Mortlake catalogue, and we know that these included a Bede, which may be Trinity College, Dublin, MS. 492, Ailred's Life of Edward the Confessor (B.M. MS. Harl. 200), inscribed 'Ioannes Dee 1575', the 'Eulogium Historiarum' (MS. Galba E. VII) and a 'Polychronicon', now at the Queen's College, Oxford (MS. 307). Humfrey Lhuyd's History of the Princes (Bodleian MS.

---

[1] *Letters of Eminent Literary Men*, p. 39.

[2] M. R. James, 'Lists of Manuscripts formerly owned by Dr. John Dee', *Trans. Bibliog. Soc. Suppt. i* (1921); cf. C. E. Wright, op. cit., p. 232.

[3] *The Private Diary of Dr. John Dee and Catalogue of his Library of Manuscripts*, ed. J. O. Halliwell, Camden Society (1842), p. 21.

[4] Evidence of this spoliation comes from Dee's own marginal notes in the Trinity College MS. of the catalogue. See M. R. James, op. cit., p. 4, n. 1.

F

Ashmole, 847) formed part of a tall folio manuscript neatly written in the hand of Robert Glover, Somerset Herald, which had been given to Dee in 1575 by his cousin, Oliver Lloyd of Welshpool. Among manuscripts not in the Mortlake catalogue is Creton's poem on the Deposition of Richard II (Lambeth MS. 598, Pt. III) which has a note at the end of the text (f. 75b) that John Dee, in 1575, 'gave for this boke a boke of the foundation of [blank] in Oxfordshyre.'

From this brief survey it may be seen that the taste for history was widespread throughout the land, shared by nobility, gentry and at least some members of almost every profession—heralds, lawyers, parsons, dons, doctors, and mathematicians. The most conspicuous absentees are the bishops, which seems surprising in view of the example set by Parker and Whitgift, but may be explicable, at least in part, by the tensions besetting the episcopate in an age of religious revolution. Numerically, the antiquaries were fairly evenly divided between the two universities; and a few of the most eminent, including Leland, Cheke, Recorde and Lawrence Nowell, had been members of both. But the names of Bale, Parker, Whitgift, Caius, and Dee lend a unique distinction to Cambridge antiquarian studies in the Tudor period. And whatever their main preoccupations—the encouragement of students, the salvaging and transcribing of manuscripts, the recovery of Old English, the editing of texts—all were united in their determination to preserve the memorials of the centuries which had made Britain what she was.

IV

ARCHIVISTS AND RECORD-SEARCHERS

RECORD-SEARCHING and appreciation of the importance of records, as distinct from chronicles, histories, and general literature, were no new discoveries in the sixteenth century. But historians like Matthew Paris in the thirteenth century, or the anonymous canon of Bridlington, in the fourteenth, who compiled books of documents to serve as appendixes to their work, were, almost without exception, writing contemporary, or near-contemporary, history; and such documents as they included were documents current in their own day, copies of which often found their way into the monastic *scriptoria*. The nearest we get, in medieval times, to an attempt to use the records of the past as an aid to its under-standing is in one or two histories of individual religious communities, such as Matthew Paris's 'Vitae Abbatum S. Albani', or Thomas Elmham's 'Historia Monasterii S. Augustini Cantuariensis' where full use is made of earlier charters and privileges, granted, or believed to have been granted, to the house. New incentives to record-searching appeared, how-ever, in the age of the Reformation. The flood of literature let loose upon the world by the dissolution of the monasteries included cartularies, correspondence, legal collections and state papers, many of which were salvaged by the antiquaries: Lord William Howard alone had more than twenty monastic cartularies in his hands.[1] The value of such material, hitherto little known outside the precincts of a particular house, now began to be more widely appreciated. Leland's *Collectanea* include extracts from archives, ancient charters, public and private monuments; and though he, Bale, and most of their contemporaries and immediate successors, may have been primarily bibliophiles, interested in collecting old books and in preserving the names of classical and medieval authors, rather than in records as such, they did not attempt to draw a firm

[1] G. R. C. Davis, *Medieval Cartularies of Great Britain* (1958), affords ample illus-tration of the point.

line between the two types of material. Again, the lively contemporary interest in English geography found expression in a new kind of study, semi-historical, semi-topographical, for which (since archaeology was still in the main a closed book) the most important evidence available was often that of written records. And the contemporary impulse (amply illustrated by the communications laid before the Society of Antiquaries) to demonstrate the antiquity of English institutions also tended to drive scholars back to the records. Many members of the Society were lawyers, and antiquity was of the essence of the common law. Their legal training did not inhibit the lawyers from swallowing myth in large doses, but it had accustomed them to the handling of record evidence and taught them some appreciation of its significance.

From the standpoint of the antiquarian record-searcher, the whole question of the custody and accessibility of the public records was obviously of the first importance. Much depended on the capacities of the custodians, for these posts were by no means sinecures, the state of the public records in the reign of Elizabeth being little short of chaotic.[1] In the chapel of the Rolls House in Chancery Lane, originally a home for converted Jews, the Chancery records had been stored until the fifteenth century, when shortage of space caused an overflow to the White Tower. Earlier attempts to turn the Tower, if not into a Record Office, at least into a clearing-house for records, had broken down, but the records of the common law courts to the end of the fourteenth century remained there, together with the later Chancery records. Subsequent records of these courts were stored in the Exchequer Treasuries in Westminster Abbey until the end of the fifteenth century, when they began to be accumulated in their own offices. A general policy of dispersal affected even the records of the Exchequer, some of which were now finding their way into various houses and offices in Westminster. In view of the prevailing confusion, it was fortunate indeed that a number of competent scholars should have been put in charge of at least some of these archives.

It was on 11 April 1567 that Lord Treasurer Winchester

[1] R. B. Wernham, 'The Public Records in the Sixteenth and Seventeenth Centuries', in *English Historical Scholarship in the Sixteenth and Seventeenth Centuries*, ed. L. Fox (1956), pp. 10–14.

wrote to Cecil asking that the records of Parliament and Chancery might be delivered to 'Mr. Bowier, Keeper of the Queen's Records in the Tower', which was large enough to house a great quantity. Mr. Bowier, the letter continues, 'will see them sorted, and kept to the Queen's honour, and common Weall of her Nobles and Subjects.' As evidence of his capacity, the Lord Treasurer had 'a book of his making for me . . . declaring my Armes and Pedigree, which I think bee well done' and which he had asked Lord Leicester to show to the Queen.[1] This was William Bowyer, owner of several valuable manuscripts, including the 'C' MS. of the Anglo-Saxon Chronicle, Laurence Nowell's transcript of the 'Vita et Mors Edwardi Secundi', William of Malmesbury's 'De Antiquitate Glastoniensis Ecclesiae'[2] and Adam Murimuth. He, it seems, was anxious to enlarge his empire by bringing the records of Parliament and Chancery under his control—possibly by way of *riposte* to an attempt made a few years before by one of the Exchequer Chamberlains to obtain a key to the records in the Tower.[3] The Queen agreed and duly sent her warrant to Sir William Cordell, master of the Rolls, ordering that the records of the Chancery be brought into the Tower and delivered to William Bowyer.[4] The order was naturally unwelcome to Cordell; and it signalized the opening of a protracted wrangle between him and Bowyer and succeeding Masters and Keepers which culminated in a Star Chamber case under James I, when it seems to have been settled in favour of the Master. Meantime, the Chancery records remained where they were, in the Rolls Chapel and the Rolls House. Bowyer did, however, make extracts from most of the Rolls of Parliament that were in his custody and, according to Roger Twysden, writing in the middle of the seventeenth century, these passed into the library of Sir Desmond D'Ewes, where he himself had consulted them.[5]

About 1578, Sir Thomas Heneage, Chancellor of the Duchy of Lancaster, was appointed Keeper, jointly with his brother Michael (1540–1600), a former Fellow of St. John's College,

---

[1] Leland, *Collectanea* II. 655.

[2] Nichols, *Bibliotheca* I. 510; M. R. James, *Catalogue of the MSS. of Trinity College Cambridge* II. 198. See C. E. Wright in *Trans. Camb. Bibliographical Soc.* III. 231–2.

[3] For details of this incident see Wernham, op. cit., pp. 16–18.

[4] *Collectanea* II. 656–7.

[5] F. Smith Fussner, *The Historical Revolution 1580–1640* (1962), p. 85.

Cambridge, who assisted Robert Hare with his collections of Cambridge records. Michael Heneage held the office of Keeper for over twenty years and he may have given expert assistance to Stow. One volume of 'Collections out of various charters, registers and instruments relating to many Noble Families in England', written in his hand, was bought by Cotton from his widow.[1] A learned clerk of the Tower records who flourished about 1580 was Thomas Talbot ('Limping Tom'), a Lancashire gentleman and possibly a member of Gray's Inn. Though Dr. Dee had 'some wordes of unkendnes' with him in the summer of 1582, their quarrel was soon composed and they 'parted frendely'.[2] Talbot was an indefatigable record-searcher to whom Camden acknowledged his indebtedness, describing him as a diligent examiner of records and perfect master of our antiquities'.[3] Cotton had some of his collections concerning abbeys and various historical matters, extracted from chronicles, rolls of noble familes and their pedigrees;[4] others were drawn from the Inquests post Mortem,[5] from the Patent, Close and a few Fine Rolls,[6] from an account of proceedings at the Court of Claims at the coronations of Richard II and his two immediate successors,[7] and from other sources as well. He was a member of the Society of Antiquaries and in 1591 joined in a discussion on the antiquity of the shires with Arthur Agarde and Francis Thynne.[8] We may also remember Peter Osborne (1521–92), whose position as Remembrancer to the Lord Treasurer of the Exchequer brought him into contact with the records. He married a niece of Sir John Cheke, the inheritor of Leland's great collections, was said to have acquired some of Bale's books, and was appointed by Parker as one of his executors. It must have been in his official capacity that he compiled for William Lambarde, probably from one of the subsidy rolls, the list of Kentish hundreds, cities, boroughs, vills and demesne lands which ends with the note, 'Hucusque extractum est per Petrum Osborne: 24 Jun: 1582'.[9]

Lambarde himself became a record-keeper in his latter years.

[1] B.M. MS, Cott., Claudius C. 1.   [2] *Diary of John Dee*, p. 16.
[3] *Britannia*, ed. Gough, I. cxlviii.   [4] B.M. MS. Cott., Vesp. D. XVII.
[5] B.M. Add. MS. 26717.   [6] Bodleian MS. Ashmole 799 ii.
[7] B.M. MS. Lansdowne 279.   [8] Hearne, *Curious Discourses* (1775), I. 27–8.
[9] Bodleian MS. Hatton 41, f. 87v.

Elizabeth made him Keeper of the Records at the Rolls Chapel in 1597 and Keeper of the Records at the Tower in 1601. This was a fitting climax to a life much of which had been devoted to the study of archives. Lambarde (1536–1601), the son of a London alderman, had migrated to Kent. He was a lawyer by profession, a member of Lincoln's Inn, and a friend of Lawrence Nowell, with whom he collaborated in some of his early work. No doubt it was his legal training which kindled his interest in Old English, for he saw, we are told, 'that he should lay the foundations of his professional knowledge deep, by going back to the customs and jurisprudence of the Saxon times.'[1] In 1568, he published, under the title *Archaionomia*,[2] a Latin translation of the laws of some of the Anglo-Saxon kings and of the treaties made with Guthrum by Alfred and Edward the Elder, some, perhaps most, of which had been collected by Nowell. To these were added the Latin laws of Edward the Confessor and William I. The collection, dedicated to Sir William Cordell, was far from complete and the translation often faulty; but Lambarde does offer his readers some explanation of Old English legal terms, like heriot, frankpledge and ordeal, an index, and a map of England under the Heptarchy. The venture is noteworthy as the first of its kind and was commended by Parker in the preface to his Asser. Nearly thirty years lay between the publication of *Archaionomia* and the author's appointment as Master of the Rolls. Much of this time was spent by Lambarde in searching records and making collections for his *Perambulation of Kent*, first published in 1576,[3] and for the topographical survey of the whole country which he had in mind for some years, as well as in the exercise of his duties as a Justice of the Peace (from August 1579) and in the collection of material for his treatises on this office,[4] and on the High Courts of Justice in England.[5] Traces of his labours may be seen in the admirable notes on *gavelkind* (now in the Parker collection at Corpus Christi College);[6] in collections such as that (now B.M. MS. Cott., Vesp. A. V.) which includes excerpts from the Perambulation of the Forests and from the

[1] Nichols, *Bibliotheca* I. 494.
[2] Printed by Day, 4to.
[3] Below pp. 135–38.
[4] *Eirenarcha* (1581).
[5] *Archeion*, published by Lambarde's grandson, Thomas Lambarde, in 1635.
[6] MS. 101, ff. 336–40.

'Textus Roffensis';[1] and among the Stowe MSS. where are preserved his transcript of the 'Dialogus de Scaccario' with its dedication to the Solicitor-General, Sir Thomas Bromley (1572) and a collection of documents relating to the Chancery.[2] For the *Perambulation of Kent* he drew freely on Domesday Book, and on royal charters such as that of Henry IV to Hythe 'which I haue seene under his seal'.[3] In his will, drawn up in 1597, the year of his appointment to the Rolls Chapel, Lambarde bequeathed to his son, 'my two severall chestes or cabynetes of evidences and wrytinges as my sondry presses and chestes of bookes of learning and of reckninges and accomptes, together with myne instrumentes of learninge and mapps.'[4] Needless to say, Lambarde's transcripts do not measure up to the standards of modern criticism. Like Parker, with whom he had occasionally collaborated, he took great liberties with his manuscripts. He altered the spelling and was guilty of many other inaccuracies.[5] Yet he was not blind to the difficulties and in the letter dated 19 December, 1587, which accompanied his Christmas present to Sir Thomas Egerton, we catch a glimpse of him as palaeographer. This present was a manuscript of the 'Dialogus de Scaccario' and, after apologizing for his inability to procure a better copy, Lambarde continues,

And yet I must acknowledge, that I have reaped some fruite in my tyme by evel writing of bookes, which (if I had mett withall in good Letters or prynte), would have escaped me. For suche is the benefite thereof, that (occasioned by earnest beholding, or iterating of the woordes, that be hardly and disordrely written) the memorie taketh a better impression, then it dothe of that, which (throughe the beawtie and facilitie therof) the eye runneth over so faste and lightly that no steppe, or sense thereof is lefte in the mynde.[6]

Lambarde's appointment as a Master in Chancery in 1592 no doubt paved the way for his friend Egerton (who became

---

[1] Lambarde saw this text in 1573, the date of an initialled note on f. 1. *Textus Roffensis*, ed. P. Sawyer (1957), p. 20.

[2] B.M. Stowe MSS. 311, 415.   [3] *Perambulation* (1576), p. 142.

[4] *Archaeologia Cantiana* V (1863), 254.

[5] For unfavourable criticisms, see Stevenson, *Asser*, p. xix; Sir F. Madden's preface to Matthew Paris, *Hist. Anglorum* I. lxx and Earle and Plummer, *Two Saxon Chronicles* II. xxxiv.

[6] V. B. Heltzel, 'Sir Thomas Egerton and William Lambard', *HLQ* XI (1947-8), 202.

Master of the Rolls in 1594 and Lord Keeper in 1596) to arrange that he should be entrusted with the custody of the records housed in the Rolls Chapel, and subsequently of those in the Tower. That he took seriously what must have been a highly congenial duty is evident from his own notes (happily preserved among his family papers) describing the audience which the Queen granted him in Greenwich Palace, only a couple of weeks before his death, when he was 64 and she was 67. This was to allow him opportunity to present his

Pandecta of all her rolls, bundells, membranes, and parcells, that be reposed in her Majesties Tower at London.[1] . . . *Her Majestie* cherrfullie received the same into her hands, saying 'You intended to present this book unto me by the Countesse of Warwicke; but I will none of that; for if any subject of mine do me a service, I will thankfully accept it from his own hands': then opening the book, said 'You shall see that I can read'; and so, with an audible voice, read over the epistle, and the title, so readily and distinctly pointed, that it might perfectly appear, that she well understood and conceived the same. Then she descended from the beginning of King John, till the end of Richard III, that is 64 pages, serving xi kings, containing 286 years: in the 1st page she demanded the meaning of *oblata, cartae, litterae clausae,* et *litterae patentes.*

W.L. He severally expounded the right meaning, and laid out the differences of every of them; her Majestie seeming well satisfied, and said, 'that she would be a scholar in her age, and thought it no scorn to learn during her life, being of the mind of that philosopher, who in his last years began with the Greek alphabet.' Then she proceeded to further pages, and asked, where she found cause of stay, as what *ordinationes, parliamenta, rotulus cambii, rediseisnes.*

W.L. He likewise expounded these all according to their original diversities, which she took in gracious and full satisfaction
. . . .[2]

Then she proceeded to the Rolls,
Romae, Vascon, Aquitaniae, Franciae, Scotiae, Walliae, et Hiberniae.

W.L. He expounded these to be records of estate, and negotiations with foreign princes or counteries.

Her Majestie demaunded again, 'if *rediseisnes* were unlawful and forcible throwing of men out of their lawful possessions?'

[1] B.M. Stowe MS, f. 55.8. Printed: Nichols, *Bibliotheca* I, App. VII, pp. 525–6.
[2] At this point came the celebrated exchanges about Richard II.

W.L. 'Yea, and therefore these be the rolls of fines assessed and levied upon such wrong doers, as well for the great and wilful contempt of the crown and royal dignity, as disturbance of common justice.'

Her Majestie. 'In those days force and arms did prevail; but now the wit of the fox is every where on foot, so as hardly a faithful and vertuouse man may be found.' Then came she to the whole total of all the membranes and parcels aforesaid ... commending the work, 'not only for the pains therein taken, but also for that she had not received since her first coming to the crown any one thing that brought therewith so great delectation unto her'; and so being called away to prayer, she put the book in her bosom, having forbidden me from the first to the last to fall upon my knee before her: concluding, 'Farewell, good and honest Lambarde!'

This, we may surmise, was Lambarde's finest hour.

The life-history of John Stow (1525–1605) shows how record-searching could cast its spell on a different type of student. Born before the dissolution of the monasteries, the son and grandson of London citizens, and surviving into the reign of James I, Stow was a member of no learned profession but for many years a working tailor, in a house by the well within Aldgate, between Leadenhall and Fenchurch Street. History and antiquities were his passion. In dedicating his *Annales of England* (1592) to Archbishop Whitgift, he wrote,

It is now more than thirtie yeeres (Right reuerende father) since I first addressed all my cares and cogitations to the studie of Histories, and search of Antiquities: the greatest part of which time I haue diligently imploied in collecting such matters of this kingdome, as I thought most worthie to be recommended both to the present and succeeding age.

This was no idle boast. For (to quote Stow's biographer, Strype), he

got into his Possession as many of the antient *English* Writers, both Prints and Manuscripts, as ever he could, by Money or Favour. ... He also became acquainted with such who increased and furthered his Knowledge in History; I mean, all the famous Studiers and Lovers of Antiquity in his Time: as Archbishop *Parker*, the Master of Antiquarians; *Lambard*, admirably skilled in the *Saxon* learning, ... Bowyer, Keeper of the Records of the *Tower* and the first Digester of them into some Method; the learned Camden; and many others of lesser Note, or less known to us.[1]

Stow was a record-searcher, if ever there was one, not only 'an unwearied Reader of all Authors of *English* History, whether printed or in MS.', but also 'a Searcher into Records, Registers, Journals, Original Charters, Instruments etc. as may be seen by the large Catalogues of them set down both in his *Annals* and *Survey*. . . . And the Rarity of his Study (library) was that it was stored not only with ancient Authors but Original Charters, Registers and Chronicles of particular places.' Strype commended him as 'a true Antiquarian, in that he was not satisfied with Reports . . . but had recourse to Originals . . . travelling on Foot to many Cathedral Churches, and other Places, where ancient Records and Charters were: and with his own Eyes to read them. . . . He often conversed in the Records of the *Tower* . . . He mentioned many ancient Wills that he read . . . He read records Four Hundred years before his own time.'[2]

Nowhere does Stow's enterprise among records show to better advantage than in the celebrated *Survey of London*, the only one of his works that has been thought worth reprinting in modern times.[3] Strype thought that he might have had some fee from the civic authorities for acting as the City Chronicler, and this may explain the complete freedom of access to the Guildhall muniments which he seems to have enjoyed. Yet the reward, if such there was, was manifestly inadequate, for, in 1590, he was driven to petition the aldermen for admission to the freedom of the City in order to reduce his expenses.[4] In addition to such famous volumes as the 'Liber Horn', the 'Liber Albus' and the 'Liber Custumarum', the last of which was in the hands, successively, of Recorder Fleetwood, Francis Tate, and Sir Robert Cotton, he shows knowledge, derived in part from the fifteenth-century miscellany known as 'Liber Dunthorne', of the London Letter-Books, the Journals, and the Husting Rolls. The City Companies were sometimes less hospitable. A request to the Vintners for leave to search their records was refused with scant courtesy:[5] and Stow may also

---

[1] *Survey of London*, ed. Strype (1720), I. v–vi.   [2] Ibid. xiv, xx.
[3] Ed. C. L. Kingsford, 2 vols. (1908). Unless otherwise stated, subsequent references to the *Survey* are to this edition.
[4] *Survey*, ed. Strype, I. vii.   [5] Ibid. I. ix.

have been rebuffed by the Fishmongers, to whom he refers as
'men ignorant of their Antiquities, not able to show a reason
why, or when they were ioyned in amitie with the Goldsmiths.'[1]
Like almost every other scholar of his age he was also indebted
to material drawn from the monastic libraries. Both the Cartulary of the Nuns' Priory at Clerkenwell,[2] and the 'Liber S.
Bartholomei'[3] bear notes in his hand. He knew the 'Liber
Papie' or Register of St. Augustine Papey, both in the original
(of which only a fragment now survives)[4] and in a partial trans-
script made about 1550;[5] the Cartulary of the Hospital of St.
John at Clerkenwell, which he describes as 'a fayre Register
booke';[6] and that of Holy Trinity Priory, Aldgate.[7] Either
directly, or through notes supplied by his friend, Francis
Thynne, he knew 'a fayre leager Booke, sometime belonging to
the Abbey of Chartsey, in the Countie of Surrey', i.e. the Chert-
sey Register compiled in the mid-thirteenth century:[8] and his
collections include notes from a Cartulary of St. Mary Overy.[9]
In addition, he consulted the Church-books of St. Andrew
Undershaft (where he was buried), St. Stephen, Coleman Street
and St. Stephen, Walbrook.[10] Assisted, no doubt, by Bowyer,
Heneage and Talbot, he made good use of the public records.
We meet references to 'a fayre Booke of Parliament recordes,
now lately restored to the Tower',[11] to the Patent Rolls, the
Inquests post Mortem and, less often, to the Charter Rolls and
Close Rolls. Stow knew of certain deeds in the Court of Aug-
mentations and he quotes (in translation) a charter of Henry I
to Battle Abbey, 'the which Charter with the Seale very faire,
remaineth in the custodie of *Ioseph Holland* Gentleman.'[12]

Needless to say, Stow's scholarship was not impeccable. The
numerous errors in his free translation of an account roll from
the household of Thomas of Lancaster may be due to his
having worked from a bad transcript, for a marginal note gives
his source as a 'Record of Pontefract, as I could obtaine of M.

---

[1] Ibid. I. 215.
[2] B.M. MS. Cott., Faust. B. ii.
[3] B.M. MS. Cott., Vesp. B. IX.
[4] B.M. MS. Cott., Vit. F. 16, ff. 113–23.
[5] B.M. MS. Harl. 604, f. 12.
[6] *Survey* I. 13. B.M. MS. Cott., Nero E. VI.
[7] Guildhall MS. 122 is a modern transcript of the original, now in the Hunterian
Museum at Glasgow.
[8] *Survey* II. 96; B.M. MS. Cott., Vit. A. XIII.
[9] In B.M. MS. Harl. 544, f. 110v.
[10] *Survey* I. 241, 227; II. 317.
[11] Ibid. I. 12.
[12] Ibid. I. 22.

Cudnor'.[1] The substance of a proclamation of Edward IV is fairly correctly transcribed from the 'Liber Dunthorne', though the grammar and spelling are modified. But his list of monuments in St. Paul's is very inaccurate, as is also, though with more excuse, his catalogue of the mayors and sheriffs of London before 1300; and his translation from the French original in the 'Liber Custumarum' of the rights that belonged to the castellan of London is likewise inexact.[2] Perhaps he attempted too much; for, though we are here concerned with him as record-searcher, it is to be remembered that he devoured the literary sources with no less enthusiasm. Yet, it is doubtful if any historian of his day knew more about records than Stow; and that, as a searcher of records he was not without honour, even in his own family, appears from an undated letter addressed to him from Warwick, on behalf of a friend, by his married daughter, Joan Foster:

. . . This is to desyer yowe, father, of all yor fryndly fryndsheppe that you can or maye to pleasure a very ffrynd of myn dwellyng here in Warwyck for to seche owt for the foundacion of a hospetall . . . founded by the earelles of Warwyck in this parte. And yf yow may healpe him ther vnto he wold reward you verye well for yor paynes, and also you shall do me great pleasure therein, for yt he is my verie ffrynd and neyghbour. It is supposed that you shall fynd the foundacion hereof yn the Tower of London, therefore good father, now agayne I pray you take some paynes therein . . . and I praye you so soon as you have found out any thing to do him good therein, send worde to me wt. as much spyd as by.[3]

Arthur Agarde (1540–1615) is less often remembered today than either Lambarde or Stow, but his claim to a place of honour among record-searchers and archivists is indisputable. He was a lawyer who spent his working life in the Elizabethan Exchequer until, at the age of 63, he succeeded to the office of Deputy-Chamberlain. Thus, he was in direct contact with important sections of the public records. But he was much more than a mere custodian and classifier. He was a genuine antiquary with a passion for seeking origins: his epitaph in the

[1] Ibid. I. 85. This roll (now P.R.O. Min. Acc. Ser. I 1/3 Mem. 20) was printed, with notes of Stow's errors, by J. F. Baldwin, 'The Household Administration of Henry Lacy and Thomas of Lancaster', *EHR* XLII (1927), 196–200.

[2] *Survey* I. 130; ibid. I. 332–3; II. 149–61; I. 62–5.

[3] Ibid. I. lxx–lxxi.

cloister of Westminster Abbey justly describes him as 'diligens scrutator' of the royal records deposited nearby. Anthony Wood tells us that 'he learned and received all his knowledge and learning in antiquities from his faithful and dear friend, Sir Robert Cotton',[1] to whom he bequeathed twenty of his notebooks and other manuscripts, together with a Latin treatise on Domesday Book. As an example of Agarde's learning and ingenuity, this is well worth attention.[2] The date of composition is uncertain but must be earlier than November 1599, when, in a paper read to the Society of Antiquaries, he attempted definition of a word (*Solin* or *Solung*) which had baffled him when writing of Domesday.[3]

In approaching Domesday Book, Agarde posed four problems. (1) The reason for its compilation. (2) The different names, or descriptions, given to the Survey. (3) The etymology of the word *Domesday*. (4) The method of compilation. His attempts to solve them led him to the two copies of the 'Discursus quidam inter Magistrum et Discipulum de Necessariis Scaccarii Observantis' which remain, respectively, in the Red and Black Books of the Exchequer. This treatise had been generally ascribed to Gervase of Tilbury; but Agarde cites the references in the Red Book to the *Tractatus* of Richard FitzNigel, Bishop of London, and seems thus to have been among the first —if not the first—of his generation to identify the author correctly. In discussing the problem of the reason for the compilation of Domesday Book, Agarde first quotes the opinion of the 'Discursus' that the book was so named because it is not permitted to question its judgements: its purpose was to settle disputes about *meum* and *tuum*; and then, with due deference, ventures to suggest another factor. Anticipating Maitland by some three hundred years, he connects the survey with Danegeld: its purpose, he hazards, was to enable the King 'to learn how much every town, vill and hamlet was bound to pay: and so, in Domesday Book are written these words, "pro v Solins, Hidis vel Carucatis se defendit", which is to say, pays Danegeld.' As has been seen, Agarde, at this date, was baffled by *Solin*; *Hida* he defines as 100 acres, or 120 by English reckoning;

1 *Athenae Oxonienses*, ed. Bliss, II. 427.
2 Printed: R. Gale, *Registrum Honoris de Richmond* (1772), App. I, pp. 1–7.
3 Below, pp. 88–90.

Carucaia as a term used in certain counties for an area of the same value as the hide. For further information on Danegeld the reader is referred to Chapter 28 of the Black Book. The second problem of the diversity of names refers to the three books in the Treasury, known as Domesday. First, there is the Great Domesday—'as great as, if not greater than, that great Bible commonly read in Churches'; then there is Little Domesday, covering Essex, Norfolk and Suffolk; and, finally, a third volume containing an epitome of both the other two. The third problem, of the etymology of the word Domesday, leads Agarde to amplify the explanation of the 'Discursus', referring to the ancient custom, in litigation over land, of directing a writ to the Treasurer and Chamberlain of the Exchequer to inform the judges on the matter from Domesday Book. 'This book was called by the poor *Domesdei, Dies Judicii,* because it was not possible to escape the sentence of this strict and terrible new examination by any sort of tergiversation.' As to the method of compilation, this, says Agarde, he learned from the 'Inquisitio Eliensis'[1] 'an ancient Register', borrowed from Sir Robert Cotton, which sets forth the questions put to the jurors. Whoever wishes to know more, let him consult the Book itself 'et Collectanea haec nostra, quae ipse multo labore, Librum scilicet ter perlegendo, in hanc formam redegi.'

Closely linked with the essay on Domesday is that on the 'Dimensions of the Land of England' which Agarde read to the Society of Antiquaries in November 1599.[2] It would be hard to find a more striking example of the combination, so characteristic of the Elizabethan antiquaries, of careful record-searching with utterly uncritical acceptance of legend when the guidance of records fails. Agarde begins with commendable caution:

Although I must confess that in this proposition I have more travelled than in any of the former, for that it concerneth me more to understand the right thereof, especially in that sundry have resorted to me thereabouts to know whether I have in my custody any records that avouch the same in certainty; yet so it fareth with me, that in perusing as well those abbreviations I have noted out of Domesday and other records since that time, as also those notes I

[1] B.M. MS. Cott., Tib. A. VI.
[2] Hearne, *Curious Discourses* (1775), I. 43–50.

have quoted out of ancient registers and books which have fallen
into my hands within these xxx years, I have found the diversity
of measurement so variable and different in every country, shire,
and places in the realm, as I was in a mammering whether it were
proper for me to write or not; for finding all things full of doubtful-
ness, and that I could not by any means reduce the question into
any certainty, I should but make a shipman's hose thereof and
therefore meant to leave it untouched by me. And yet, lest I should
be deemed one that should begin to break order, I thought good to
put myself to the censure of your wise judgements rather than by
silence to draw upon me your harder conceits in that behalf.

Yet, before attempting definitions, the all-important question of
'antiquity', or origins, has to be tackled; and, for Agarde, as for
most of his contemporaries, antiquity meant Trojans. 'Hide' is,
admittedly, a puzzling word, 'for you shall not find that word
in any other language than ours, neither French, Latin,
Italian etc.' But

I do think that our nation drawing first our original from the Trojans
. . . could not but bring from thence the same order which was
observed in those countries of measuring their lands, as appeareth by
Dido in Virgil, who was the founder of Carthage, and coming
thither by sea bought of the prince of that country so much ground,
as she could compass with an hide, to build a city for herself and her
subjects; which being granted, she caused the same to be cut into
small shreds, and so compassed a mighty deal of land more than was
expected; so our forefathers, as it should seem, did collop out of the
countries they dwelt in in like sort.

There follow some astute comments on the meaning of 'Solin'
('after English account containeth 216 acres'), 'Hide' which,
defined in the 'Discursus' as consisting originally of 100 acres,
Agarde again identifies correctly with the 'long hundred' of
120 acres and quotes Knighton[1] in support of his view that, in
those shires in Domesday where no hides are named, *hida* and
carucata are synonymous terms. Where both are named,
however, he judges the carucate to be a ploughland of about
60 acres. Further authorities are cited and then, with a murmur
of apology—'Thus much, if not too much, for *Hida* and

[1] *Chronicon* I. 181. The manuscript consulted by Agarde was 'in the custody of a
gentleman in Leicester named Mr. John Hunt.' John Hunt (d. 1613) held the
manor of Cold Newton. See L. A. Parker, 'The Depopulation Returns for Leicestershire in 1607', *Trans. Leics. Arch. Soc.* XXIII (1946–7), 263.

Carucata terrae',—he proceeds to define *jugum, virgate*, and *bovate* with equal precision. As for *ferling*, 'that word is only used in the west parts, wherein I remit myself to the opinion of those countrymen: but I could never find it expounded.' Subject to correction, he suggests that it may be much the same as bovate. Finally, the acre, though defined by law as 40 × 4 poles, seems to differ from place to place, since it is not clear how many feet should go to a pole. Examples are drawn from four sources—a table made in the Star Chamber under Henry VII, assessments of Forest assarts under Henry III and Edward I, Knighton, and the 'Dialogus de Scaccario'—and the speaker ends with a plea to his hearers to accept what he has said in good part, 'having omitted sundry notes for confirmation of this, which I had set down, because I would not be excessive tedious, as I fear I have been.'

Many of Agarde's numerous other addresses to the Society of Antiquaries were inspired by this same insatiable curiosity about origins: the 'antiquity' of the subject, be it Dukes or Epitaphs, is the guiding theme. The quality of the papers is uneven. Few reach the standard of that on land dimensions, though the studies of 'The Etymology, Antiquity, and Privileges of Castles' (1598), of 'The Antiquity, Use and Ceremony of Lawful Combat' and of 'The Antiquity of Epitaphs' (1600),[1] reveal both sound learning and good judgement. By contrast, those on 'The Etymology, Dignity, and Antiquity of Dukes in England' (1590), on 'The Antiquity of Shires' (1591), and on 'The Authority, Office, and Privilege of Heralds' (1601) are slight and very general.[2] Citations from literary sources are not very numerous, though Agarde does quote from Jocelin de Brakelond, a chronicler not widely read in the sixteenth century, and he makes good use of collections, like those of Sir Henry Savile, published in his own lifetime. Robert Hare, 'that worthy antiquary,' lent him 'a large booke of St. Augustines of Canterbury, wherein was a full story of our island',[3] and he made good use of one of the metrical lives of the Archbishops of York.[4] But the references to records are wide-ranging and impressive, drawn from monastic registers and private charters, from the

---

[1] Hearne, *Curious Discourses* I. 186–91; II. 215–22; I. 246–51.
[2] Ibid. I. 184–6; 19–21; 61–3.   [3] Ibid. II. 160.
[4] *Historians of the Church of York*, ed. J. Raine, R.S. II. (1886), 464–87.

G

Parliament and Statute Rolls, the Liberate Rolls, Feet of Fines, King's Bench and Common Bench proceedings and Final Concords. The superstitions are there, of course. Julius Caesar built the Tower of London; Joseph of Arimathaea first preached Christianity in Britain.[1] But so, too, are such shrewd comments as those on the derivation of the word 'sterling', the antiquity of the Inns of Court, and the conclusion that 'the best time and chief rising' of heralds was under Edward III.[2] Some interesting personal reminiscences emerge—of the castle in Cambridge 'where I, being a scholar there, saw the *Juillet* [i.e. Keep] standing, but it hath been since in my tyme defaced'; of the standing stones at Boroughbridge which Agarde saw 'xxxiiij years agoe, when I was attendinge on Sir Nich. Throkemton, who wayeted on the duke of Richemount.'[3] His patriotism, the mainspring of so much of the learned activity of the age, reveals itself in a passage from the paper on 'The Diversity of Names of this Island': 'And surely that sweet name of England hath been of singular estimation among and above all other nations; insomuch as let an Englishman be in company among people of sundry other nations, you shall have him admired of them all, yea, and both of man and woman more favoured and respected, than any other in the company, as one that carrieth more courteous, friendly and lovely countenance before all other people.'[4] His protestantism emerges from the approval with which he quotes Wyclif's denunciation of the idolatrous oaths of the Middle Ages,[5] and his personal piety from the moving conclusion to his paper on Epitaphs. As the monuments of our Kings from Edward I's time onwards are to be seen at Westminster, 'I shall leave them to receive that fate which all corruptible things doo, and will desire of God to have but that wrytinge imprinted in and upon all our soules, whereof Christe speaketh in the xth chapter of St. Luke's gospel, Rejoice, because your names are wrytten in heaven. *Hic mihi Finis erit Studiorum atque Laborum.*'[6]

Agarde was sixty when these words were written; but the end of his labours was not yet. His enduring monument to posterity consists less in his essays in interpretation, remarkable

---

[1] *Curious Discourses* I. 187; II. 161.
[2] Ibid. II. 316–17; I. 64–5; I. 60.
[3] Ibid. I. 187, 212.
[4] Ibid. I. 97.
[5] Ibid. I. 261.
[6] Ibid. I. 251.

though these are, than in his collections and classifications of the raw materials of history. He put together an 'Abbreviatio Placitorum in Banco Regis' for the reign of Edward I:[1] he was responsible for most, if not all, of five massive volumes of miscellanea which include voluminous extracts from the public records and from private collections;[2] and for many other transcripts; and, with the help of Cotton and Sir Walter Cope, he compiled a catalogue, completed in 1610, when he was seventy, of the records in the four Treasuries of the Exchequer.[3] Not the least interesting aspect of this fascinating document is the light it throws on the archivist at work and on the difficulties that beset him.

The catalogue is a model of clarity, intended, in the main, as a guide to searchers. Agarde is impelled, however, to begin with some words of warning and admonition to those that have the custody of records: 'beseeching all them yt [that] shall succeed me in the name of God for the service of the Prince, satisfyinge of the Subject and discharginge of their owne duty, with a good conscience, to have a speciall regard to observe some instructions (I presume soe to call them, because by longe experience I have learned and noted them,) whiche I shall lay downe heareunder, both for the preservacion of the same recordes and for the ready findinge of them.' The four enemies to be guarded against are Fire; Water; Rats and Mice; Misplacing. The first may be avoided if the records are stored in vaults and no candles brought in except in lanterns. As to the second, it is the duty of the officers, after a heavy fall of rain or snow, to discover if any damage has been done and, if necessary, 'to lay abroad the same recordes soe wett to the end they may drie by aire especially (or els before a fire, which is both dangerous and hurtfull).' Boxes, chests and strong presses are the best protection against rats and mice, though they 'will pearce through with gnawinge the presses of timber' if these are not regularly inspected. As for misplacing, 'it is an enemye to all good ordre, and the bringer in of all horror and inconvenience amonge records.' But there is a last and worse enemy to be feared

---

[1] B.M. Add MS. 25, 160.   [2] B.M. Stowe MSS. 527–31.
[3] *The Antient Kalendars and Inventories of the Treasury of His Majesty's Exchequer,* ed. F. Palgrave (1836), II. 311–35.

' . . . there followeth yet a last daunger woorse than some of the former, that is even plaine takinge of them away.' This may occur, either when a warrant is issued for the production of certain records in the council or one of the courts, and afterwards, 'although the officers come for them and demaund them never soe oft, yet shall he seldome or never gett them out of their handes, as by experience I have found'; or else, when records are lent to officials or others, 'wherein it appeared to me that sundry have failed.'

These warnings uttered, Agarde then conducts his readers through the four Treasuries, noting as he goes some of the fruits of his own labours. Thus, in a little room adjoining the Court of Receipt are three chests containing Quo Warranto and other pleadings of the reign of Edward I, 'put by me, some two shires in a bagge, and some one shire, for the more easy findinge and preservacion where before they lay confused togither.' In the next chest are to be found 'a bagge of sondry Charters . . . whereof I have in a blacke booke in paper abbreviated, intituled *Carte tangeñ diverš libertates de diversis Monasteriis et aliis*'; 'a great bagg of Roles of Assis. in H.3 time; E.1 : E.3 : et H.4. all abbreviated by me into bookes, very redie to be found by the number rolle'; and 'a bagg of such Pliamt [Parliament] Rolls as I could find in my time and collect togeither, beeinge especially in E.1. time, which I have abbreviated into a booke, and they bee very worthy records.' Records in the second Treasury 'which is in the newe Pallace of Westm̃. over the little Gatehouse there, locked with 3 lockes and keyes', include '*Robt. Catesby* the treator's evidence, selected out of twoe great hamps [hampers] delivered in to me by my late Lord Threasaurer, th Earle of *Dorset* . . . which cost me a quarter of a yeare's worke.' In the third Treasury, in the old Chapter House of the Abbey, the first and second chests contain Feet of Fine and Plea Rolls of the time of Richard I, John, and Henry III, 'put into order by me, in a summer spent onely therein';[1] the twenty-third chest, pleas *coram rege* of Henry V, 'abbreviated by me 1607'. Only when he comes to the fourth Treasury, in the cloister of the Abbey, 'locked with 5 stronge keyes and within two stronge double dores', is Agarde forced to be less explicit

[1] Cf. B.M. MS. Harl. 94.8. 'a note of Pedes Finium of H 111d's Tyme . . . by Arthur Agarde in the Great Vacation 1602, Reviewed, Repaired & Sorted. etc.'

about the records, 'because I tooke notes but on a suddaine, by reason I could not make any stay there. . . .'

Valuable as this catalogue must have been to searchers, the systematic arrangement which it suggests was largely super-ficial. Despite his heroic efforts to reduce it, confusion still reigned among the public records when Agarde died in 1615. Many were still inaccessible to historians, few of whom, indeed, were much disposed to follow Stow's example in consulting them; and the day of systematic publication was far distant. Yet the work of men like Agarde and William Bowyer had at least served to draw attention to the dangers which threatened the records and to the need for care in their preservation. Nor was it only the national records that excited interest. In far-away Exeter, John Hooker devoted many years to the arrange-ment and study of the city's muniments and, as he informed the mayor and alderman, he had 'Caused places to be appointed and presses to be made wth Kayes and lockes and wth a booke wherin I haue Registred euery writinge and Rools of all such evidences as then Remayned all wch nowe I haue Caused to be locked vp in salfitie wthout farther spoyle and the keyes to Remayne in your owne Custodye.'[1] And, though too many historians still contented themselves with re-reading and re-writing the older histories, the topographical studies of scholars like Lambarde and Stow, and the papers presented by Agarde and others to the Society of Antiquaries were pointing the way to a new kind of social and constitutional history which, sooner or later, must drive scholars back to the records. A fortunate chance has preserved for us a glimpse of an early scholar engaged in the kind of searches that Agarde and his friends were seeking to assist—at a price.

On 29 May 1589, George Owen, of Henllys in Pembroke-shire, presented himself at the Exchequer, in the hope of finding material relevant to the early history of the Lordship of Kemes. There, he tells us, he searched 'the booke of Domesdaye wch Remayneth with mr Agar and mr fenton in the Cellers office', but the way was not easy and he could find nothing: '. . . the boke is very ancient & hard to be redd & whosoe findethe any things must pay for the copy of euery line iiijd for yt must be exemplified in the selfe same Correctnes as yt ys wrytten in

---

[1] *Trans. Devon & Cornwall Record Society* (1919), II. 2.

the booke wch is strange and hard for any man to Rede also the
serche is vjs viijd whether yow finde or not.' Owen also searched
the Quo Warranto rolls for Herefordshire for the reign of
Edward I and, for a further payment of 8s., he obtained leave
to continue to search there for the whole of Trinity Term.
The officials were evidently anxious to be helpful. The unknown
'Mr. Fenton'[1] told Owen that within the past week he had found
a reference to Kemes '& yf I wowld com on Sundaye next in the
afternoone to his howse by hide parke called knightes bridge I
shold see yt.' Mr. Fenton also told him that he had much
material touching the Lordship of Gower, and he and other
officers showed him 'diuerse Records particular for Wales &
hadd a grete canvas bagg full of Recordes for south Wales
wherein were bundells Indorsedd com penbr/ cardigan
Carmardyn/ wch I am promised to haue the perusall of.' A
fellow-searcher, James Strangman, who was engaged in making
collections for Essex, told him that while he was searching the
Red Book of the Exchequer, 'in Mr Saluweyes custodye', he
'found somthing toching Kemes.'[2] On 31 May, Owen himself
obtained access to the Red Book 'in mr Saloweyes office wherin
ar many thinges of very ancient tyme . . . but I cowld as yett
find nothing toching Kemes.'[3]

[1] He cannot have been Geoffrey Fenton, the translator of Guicciardini, who was
in Ireland at this time.
[2] The only reference to Kemes in the Red Book of the Exchequer is in the list of
Welsh Cantreds. This had already been transcribed for Sir John Price in 1539 by
Thomas Soleman. See *Red Book of the Exchequer*, ed. H. Hall R.S. II (1896), cclxii,
762.
[3] *Cymmrodorion Record Series* (1897), pp. 370–3.

V

GENERAL HISTORIES OF BRITAIN

ROBERT FABYAN, who was born about the middle of the
fifteenth century and died in 1513, may fairly be regarded
as the doyen of those historians who were seeking to
preserve the memory of the medieval world for the new age of
the Tudors. A prosperous London draper, Alderman of the
ward of Faringdon Without, and later one of the Sheriffs of the
City, he was first and foremost the heir of the London Chroniclers and in his *New Chronicles of England and France*, published
posthumously in 1516,[1] he adopted the traditional method of
dating by the years of the mayoralty, from the end of the twelfth
century. Beginning with the arrival of Brutus in 1106 B.C., the
chronicle provides a general survey of the affairs of England
and, later, of France, to the end of the reign of Richard III.
Fabyan cites the standard medieval authors, from Bede to
Caxton, and seems to have had some idea of trying to reconcile
them, but the task was beyond his powers:

> The auctours so rawe, and so ferre to culle:
> Dymme and derke, and straunge to vnderstonde;
> And ferre oute of tune, to make trewe songe,
> The storyes and yeres to make accordaunt.[2]

—and, as he modestly admits, his education had been limited,

> For by hymn that neuer yet ordre toke,
> Or gre of Scole, or sought for great cunnynge,
> This werke is gaderyd, with small vnderstandynge.[3]

The only original features of the book are his questioning of the
traditional account of Arthur's victories in France,[4] a few interpolations relating chiefly to the history of London after 1440,

---

[1] There appears to be no external evidence for Fabyan's authorship earlier than
the edition of 1533, but nothing in his career militates against the traditional ascription
of the *Chronicles* to him. See *The Great Chronicle of London*, ed. A. H. Thomas and
I. D. Thornley (1938), pp. xliv seq.

[2] *The Chronicle of Fabian*, ed. Sir H. Ellis (1811), p. 239.

[3] Ibid., p. 3.   [4] T. D. Kendrick, *British Antiquity*, p.41.

and a tinge of Lancastrian sympathy which sometimes colours the traditional Yorkist version of events.[1]

In one of the execrable verses which appeared as a Prologue to the first edition, Fabyan explains his motive in undertaking this massive compilation:

> Nat for any pompe, or yet for great mede
> This werke I haue taken on hande to compyle;
> But of cause oonly for that I wolde sprede
> The famous honour of this Fertyle Ile,
> That hath contynyed, by many a longe whyle,
> In excellent honour, with many a royall guyde,
> Of whom the dedes haue spronge to the worlde wyde.[2]

This much he has in common with his successors: the glory of Britain is his theme and to it even the glory of London is secondary. It was a theme, much to the taste of the sixteenth century. But, as Fabyan's book was composed under the old regime, before the breach with Rome, certain alterations in the text were necessary before it could become wholly acceptable to the new. Significant changes appear in the editions of 1542 and 1559, where many passages relating to miracles, relics, and pilgrimages were deleted, where the Pope becomes the Bishop of Rome, where Becket is demoted from 'blessyd archebisshop' to 'trayterous byshoppe', he is slain, not 'martyyred' and most of his history is cut out.[3] In this amended version, the book was very popular and it became the principal medium through which the London chronicles were known to the Elizabethans. There was, however, fairly general recognition of its defects. The speech put into the mouth of John Tiptoft, Earl of Worcester, by one of the authors of the *Mirror for Magistrates*, alleges that

> Vnfruytfull Fabyan folowed the face
> Of time and dedes, but let the causes slip;
>
> .   .   .   .
>
> But seing causes are the chiefest thinges
> That should be noted of the story wryters,
> That men may lerne what endes al causes bringes

---

[1] C. L. Kingsford, *English Historical Literature in the Fifteenth Century* (1913), pp. 103–6. It is noteworthy that the passage stating Crouchback to have been the elder son of Henry III (*Chronicles*, p. 330) was omitted in the later editions.
[2] *Chronicles*, p. 3.   [3] Ibid., pp. xx, 273, 275–6.

They be unwurthy the name of Croniclers,
That leave them cleane out of the registers,
Or doubtfully report them. . . . .[1]

This was fairly acute criticism; but it did not stop the Elizabethans from reading Fabyan. The book, is, indeed, readable;
and, derivative though it is, it remains significant as the summing-up of a century of previous development and as the first
of the many general narrative Histories of England to appear in
print during the sixteenth century.

Another Londoner with a taste for history was Richard
Arnold, whose misleadingly named *London Chronicle* was
printed at Antwerp early in the century and republished at
Southwark in 1521. 'In this boke', runs the preface, 'is con-
teined ye names of the baylyfs, Custos, mayers and sherefs of
ye cyte of London from the tyme of kynge Richard the fyrst &
also the articles of ye Chartour & lybartyes of the same Cyte.
And of the chartour and lybartyes of England with other
dyuers maters good and necessary for euery cytezen to under-
stond and knowe. . . .' The book is, in fact, a curious miscellany
of historical raw materials, much of it bearing little or no
relation to the history of London.

Fabyan soon found a successor in John Rastell, the lawyer-
printer, brother-in-law to Sir Thomas More, who, in 1529,
published *The Pastyme of People*, a work designed to suit the
taste of commoners and to include the history of other lands
besides Britain and therefore in some respects inevitably more
superficial than Fabyan.[2] Yet Rastell's achievement was greater
than has always been recognized. Even Fabyan had been
unable to swallow Arthur whole, but Rastell went much further.
Respectful of 'holy Beda' and highly suspicious of Geoffrey of
Monmouth, he was dubious, not only about the supposed
exploits of Arthur,[3] but also about the entire Brutus myth—
though he did decide to summarize the accepted version
because of the moral lesson it had to teach. His keen critical
sense reveals itself in his summary of the arguments against the

---

[1] *The Mirror for Magistrates*, ed. L. B. Campbell (1938), p. 198.
[2] The most recent edition is that of T. F. Dibdin (1811). See L. B. Wright,
Middle-Class Culture in Elizabethan England (1935), p. 303.
[3] W. R. Trimble, 'Early Tudor Historiography 1485–1548', *Journal of the History
of Ideas* XI (1950), 34.

authenticity of Arthur's supposed seal at the shrine of St. Edward in Westminster Abbey, around the border of which were the words 'Arthurus patricius Britannie Gallie and Dacie imperatur.' This was said to have been attached to a deed of gift, 'wherof ye perchement & wryting for age is wastyd & putrefyed'. Some, however, deny this on the grounds that Westminster was not founded in the (supposed) time of Arthur; that it was impossible that wax should survive for about a thousand years; and that the custom of affixing seals to documents began with William I: '. . . let euery man be at his lyberte to beleue ther in what he lyste.'[1] Rastell likewise mentions, but does not commit himself to, the view that King Ethelwulf 'foundyd furst ye unyuersyte of Oxenford'.[2] He demonstrates the correct date of Westminster Hall from the evidence of the royal arms in the timber and stonework. He notes, not only the grant of Magna Carta, 'besyde Stanys, at a place called Rumney Mede',[3] but also the amended versions issued under Henry III. If the affairs of London appear to occupy a disproportionate amount of space, this was in the fifteenth-century tradition. *The Pastyme of People* affords clear evidence that the spirit of historical criticism, most commonly associated with Polydore Vergil, was already active in a native author.[4]

Born at Urbino about 1470, Polydore Vergil had already won something of a reputation as a scholar when he came to England in 1502.[5] He had published *Adagia* (a collection of proverbs) and *De Inventoribus Rerum* (a treatise on inventors) and he enjoyed the friendship of Erasmus. His world was the cultivated world of Renaissance Europe, still only palely reflected in England at the beginning of the sixteenth century. Polydore had obtained papal appointment as a deputy-collector of Peter's Pence and he worked in close collaboration with his Italian patron, Adriano Castelli, who held two English sees (Bath and Wells, and Hereford) in succession. Through Castelli's influence Polydore himself obtained a number of ecclesiastical preferments, including a prebend in St. Paul's. Henry VII regarded him with favour, and it was on

---

[1] *The Pastyme of People* (1811), pp. 106–7.   [2] Ibid., p. 124.   [3] Ibid., p. 178.
[4] F. J. Levy (op. cit., pp. 72–3) suggests that the two may have been acquainted though no evidence of this survives.
[5] For his biography, see D. Hay, *Polydore Vergil* (1952), pp. 1–21.

this King's invitation that he agreed to write a history of England. For a time, both he and Castelli enjoyed the favour of Wolsey; but, by 1515, they were in disgrace—probably because they had not shown enough enthusiasm in support of Wolsey's ambitions—and Polydore even suffered a period of imprisonment though, when he was released, his preferments were restored. The religious changes of Henry VIII's reign were undoubtedly distasteful to him and he seems to have decided to ignore the dissolution of the monasteries;[1] but, according to Burnet, as a member of Convocation he signed the articles of 1536 and the declaration of 1547 for communion in both kinds.[2] He found it convenient, however, to pay two long visits to Italy in the last decade of Henry VIII's reign, and it was in 1550, when Northumberland's government was beginning to move firmly in the direction of Protestantism, that he sought and obtained leave to return home for good. His latest known composition is a letter of congratulation to Mary Tudor on her accession, expressing the hope that she will find it possible to restore the realm to its former state and to correct its sins and errors.[3] Polydore thus stands apart from most other historians of the Tudor period, because he was a foreigner and always, at heart, a Catholic. Though he loved England well enough to make it his home and to seek naturalization, his work was intended primarily for consumption abroad. He was inevitably detached from the ebullient patriotism of the English writers, and it is significant that in old age he should have felt again the pull of his native land.

Polydore Vergil's first significant contribution to British history was his edition of Gildas based on the collation of two manuscripts and printed, probably, in Antwerp in 1525.[4] The *Anglica Historia*, covering the history of England to 1509, was first published in 1534; a second edition appeared in 1546 and a third (with a continuation to 1538) in 1555, all printed at Basle. Several later editions followed, the last version of the original Latin text being printed at Leyden in 1651. The decision to use Latin, though doubtless inevitable, has ultimately proved somewhat unfortunate, for it has meant that

---

[1] Ibid., pp. 114–15.
[2] *Polydore Vergil's English History*, ed. Sir H. Ellis (1884), p. xv.
[3] Ibid., pp. xxxviii–xxxix.   [4] D. Hay, op. cit., pp. 29–31.

much of the *Historia* is hard to come by. Copies of the early editions are comparatively rare and only the last section (1485–1537) has been critically edited.[1] And, though an English translation had been made before the end of the reign of Henry VIII, only Books 23–5 (1422–85) and the first 8 books (pre 1066) have ever been printed.[2]

In an early draft of his epistle dedicatory to Henry VIII, Polydore Vergil allows us a glimpse of his preparatory labours:

I first began to spend the hours of my night and day in searching the pages of English and foreign histories . . . I spent six whole years in reading these annals and histories during which, imitating the bees which laboriously gather their honey from every flower, I collected with discretion material proper for a true history. When on approaching our own times, I could find no such annals . . . I betook myself to every man of age, who was pointed out to me as having been formerly occupied in important and public affairs, and from all such I obtained information about events up to the year 1500. From that time—since I came to England immediately after that date—I have myself noted down day to day everything of importance.[3]

Here we have one clue to the great difference between Polydore Vergil and Fabyan. Polydore collected his materials (which included official as well as literary sources) with discretion. He used discrimination in judging the qualities of different authors and finally declared only three of them to be worth much attention—Bede ('then whome I have seene nothing more sounde, sincere, or trewe'),[4] William of Malmesbury, and Matthew Paris. The rest he dismisses as mere annals, often inconsistent and often erroneous, *nudi, rudes, indigesti ac mendosi*. In particular, Polydore found the work of that popular author, Geoffrey of Monmouth, to contain a mingling of legend and fiction that was altogether unworthy of belief.

It is evident that this represents a breakaway from the traditional methods of Fabyan and his predecessors. Polydore was as sceptical as they were credulous and he brought a spirit of scepticism to his reading of historical sources. In the first book

[1] By Professor D. Hay for the Camden Society (1950).
[2] Sir H. Ellis edited them for the Camden Society in 1844 (vol. xxix) and 1846 (vol. xxxvi).
[3] F. A. Gasquet, 'Polydore Vergil', *TRHS* n.s. XVI (1902), 11.
[4] Camden Society XXXVI, 27.

of the *Anglica Historia*, he avers that 'an Historie is a full rehear-
sall and declaration of things don, not a gesse or divination.'[1]
His scepticism led him to reject Brutus, even more firmly than
Rastell had rejected him, and to recognize that 'Trulie ther is
nothinge more obscure, more uncertaine, or unknowne then the
affaires of the Brittons from the beginninge.'[2] It led him, in
short, to undermine the whole fabric of legend erected by his
predecessors and embellished by his contemporaries in order to
explain the ancestry of the race.[3] It is true that in the latter part
of his work he suggests the outline of the peculiar pattern of
English history which was to gain widespread acceptance
through its popularization by Hall, that he sees the disasters of
the fifteenth century as a series of moral judgements and the
accession of Henry Tudor as the providential climax. But he is
always cooler than Hall and he has no taste for melodrama.
And, though Hall and his successors were all too ready to
criticize the monastic historians, what makes Polydore's judgements much more remarkable is that they sprang, not from
Protestant prejudice, but from the impact of the inferior annals
and semi-fictitious histories of the Middle Ages on a mind bred
in the classical tradition and accustomed to new methods of
criticism.

Polydore's classical training led him to write in a Latin style
which, albeit rhetorical, is much more precise than that of the
late medieval chroniclers; and he had little use for the language
of medieval common law 'quam neque Galli nec Angli recte
callebant.'[4] The *Historia* from 1066 has been described as a
series of royal biographies placed end to end,[5] but Polydore did
make some attempt to break away from the purely annalistic
method and to offer summaries of historical situations, and
judgements which often hit the nail on the head. Of the position of the English in France after the burning of Joan of Arc, he
writes:

The affaires of England grewe by this meane, from day to day,
through Fraunce, woorse and woorse, which did diversly affect the
nobilitie: for some, very pensife in mind, deemed the distresse of the
present time light, in comparison of that which they forsawe to be
imminent: others thought that woorse could not chaunce than had

---

[1] Ibid., p. 26. [2] Ibid., p. 33. [3] Kendrick, op. cit., *passim.*
[4] *Anglica Historia* (1649), p. 203. [5] D. Hay, op. cit., p. 99.

alreadie chaunced, for they sawe the forces of thenemy augmented
and their owne diminished: wherefore every man, much musing
with ardent affection, considered with himselfe particularly whether
it were possible to remedie the state of thinges almost utterly
decayed.[1]

And of the end of the Hundred Years War he writes,

This, finally, was the ende of forreyne warre, and likewise the
renewing of civill calamitie: for when the feare of outwarde enemy,
which as yet kept the kingdome in good exercise, was gone from
the nobilitie, such was the contention amongst them for glorie
and soveraintie, that even then the people were apparently divided
into two factions, according as it fell out afterwards, when those two,
that is to say, king Henry, who derived his pedigree from the house
of Lancaster, and Richard duke of Yorke, who conveied himselfe by
his mothers side from Lyonell, sonne to Edwarde the Thirde, con-
tended mutually for the kingdome. By meane whereof there two
factions grewe shortly so great through the whole realme, that,
while thone sought by happ or nap to subdue thother, and raged in
revenge upon the subdued, many men were utterly destroyed, and
the whole realme brought to ruine and decay.[2]

It is important, however, not to exaggerate Polydore Vergil's
achievement. Though far in advance of Fabyan, he was not
entirely original. Both Tito Livio, the biographer of Henry V,
and Sir Thomas More, in his *Richard III*, had attempted to
write history from a critical standpoint and in an elegant
literary style. Though no one before him had tried to apply
these standards to a complete English history, the standards
themselves were not unknown, even in England. His near-
contemporary, Sir Thomas Elyot, whose substantial *Bibliotheca*
appeared in 1545 with a dedication to Henry VIII, was highly
sceptical of some current historical concepts. Under the heading
Britannia he wrote '. . . . neyther the Romans nor the Grekes
do write of any man called Brutus'; and that the ancestors of
the Britons were Trojans is dismissed as a fantasy 'which among
wise men, maie be well laughed at.' Polydore's range of reading,
though wide, was not, and could not be, comprehensive, even
as regards the literary sources, since very few of the chronicles
were yet in print and many were inaccessible; for the fifteenth
century, in particular, he seems to have read little beyond Tito

---

[1] Camden Society XXIX, 39.   [2] Ibid., pp. 93-4.

Livio, Fabyan and the *Brut*. And, as was inevitable in a work on this scale, he made many mistakes. He thought that sheriffs, justices of the peace and juries were all introduced by William I; he seems to have originated the curious notion, which was taken up by almost all his successors, that the representative parliament was the invention of Henry I; and he read *scaccarium* as a corruption of *statarium*. The characterization, though sometimes acute, is often very conventional. Henry V is a pasteboard figure, compounded of all the virtues; Henry VII is highly idealized. Yet, despite its weaknesses, the fact remains that Polydore Vergil's was the first general history of England to be written in a judicious and critical spirit and in a deliberately literary style.

Most of his contemporaries and successors conceded these points; but few of them cared for his conclusions. Not many historians have been more harshly criticized; and, indeed, the storm which it provoked may well be a measure of the importance of his achievement. The mainspring of all the abuse was indignation that Vergil, a foreigner, had 'pitched somewhat smartly upon the antiquity of Britain.' Leland wrote his *Assertio Arturii* to defend Geoffrey of Monmouth against Vergil's strictures; another critic called him 'that most rascall dogge knave in the worlde'.[1] Sir Henry Savile censured him as an ignorant foreigner; Dr. Caius alleged that he had burned the manuscripts of ancient historians so that his own errors might not be perceived; and, in the next century, Gale and Wood declared that he had pillaged a number of libraries in Oxford and elsewhere and sent a whole shipload of manuscripts to Rome.[2] Wild though these accusations were, they had their uses: for the effect was to stimulate, not only enquiry into the early history of Britain but also the publication of some of the sources.[3]

Two further essays in medieval history were published early in the reign of Edward VI. George Lily's *Chronicon sive . . . enumeratio Regum*, which was subsequently bound up with an edition of Vergil's history, appeared first in the *Descriptio Britanniae* of Paulus Jovius, printed at Venice in 1548. A Catholic, like Vergil, Lily may fairly be regarded as his disciple,

[1] Quoted by D. Hay, op. cit., p. 159.
[2] Kingsford, op. cit., p. 257.   [3] See p. 65 above.

in that he too wrote in Latin, demolished the Trojans and made Henry I the founder of parliament. But the book is much slighter than Vergil's, and Lily, who was the son of the famous grammarian and had himself been a student at Magdalen College, Oxford, before he became chaplain to Cardinal Pole, was interested, above all, in religious and, more particularly, in academic foundations. By stressing the munificence of kings and bishops in this respect he doubtless hoped to restore the reputation of England in the eyes of Catholic Europe. He has no entry for the year 1215, and Mortmain is the only one of Edward I's statutes that appears to interest him. *An Epitome of Chronicles*, published in 1549 with a dedication to Somerset by Thomas Cooper, Master of Magdalen College School at Oxford and afterwards Dean of Christ Church and Bishop successively of Lincoln and Winchester, made for itself in its title the ambitious claim that it contained 'the whole discourse of the histories as well of this realme of England, as all other countreis, with the succession of their kynges, the tyme of their reigne, & what notables actes thei did'; and Cooper explains that the work was begun, not many years past, by 'a studious yonge man named Thomas Lanquet', who had covered the pre-Christian era, and that he himself had continued it, from A.D. 17 to the second year of Edward VI.[1] In the section ascribed to him, Lanquet (who, no doubt, knew both his Rastell and his Vergil) reveals himself as commendably sceptical, writing of the history of pre-Roman Britain that it 'is full of errours, and hath in it no manifest apparence of truthe, as beyng written neither of no ancient tyme, nor yet by noo credible hystorian. For, if there had remained any veritable monument of these tymes, surely the worshypful Beda and Gildas, our countreie men, yea and Caesar, the conquerour therof, wolde not haue omitted them.' But, having said so much, Lanquet's courage failed and he reached the lame conclusion, 'Neuer the lesse I wil not doscent from the common opinion therof, but wil also folow it as nere as I may, obseruing the iust computacion of the yeres, and the conferment of histories.'[2] Neither author quotes many of his sources (though Cooper acknowledges his indebtedness to Fabyan) and the book emerges as a bald record of the supposed history of events in western Europe.

[1] From the Preface.   [2] *An Epitome of Chronicles*, p. 32.

Edward Hall, who died in 1547, was a Londoner, like Fabyan, but of very different background. Educated at Eton and King's College, Cambridge, he entered Gray's Inn and became Common Serjeant and Under-Sheriff of the City of London. He was a member of several of Henry VIII's parliaments and always showed himself a strong supporter of the government. His is the first essay on a period of general English history to be written in the spirit of the Reformation; and the glorification of the House of Tudor, already suggested by Polydore Vergil, is stated by him in its most extravagant form. The title of the work, published by Grafton in 1548, affords a clear indication of its scope and argument:

> The Vnion of the two noble and illustre famelies of Lancastre & Yorke, beeyng long in continual discension for the Croune of this noble realme, with all the actes done in bothe the tymes of the Princes, bothe of the one Linage and of the other, beginnyng at the tyme of Kyng Henry the Fowerth, the first aucthor of this Deuision, and so successively proceading to the Reigne of the high and prudent Prince Kyng Henry the Eight, the vndubitate flower and very heire of both the sayd Linages.

Though the bulk of his material is derived directly from Vergil, Hall, as a distinguished critic has observed, introduced a new concept of drama into English history:[1] and the titles of the eight chapters of his book suggest the unfolding of a play:

   i. The vnquiet tyme of kyng Henry the Fowerth.
   ii. The victorious actes of kyng Henry the v
   iii. The troubleous season of kyng Henry the vj
   iv. The prosperous reigne of kyng Edward the iiij
   v. The pitifull life of kyng Edward the V
   vi. The tragicall doynges of kyng Richard the iij
   vii. The politike gouernaunce of kyng Henry the vij
   viii. The triumphant reigne of kyng Henry the viij

These are the acts of the great moral drama which begins with a dark deed of usurpation and moves through a series of triumphs and disasters to its high climax in the age of the Tudors. In the preface, which takes the form of a dedication to Edward VI, Hall reveals something of his motives in writing this history. Every nation, he says, is desirous 'to enhaunce lady

---

[1] E. M. W. Tillyard, *Shakespeare's History Plays* (1944), pp. 40–50.

Fame, and to suppresse that dedly beast, Obliuion. For what diuersitie is betwene a noble prince & a poore begger, ye a reasonable man and a brute beast, if after their death there be left of theim no remembrance or token.'[1] Princes are under a debt of gratitude to those that set forth the lives and acts of their forebears, for 'writing is the key to induce virtue and repress vice.' In other words, history is the story of great men and its purpose is to teach moral lessons. Hall then goes on to lament the loss of much of our early history because of men's failure to record contemporary events:

. . . my herte lamenteth to knowe and remembre what rule this tyrante Obliuion bare in this realme, in the tyme of the Britons. For from the first habitacion of this land, no man of the Britons either set furthe historie of their begynnyng, or wrote the hole liues of their princes & kynges, excepte Gildas whiche inueighed against the euill doynges of a few tyrantes and euill gouernours. In so muche that Cesar writeth, that when he was in this realme, the people could not tel their linage, nor their begynnyng. But one Geffrey of Monmothe a thousand yere and more after Iulius Cesar, translated a certayn Britishe or Welshe boke, conteinyng the commyng of Brute with the sequele of his linage, till the tyme of Cadwalader, whiche Britishe boke if it had slept a little lenger, Brute with al his posteritie had been buried in the poke of Obliuion, for lacke of writyng.[2]

The Saxon and medieval periods were better furnished with historians:

The strong Saxons, after thei had gayned this lande, set vp the banner of Fame, and had their liues notably written by diuerse and sundrey famous clerkes, euen from their firste entery into this lande, till the firste Monarchy, and so successyuely. In the Normans tyme, many notable workes hath been set furthe, some of one prince perticulerly & some of mo: So that in fine, all the stories of kynges, from kyng Willyam the firste, to kyng Edward the third, bee set furthe at length by diuerse authours in the Latin tonngue, as by Matthewe of Paris, sometyme religious in sancte Albons and other. After whome Iohn Frossart wrote the liues of Kyng Edward the third, and Kyng Richard the seconde. . . .

It is the fifteenth century which has suffered most from lack of historians:

---

[1] *Hall's Chronicle*, ed. Sir. H. Ellis (1809), p. v.   [2] Ibid., p. vi.

Sithe the ende of Frossarte whiche endeth at the begynnyng of king Henry the fourthe, no man in the Englishe tonngue, hath either set furth their honors according to their desertes, nor yet declared many notable actes worthy of memorie dooen in the tyme of seuen Kynges, whiche after Kyng Richarde succeded: Excepte Robert Fabian and one[1] with out name, whiche wrote the common English Chronicle, men worthy to be praysed for their diligence, but farre shotyng wide from the butte of an historie.

This brings Hall to exposition of his own purpose:

Wherfore . . . lest cancarde Obliuion should deface the glory of these seuen Princes . . . I haue compiled and gathered (and not made) out of diuerse writers, as well forayn as Englishe, this simple treatise whiche I haue named the vnion of the noble houses of Lancaster and Yorke. For as kyng henry the fourthe was the beginnyng and rote of the great discord and deuision: so was the godly matrimony, the final ende of all discensions, titles and debates.[2]

Hall's purpose, then, was to improve on Fabyan, and that he did so can hardly be denied. His reading was far wider, his sense of historical development much more acute. His treatment of the fifteenth century was more elaborate than Polydore Vergil's—though he borrowed more freely from him than his readers might suspect. He used Polydore when it suited him, but did not hesitate to discard him at will. Thus, he expressed no doubts about the veracity of Geoffrey of Monmouth; but he is ready enough to suspect the motives of the monastic historians. A characteristic comment, far from charitable, but not, it must be admitted, altogether wide of the mark, runs as follows:

For you muste vnderstande that these monasticall persones, lerned and vnliterate, better fed than taught, toke on them to write & register in the boke of fame, the noble actes, the wise dooynges, and politike gouernances of kynges and princes, in whiche chrono-graphie, if a kyng gaue to them possessions, or graunted them liberties or exalted them to honor & wordly dignitee, he was called a sainct he was praised without any deserte aboue the Moone . . . But if a christian prince had touched their liberties or claimed any part iustly of their possessions, . . . Then tonges talked and pennes wrote, that he was a tirant a depresser of holy religion, an enemie to

---

[1] He means the *Brut*.　　　　　[2] *Chronicle*, ed. Ellis, pp. vi–vii.

Christes Churche and his holy flocke, and a damned and accursed persone. . . .[1]

But when it comes to human character, an uncritical tendency to see men and women as black or white at once reveals itself. Thus, to heighten the contrast between Henry as prince and Henry as king, Hall gives full credence to the tales of his riotous youth, even adding some details such as the story of Henry striking the Chief Justice, which may have derived from legend, or from some source now lost.[2] For Henry's qualities as king, however, the author can hardly find synonyms enough:

. . . the blasyng comete and apparent lanterne in his daies, he was the mirror of Christendome & the glory of his countrey. he was the floure of kynges passed and a glasse to them that should succede . . . this noble and puissant prince . . . whose life although cruel Atropos before his tyme abbreuiated, yet neither fyre, rust, nor fretting tynne [*sic*] shal amongest Englishmen ether appall his honoure or obliterate his glorye which in so fewe yeres and brief dayes achived to high aduentures and made so great a conquest.[3]

His judgement on Cardinal Beaufort, intended, perhaps, to awaken in his readers unfavourable memories of another Cardinal, reveals the same want of balance:

. . . haut in stomacke and hygh in countenaunce, ryche aboue measure of all men & to fewe liberal . . . preferrynge money before frendshippe . . . His couetous insaciable, and hope of long lyfe, made him bothe to forget God, hys Prynce and hymselfe in his latter daies . . . Of the gettyng of this mannes goodes. . . . I wil not speake: but the kepinge of them for his ambycious purpose, aspiryng to ascend to the papisticall sea, was bothe great losse to his naturall Prince, and natyue countrey: for his . . . secrete treasure mught haue releved the commonaltie, when money was scante and importunate charges were daily imminent.[4]

Or again, the most unfortunate of all Hall's character-sketches, his judgement on Joan of Arc:

. . . a mayd of the age of xx yeres, and in mans apparell . . . a chamberleyn in a common hostery, and was a rampe of suche boldness, that she would course horsses and ride theim to water, and do thynges, that other yong maidens bothe abhorred & wer ashamed to do . . . She (as a monster) was sent to the Dolphin. . . .[5]

[1] Ibid., pp. 15–16.   [2] Ibid., p. 46.   [3] Ibid., pp. 113–14.
[4] Ibid., pp. 210–11.   [5] Ibid., p. 148.

Contemporary comment on the Maid of Orleans had been bald and non-committal: it was Hall who, relying on the Burgundian chronicler, Monstrelet, introduced the fiction of a female monstrosity which was taken over from him by Stow and is responsible for the distorted picture which appears in Shakespeare's *King Henry VI*.[1]

Many passages in Hall's chronicle reflect that profound respect for the secular power natural in a good subject of Henry VIII, a respect which, in Hall, even outweighs his prejudices. In his account of the riots at Norwich in 1446, he makes it plain that civil disorder is to be condemned, even when provoked by monastic tyranny; and the revolt of Jack Cade, with which, since it was a move in favour of York, Hall might have been expected to have some sympathy, is condemned outright: 'one Alexander Iden . . . manfully slewe the caitife Cade, & brought his ded body to London, whose hed was set on London bridge. This is the success of all rebelles, and this fortune chaunceth euer to traytors. For where men striue against the streame, their bote neuer cometh to his pretensed porte.'[2]

Roger Ascham once charged Hall with having made excessive use of what he called 'indenture English', that is, of synonyms and equivalent phrases; and it is certainly true that he was prodigal in his expenditure of words. He seldom hesitates to use two phrases where one would do—'few yeres and brief dayes', 'haut in stomache and hygh in countenaunce', 'erred and went out of the way'. Yet this manner of writing (which reached its highest level in the Book of Common Prayer) was characteristic of the age and adds colour and rhythm to the narrative.[3] Hall had a sensitive ear for language and he was a master of the vivid phrase. After Henry V's decision to send an expeditionary force across the Channel '. . . now all men cried, warre, warre, warre, Fraunce, Fraunce'. The King of Scots, 'After he had once taken the ayre and smelt the sent of the Scottishe soyle became like his falce, fraudulent forfathers . . .'. When news came of the arrival of the Earls of Pembroke and Richard in Brittany, 'this thyng nipped kyng Edwarde hardly at the verie stomacke.'[4]

[1] Kingsford, op. cit., p. 264. [2] *Chronicle*, p. 222.
[3] See E. M. W. Tillyard, op. cit., p. 41. [4] *Chronicle*, pp. 56, 119–20, 305.

As has often been remarked, Hall took great liberties with his sources, inventing at will the lengthy speeches which he puts into the mouths of his characters. Such are the supposed orations of Archbishop Chichele, the Earl of Westmorland, and the Duke of Exeter at the Leicester parliament of 1414.[1] Speeches of this kind were in the classical tradition, and, though not always approved, were generally recognized for what they were. Many of Hall's are brilliantly composed and nearly all of them were essential to his dramatic purpose. Yet it must be admitted that his introduction of them into what purports to be a historical narrative adds a fictitious element and has tended to increase the confusion of readers unfamiliar with the sources on which Hall drew.

Hall's permanent importance lies in his influence on those who came after him. Passing through Holinshed (or, possibly, directly) to Shakespeare, his version of fifteenth-century history implanted itself firmly, and it may be ineradicably, in the minds of ordinary Englishmen. In its dramatic alternations of prosperity and disaster, the fifteenth century was seen as an aberration from the norm of good governance, as a series of moral judgements, deriving from the dark deeds of 1399, and serving as a prelude to 1485. Henry V is the pattern of chivalry; Gloucester, 'the Good Duke', is the wise and patriotic statesman; Henry Beaufort, the proud and crafty prelate; Margaret of Anjou, the she-wolf of France and Suffolk her lover; Richard III, a malignant figure of darkness. More than this, Hall expounds what has been called 'the Tudor myth' and raises it to heights undreamed of by Polydore Vergil. Polydore did, indeed, pay solemn tribute to the achievement of Henry VII, seeing him as the instrument of Providence; but Hall, in writing of his marriage to Elizabeth of York, does not hesitate to use such a synonym as the union of the Godhead with the manhood.[2] No qualms or scruples seem to have disturbed him in working out his theme. He does not ask himself why such notable triumphs should have been allowed to Henry V, the son of a usurper, still less whether the renewal of the war in France was in the best interests of the nation. He turns a blind eye alike to Gloucester's irresponsible bellicosity, and to the far-seeing statesmanship of Cardinal Beaufort. He does not recoil

[1] Ibid., pp. 50–6.   [2] Ibid., p. 2.

from the spectacle of Edward of York wading through blood to the throne. With eloquence and conviction he presents his readers with the Yorkist version of conflicting politics, heightened and coloured in the Tudor interest. It is a version nearly as false as it is dramatic: but it had come to stay.

Hall had bequeathed the manuscript of his Chronicle to Richard Grafton, who had been publishing under Henry VIII and, under Edward VI, held the office of Printer to the King. Grafton's rash venture in printing the proclamation of Lady Jane Grey as Queen resulted in his imprisonment under Mary; and the beginning of Elizabeth's reign saw him an elderly, impoverished, and somewhat embittered man. His activities as printer and publisher, and his connections with many notable contemporaries, led him to be much spoken of; but he has small claim to distinction as a historian, being little more than a purveyor and not always, it seems, quite an honest purveyor, of other men's goods. In 1543, he had published Hardyng's verse chronicle with a prose continuation of his own, borrowing freely from Polydore Vergil and Sir Thomas More without acknowledging his indebtedness to either. He also produced, in 1548, an inferior continuation to Hall's chronicle. But his most substantial ventures in historiography belong to the reign of Elizabeth.

Grafton's two histories—*An Abridgement of the Chronicles of England* (1563), and *A Chronicle at Large and Meere History of the Affayres of England* (1568), though of little value in themselves, are interesting if only because they gave rise to a scholarly wrangle which throws some light on contemporary standards and methods. For details of the quarrel we are indebted to Grafton's adversary, John Stow, according to whom the first edition of the *Abridgement* (which sold out rapidly) contained a number of glaring mistakes. In the second edition, published within a year, Grafton declared these to have been misprints; but many errors still remained. Stow said that Grafton 'had not only mysplacyd all moaste all ye yeares of our lord god, but also ye yeres of ye begynengs and endyngs of all ye kyngs of the realme.' He had misplaced, or omitted, many of the mayors and sheriffs of London; he had derived the word 'sterling' from starling because he supposed such a bird to have been engraved on the coins; and, after stating that Henry IV ended his life in the twelfth year of his reign, he 'then declarethe what was done in ye 13 and 14 yerese of his reigne, for yt he makyth hym to raygne ij yeres aftar he was dede and beryed.' Widespread recognition of these and other errors caused a number of London citizens and others to ask Stow to produce a better history and also to 'write agaynst & reprove Richard Grafton.' Stow declined the first invitation but accepted the second. He went to call on Grafton and pointed out some of his more glaring mistakes. Grafton apparently succeeded in concealing his rage at what must have seemed to him the impudent criticisms of a much younger man, still unknown as a writer. For his own mistakes he blamed Fabyan, 'which was a very nowghty cronycle' and 'Coper whiche was x tymes worse'. With what may well have been intended for heavy irony, Grafton asked Stow to concede that at least his style was better than Cooper's. '. . . he shewyd me', said Stow, 'wher Coper had written ij negatyves in on sentence, which was not ye part of a learnyd man; he addyd forther, "I do not" (quod he) "write ij negatives in one sentence: I can tell how to wryte, I trowe etc." To be short, he gave me thankes & professyd his friendshype in eny thinge that lay in hym to do & so we partyd.' But it was hardly in human nature, and certainly not in Grafton's, to take such criticisms lying down. When Stow's *Summarie of English Chronicles* appeared in 1565, Grafton made an abridgement of it which he prefaced with the blunt accusation that Stow had 'counterfeacted my volume . . . & hathe made my trvayle to passe vnder his name', and demanded that the Stationers' Company should withdraw their licence for the publication of the book. In the end, the Stationers invited both Stow and Grafton to appear before them and argue their case. Stow appeared, but Grafon could not face it. He 'allways made excusys & drave them of from tyme to tyme & nevar came at them', so that the Company was obliged to drop the matter and apologize to Stow.

Grafton continued, however, to abuse Stow in print, denouncing his work as 'superstitious foundations, fables and lies foolishly *stowed* together', to which Stow replied with references to 'unfruitful *grafts*'. When Grafton's *Chronicle at Large* appeared, Stow not only declared that he had taken it all from Froissart, Fabyan, Hall, and Cooper; he also made the more serious allegation that Grafton had taken his list of authorities from him (Stow) without ever having read them, and that, in order to make the list look more impressive, he often cited the same name twice, 'as in ye letter A. he writes Antoninus, in ye letter B, byshope, which is all one &c.' The last word lay with Stow, for Grafton died before he could produce his defence. Though not all Stow's criticisms were substantial, there can be little doubt that, in the main, his judgement of Grafton was sound. It did not, however, detract from the popularity of Grafton's histories which went into several editions, the *Abridgement of Chronicles* continuing to be regarded as the standard History of England. But the controversy had at least revealed that a section of informed opinion was beginning to demand from the historian a certain standard of accuracy and independent reading of the sources, if nothing more.[1]

John Stow made two further ventures into the general history of England after the publication of his *Summarie. The Chronicles of England* appeared in 1580 and the *Annales of England* in 1592, each representing an enlargement of its predecessor. Though much less readable than Hall, Stow was unquestionably a better historian, not only (as has been seen) more alive than any contemporary historian to the importance of records,[2] but also so well acquainted with the medieval chronicles as to reproduce them, with almost too great fidelity, in his own work. His laudable conviction that 'in hystories the chiefe thyng that is to be desyred is truthe'[3] led him to write with a kind of dry detachment that comes near to being dull. He preserved the annalistic form: and at times it seems as though the sheer volume of his material had overwhelmed him and deprived him of all power of discrimination. For this diligent searcher in the public records swallowed Geoffrey of Monmouth whole, and offers us Brutus, Joseph of Arimathaea, Arthur and the rest as sober history. He follows Hall in putting fictitious speeches into the mouths of his characters (though, lacking Hall's sense of drama, he does not do this well); he follows Polydore in making Henry I the creator of parliament; he gives us human and animal monstrosities, comets, floods, and pillars of fire in

---

[1] The text of Stow's version of the controversy is printed by C. L. Kingsford in his Introduction to the *Survey of London* (1908), I. xlviii–liii.

[2] Above, pp. 83–86.

[3] From the Epistle to the Reader prefaced to the *Summarie* (1565).

generous measure; but it is hard to discover his opinions of either events or persons. He writes with complete detachment of such controversial figures as Becket, King John, and John Wyclif. His work, as a whole, lacks light and shade. He had little sense of language and he writes less lucidly than Polydore and less rhythmically than Hall. The oblivion into which his *Chronicles* and *Annales* have passed is not wholly undeserved; for what he gives readers is the raw bones of history, rather than history alive. It was not until he set to work on the history of his native city that his talents found full scope. *The Survey of London* is a very different matter.[1]

It was in 1563 that John Day published, in one folio volume, the first edition of what was to prove an Elizabethan best-seller —John Foxe's *Actes and Monuments of these latter and perilous dayes, touching matters of the church*. Seven years later (1570), the scope of the work was extended and it appeared in three volumes, with the new title—*Ecclesiasticall history, contayning the actes and monumentes of thynges passed in euery kynges tyme in this realme*, to which, in 1576, was added, *especially in the Churche of England*. Two further editions of the work which came to be most commonly designated as *The Book of Martyrs* appeared (1583 and 1598) before the end of the Tudor period. Though the book is valuable chiefly to the historian of sixteenth-century Protestantism, Foxe brought the right ideas to his study of the medieval period. For the historian, he wrote,

diligence is required, and great searching out of bookes and autors, not onely of our time, but of all ages. And especially where matters of religion are touched perteyning to the church: it is not sufficient to see what Fabian or what Halle saith; but the recordes must be sought, the registers must be turned ouer, letters also & auncient instrumentes ought to be perused, and autors with the same compared; finally, the writers among them selues are to be conferred with another: And so with iudgement (matters are) to be wayed; with diligence to be labored; and with simplicitie, pure from all addiction and partialitie, to be uttered.[2]

Though very far from impartial, Foxe spared no pains to explore medieval primary sources, from many of which he quotes at great length. He knew Gildas, Bede, and the standard medieval chronicles; he owned the manuscript of the Great Chronicle of London, before Stow acquired it;[1] and he also made use of charters of William I, letters of Anselm and Becket, and episcopal registers from Canterbury, Norwich, and Hereford, together with legends innumerable, to support his thesis of 'the proud and misordered reign of Antichrist, beginning to stir in the Church of Christ', about the time of the Norman Conquest. Wyclif is his medieval hero; and it was from his friend, John Bale, that he obtained the only surviving copy of the 'Fasciculi Zizaniorum'.[2] His book displays impressive knowledge of the names and opinions of fifteenth-century Lollards, including Margery Baxter, who receives more attention than many of her male counterparts.[3]

The attitude of the much less well-known Francis Godwin (1562–1633) contrasted sharply with that of Foxe. Godwin, who was a friend of Camden's and subsequently Bishop of Llandaff, published in 1601 his *Catalogue of the Bishops of England since the first planting of Christian religion in this Island, together with a briefe History of their liues and memorable actions, so neere as can be gathered out of antiquity*. Few traces of hysterical Protestantism appear in these solid and generally well-balanced (though not very well-documented) biographies, and it is notably absent in that of Thomas Becket; and in his Address to the Reader, Godwin offers a fair enough judgement on the effects of the writings of Foxe and his like:

... For it is not to be denied, that the most part of the Chroniclers & historiographers of our age, haue borne a hand hard ynough at least upon the Prelates and Cleargy of former times. ... For in the vulgar sort ... is bred a conceit, not onely that the men were wicked, and so their doctrine corrupt ... but also their functions and callings to be utterly unlawful and Antichristian. ...

It is not, therefore, surprising that the firmly Catholic standpoint of Nicholas Harpsfield (1519–75) should have landed him in the Tower for the last sixteen years of his life, and that it was not until 1622 that his *Historia Anglicana Ecclesiastica . . . in*

[1] Thomas and Thornley, *The Great Chronicle of London*, pp. xvi–xvii.
[2] Described as 'a certaine old written boke in parchment, borrowed once of J.B.' (Foxe, I. 653).
[3] Two useful recent studies of Foxe are those of J. F. Mozley, *John Foxe and his Book* (1940), and W. Haller, *Foxe's Book of Martyrs* (1963).

Quindecim Centuriis Distributa, edited by Richard Gibbons, S.J., was published in Douai. In the Address to the Reader which prefaces this substantial work, the author cites an impressive list of sources, both English and foreign, and, needless to say, the *Historia Wicleffiana,* with which the book concludes, presents Foxe's hero in a very different light.

That the chronicle known as Holinshed's did not suffer the same fate as Stow's general histories was due less to its intrinsic merits than to its use by Shakespeare. As is well known, it originated in the printing-house of Reyne Wolfe, who had envisaged an ambitious scheme for a universal history and cosmography and, for twenty-five years before his death in 1573, had been at work (assisted by Ralph Holinshed, a native of Cheshire, who had studied at Cambridge) on the part of it relating to the British Isles. After Wolfe's death, three other established printers—John and Luke Harrison and George Bishop—took it over, and Holinshed continued his labours in their service. It soon became clear that the project of a universal history was too vast to be practicable, and the publishers decided to limit themselves to histories and descriptions of England, Scotland, and Ireland and to omit the maps. William Harrison, a chaplain in the service of Lord Brooke, was engaged to assist Holinshed in the descriptions of England and Scotland; and Richard Stanyhurst undertook to complete the history of Ireland, which Holinshed, drawing mainly on a manuscript by Edmund Campion, had already brought down to 1509. In July 1578, the printers obtained licence for the publication of 'Ralph Hollingshed's Cronycle' in two large folio volumes, which were well received. Holinshed himself did not long survive the publication. He died in 1580, and the printers then decided to prepare a new edition, John Hooker of Exeter being employed as general editor, assisted by Francis Thynne, Abraham Fleming, and John Stow. Hooker supervised the revision of the work, making many additions and alterations; and the new edition which appeared in 1587 was used by Shakespeare.

Thus, Holinshed's Chronicle was really the work of a syndicate. Harrison, Stanyhurst, and Hooker, as well as Holinshed himself, all contributed to the first volume which contains descriptions of England, Scotland, and Ireland, the history of

England to 1066 and the histories of Scotland and Ireland. Volume II (1,590 pages) contains the history of England from 1066 to 1586, written partly by Holinshed and partly by 'John Stow and others'. Not much in the way of literary artistry is to be looked for in work of this kind, compiled by many hands over a long period of years; and in their various epistles and prefaces the authors expressly disclaim any pretension to elegance of composition. 'Certes, I protest before God and your Highness', wrote Harrison in his Epistle Dedicatory,

> that I neuer made any choise of stile, or words, neither regarded to handle this Treatise in such precise order and method as manie other would haue done, thinking it sufficient, truelie and plainelie to set foorth such things as I minded to intreat of, rather than with vaine affectation of eloquence to paint out a rotten sepulcre . . . but howsoeuer it be done, & whatsoeuer I haue done, I haue had an especiall eye vnto the truth of things, and for the rest, I hope that this foule frizeled Treatise of mine will proue a spur to others better learned . . . and of greater iudgement in choise of matter. . . .[1]

Holinshed, in his Epistle Dedicatory to Cecil, explains that he has preferred comprehensiveness to order and selection in the arrangement of his materials:

> The histories I haue gathered according to my skill, and conferred the greatest part with Maister Wolfe in his life time, to his liking, who procured me so manie helpes to the furtherance thereof, that I was loth to omit anie thing that might increase the readers knowledge, which causeth the booke to grow so great. But receiuing them by parts, and at seuerall times (as I might get them) it may be, that hauing had more regard to the matter than the apt penning, I haue not so orderlie disposed them, as otherwise I ought; choosing rather to want order, than to defraud the reader of that which for his further understanding might seeme to satisfie his expectation.[2]

The book does, indeed, 'want order', not only in the arrangement of the several sections but in the lack of any selective principle governing the composition of the histories themselves. Holinshed and his associates suffered from the characteristic weakness of the inferior historian, inability to leave things out; and the modern reader who has to handle these weighty tomes may well regret that the editors allowed the work to 'grow so

[1] *Holinshed's Chronicle*, ed. (1807–8), I. vii. [2] Ibid. II.

great'. He cannot, however, withhold praise from the industry of the compilers. Though they borrowed freely from Hall and others, they were by no means mere plagiarists. They had read extensively and independently in the medieval literary sources; they knew the 'Dialogus de Scaccario'; they had consulted the registers of one or two religious houses, such as Bermondsey and Battle; and their list of authorities includes 'Recordes and Rolles diverse'. But in their approach to historical problems they show the same lack of critical discrimination that characterizes Stow's general histories. Britain was inhabited by the sons of Japhet shortly after the Flood; later came Albion the Giant who was slain by Hercules; then Brutus the Trojan (we are given the text of one of his letters, taken from Gerald of Wales) seized control with the help of Gogmagog; and after him followed a long succession of kings until the coming of the Romans; Joseph of Arimathaea brought Christianity, though some doubts are expressed as to whether St. Paul, or Simon Zelotes, or both, accompanied him.[1] When the Romans departed, the Saxons arrived. Arthur, 'a yoong, towardlie gentleman', put up heroic resistance to their incursions, winning twelve great victories, though in justice to Holinshed it must be noted that he admits 'Of this Arthur manie things are written beyond credit.'[2] So the familiar tale follows its accustomed course up to the Norman Conquest, where the first part of the History of England ends with an appropriate moral:

Now let these alterations of regiments be remembred . . . and teach vs that therein the iudgements of God reuealed themselues to speciall purposes. And whatsoeuer hath beene mentioned before . . . let vs I say as manie as will reape fruit by the reading of chronicles, imagine the matters which were so manie yeeres past to be present, and applie the profit and commoditie of the same vnto our selues; knowing . . . that, next vnto the holie scripture, chronicles doo carie credit.[3]

In the volume devoted to the post-Conquest period the annalistic form is maintained. We are taken through the reigns of successive rulers, year by year, in the manner of a medieval chronicle, and presented with a mass of detail, part fact, part fiction, with battle, murder and sudden death as the most

---

[1] Ibid. I. 486–7.   [2] Ibid. I. 574.   [3] Ibid. I. 766.

conspicuous features of the narrative. There is little characterization, though at the end of each reign we are given a brief
estimate of the ruler and invited to consider the appropriate
moral; and this is usually followed by a list of the learned men
who flourished in those days. The sources are quoted fully but,
as a rule, parrotwise; where conflicting accounts of the same
event are brought together, Holinshed follows his own precept
of leaving the reader to decide between them. He seems hardly
aware of any difference in value between (for example) the
testimony of Matthew Paris and of Fabyan for an event in the
thirteenth century. As it approaches the later Middle Ages,
the work increases in value because of the authors' use of
independent sources; but little remains of the dramatic tensions
to be found in Hall. Though he accepted it, Holinshed 'blurs
the great Tudor myth.'[1] He is pedestrian where Hall is eloquent
and laboured where Polydore is lucid.

A virulent form of Protestantism clouds Holinshed's understanding of the Middle Ages. Becket's mother, we are told, was a
Syrian born and a Saracen by religion and the moral of her son's
end is summarized as follows:

Thus you haue heard the tragicall discourse of ambitious Becket,
a man of meane parentage, and yet through the princes fauour
verie fortunate, if he had not abused the beneuolence of so gratious
a souereigne by his insolencie and presumption. Wherein we haue to
note, how unseemlie a thing it was for him, being called to so sacred
a function, to lead so secular and prophane a life. . . . We are also
taught, that promotions atchived by ambition are not permanent,
and are so farre from procuring fame and renowne to the obteiners,
that they turne them in the end to shame, infamie and reproch, after
losse of life and effusion of bloud.[2]

John is blamed severely for consenting to become a papal
vassal after hearing 'the sawcie speech of proud Pandulph the
popes lewd legat', and the moral of his reign is 'to shew the
palpable blindnes of that age wherein King John liued, as
also the religion which they reposed in a rotten rag . . .'. But
of Edward I we read 'wise he was and vertuous, an earnest
enimie of the high and presumptuous insolencie of preests, the
which he iudged to proceed cheeflie of too much wealthe and
riches: and therefore, he deuised to establish the statute of

[1] E. M. W. Tillyard, op. cit., p. 51.   [2] *Chronicle* II. 136–7.

Mortmaine, to be a bridle to their inordinate lusts and riotous excesse.'[1]

Protestant prejudice must certainly be reckoned among the major handicaps of the Elizabethan historians; and the study of late medieval history, in particular, was subject to all the drawbacks that normally attend study of the recent past. Many of the subjects of Henry VIII and of Elizabeth were acutely conscious of living in an age of enlightenment, feeling themselves to have passed from the darkness of popery to the dawn of true religion, from the horror and confusion of civil war to the beneficent rule of strong monarchy. Enthusiasts for the revival of classical studies tended to see the medieval period as an age of barbarism, riddled with every kind of irrational super-stition. And almost all the scholars and historians felt it neces-sary to apologize for the style of the medieval chroniclers. Leland deplored their lack of 'eloquence'; Parker had to argue that valuable historical material should not be neglected merely because it was written in rough Latin. Few appreciated the merits of historians like William of Malmesbury, jurists like Bracton, or humanists like John of Salisbury. Fewer still understood the degree to which classical poetry and rhetoric were loved and studied in the Middle Ages. The prevailing attitude was denounced by Samuel Daniel, writing in 1602:

Nor can it be but a touch of arrogant ignorance to hold this or that nation barbarous, these or those times gross, considering how this manifold creature man, wheresoever he stand in the world, hath always some disposition of worth. . . . Is it not a most apparent ignorance, both of the succession of learning in Europe and of the general course of things to say that all lay pitifully deformed in those lack-learning times from the declining of the Roman Empire till the light of the Latin tongue was revived by Reuchlin, Erasmus and More? . . . And yet long before all these our nation was not behind in her portion of spirit and worthiness but concurrent with the best of all this lettered world: witness, Venerable Bede that flourished above a thousand years since . . . what should I name Walter Map, Gervase Tilburiensis, Bracton, Bacon, Ockham and an infinite catalogue of excellent men . . . that have left behind them monu-ments of most profound learning in all sciences. So that it is but the clouds gathered about our own judgements that makes us think all other ages wrapt up in mists and the great distance betwixt us that

[1] Ibid. II. 306, 338, 544.

causes us to imagine men to far off to be so little in respect of our-
selves. . . . The distribution of gifts is universal and all seasons hath
them in some sort. We must not think but that there were Scipioes,
Caesars, Catoes and Pompeys born elsewhere than at Rome.[1]

Yet if medieval history appeared to many as a story of
decline, it continued to be read, and to be read with increasing
interest as the century advanced: as has been seen, the historians received encouragement from some of the highest in the
land. The reasons are not far to seek. A long and glorious past
was an indispensable asset to any nation desirous of making
its influence felt in Europe; and, though it was none too easy
to declare with conviction that the long centuries of the Middle
Ages were centuries of barbarism and superstition, and in the
same breath to claim for Britain a glorious history, the difficulty
did not prove insurmountable. Stress could be laid on the very
early chapters of British history, before the establishment of the
primacy of Rome. The story of Brutus could be used as evidence
of direct connection with classical antiquity, and the conversion
of the Britons by Joseph of Arimathaea or St. Paul as evidence
of the purity of British ecclesiastical traditions. In telling the
story of succeeding ages, stress could be laid on the anti-papal
activities of kings, like Henry II or Edward I, ecclesiastics,
like Grosseteste or Wyclif, politicians, like Gaunt or Oldcastle.
Or again, English history could be written and read mainly as
the history of great men of action. Attention could be directed
to victories in the field; the ecclesiastical aspect of history could
be, if not altogether ignored, at any rate minimized as it was in
so many of the histories written in this century. Arthur and
Alfred, Richard I and Edward III, the Black Prince and Henry
V, could readily be admitted as heroes: Becket and his like
could no less readily be allotted the role of minor villains.
Studied in this spirit, medieval history ceased to be dangerous
and became a valuable asset to the enthusiastic nationalist.
And, in many respects, it remained conservative.

Medieval historians wrote within a theological framework;
they regarded history as exemplarist and society as by nature
hierarchical; and, though these concepts suffered some modi-
fication, they were by no means abandoned in sixteenth-
century England. The view of history which saw men not as the

[1] Samuel Daniel, *Poems and a Defence of Ryme*, ed. A. C. Sprague (1930), pp. 140–4.

I

instrument of God but as the plaything of fate, which pointed to blind Fortune, not to divine Providence, as the motive force, had not struck roots in English thought. Machiavelli's ideas were considered, but, in the main, rejected. ' . . . that which seemeth most casual and subject to fortune', wrote Sir Walter Raleigh, 'is yet disposed by the ordnance of God, as all things else.'[1] Like their medieval forefathers, most Elizabethans see history as the reflection of a divine plan. It is still providentially ordered and, in that sense, theocentric. Yet it is providential with a difference. The Divine Being is reflected in the order of created nature, in the majesty of law and, in human history, in the rise and fall of nations, races, dynasties, and individuals. For the prevailing view of history is cyclic: it is seen to consist in alternations of good and evil fortune, though these alternations are believed to be the result, not of blind chance, but of divine planning. And, perhaps because of this emphasis on the cyclic aspect of history, on the pattern that endlessly repeats itself, the Tudor concept of history is less eschatological than was the medieval, attention is drawn to God's judgements as given in time, rather than to the final judgement in eternity. Amiot's preface to Plutarch's *Lives*, translated from the French by Sir Thomas North and published in 1579, declares that the historian

is but as a register to set downe the iudgements and definitiue sentences of Gods Court, whereof some are geuen according to the ordinarie course and capacitie of our weake naturall reason, and other some goe according to Gods infinite power and incomprehensible wisedom, aboue and against all discourse of mans understanding, who being unable to reach to the bottome of his iudgements, and to finde out the first motions and groundes thereof, do impute the cause of them to a certaine fortune, which is nought else but a fained deuice of mans wit, dazeled at the beholding of such brightnesse, and confounded at the gaging of so bottomlesse a deepe, howbeit nothing commeth to passe nor is done without the leaue of him that is the verie right and trueth it selfe. . . .

The moral element underlying much medieval historiography persists in the sixteenth century, intensified rather than diminished. In the first place, history is the school of private virtue 'So that it is as hard a matter', wrote Stow in the preface

[1] *History of the World.* (1736 edn.), I. 14.

to *The Chronicles of England* (1580), 'for the Readers of Chronicles, in my fansie, to passe without some colours of wisedome, invitements to vertue, and loathing of naughtie factes, as it is for a welfauoured man to walke up and downe in the hot parching Sunne & not to be therewith sunburned.' Heavy moralizing is a characteristic common to nearly all the sixteenth-century historians. They labour the rewards of virtue and the penalties of vice, and few, even of the subtler minds among them, seem to have been troubled by doubts as to the validity of this kind of argument. And history was much more than a school of private virtue. For princes and their people it was, above all, a school of public duty; and here, in the political lessons that it had to teach, lay its supreme virtue for the Tudor age. First, and most obvious, was its value for princes whom it instructed without flattery. The main intention of *The Mirror for Magistrates*, one of the most popular and influential compilations of the age, was to teach rulers their duty by showing them examples of the awful fate of tyrants in the past. The history of Richard II affords a good example,

> Happy is the prince that hath in welth the grace
> To folowe vertue, keping vices under,
> But wo to him whose Will hath wisedomes place:
> For who so renteth ryght and law a sunder
> On him at length loe, al the world shall wunder,
>
> .   .   .   .
>
> Let Princes, therfore vertuous life embrace
> That wilful pleasures cause them not to blunder.[1]

Princes are warned that their dynastic claims can never excuse the miseries of civil war:

> Farre better it wer to loose a piece of right,
> Than limmes and life in sousing for the same,
>
> .   .   .   .
>
> Wherfore warne princes not to wade in warre,
> For any cause, except the realmes defence:
> Their troublous titles are vnwurthy farre,
> The blud, the life, the spoyle of innocence.[2]

And on Bosworth field, Richard III is made to point the moral of his own misdeeds:

---

[1] *The Mirror for Magistrates*, ed. L. B. Campbell (1938), pp. 111–12.
[2] Ibid., p. 190.

Loe here you may beholde the due and iust rewarde
Of tiranny and treason which God doth most detest
For if vnto my duety I had taken regarde,
I myght haue lived stil in honour with the best.[1]

No less important was the moral value of history for the subjects of the prince, the duty of obedience and the wickedness of rebellion being the dominant themes. *The Mirror for Magistrates* echoes the moralizings of Hall and Holinshed. Thus, Jack Cade is made to exclaim,

Full litell knowe we wretches what we do,
When we presume our princes to resist.
We war with God, against his glory to
That placeth in his office whom he list,
Therefore was never traytour yet but mist
The marke he shot, and came to shamefull ende

.   .   .   .

God hath ordayned the power, all princes be
His Lieutenants, or debities in realmes.'[2]

Tyranny is sinful; princes should obey the law; but history teaches that no tyranny, however cruel, justifies rebellion. The moral is well put in one of the official Homilies issued in 1569: 'Turn over and read the histories of all nations; look over the chronicles of our own country: call to mind so many rebellions of old time and some yet fresh in memory: ye shall not find that God ever prospered any rebellion against their natural and lawful prince, but contrariwise that the rebels were overthrown and slain and such as were taken prisoners dreadfully executed.'[3] This was government propaganda; but there can be little doubt that it affords a fair enough reflection of the common opinion of the age. It explains the misfortunes of John Hayward, whose rash dedication to the suspect Earl of Essex of *The first Part of the life and raigne of Henrie IIII, Extending to the end of the first yeare of his raigne* (an account of the overthrow of Richard II by Henry Bolingbroke, published in 1599), together with his emphasis in the preface on the exemplarist value of history, 'both for private directions and for affairs of state', landed him

[1] Ibid., p. 370.   [2] Ibid., pp. 176-7.
[3] Quoted by E. M. W. Tillyard, op. cit., p. 69.

in the Tower.[1] Sir Philip Sidney did, indeed, venture to question the historian's competence to act as the schoolmaster of mankind. In his *Apologie for Poetrie* (*c.* 1583) he wrote that the historian 'denieth in a great chafe, than any man for teaching of vertue, and vertuous actions, is comparable to him', but he 'is so tyed, not to what shoulde bee but to what is, to the particular truth of things and not to the genral reason of things, that hys example draweth no necessary consequence, and therefore a lesse fruitfull doctrine.' But Amiot had already provided an answer in his assertion that history 'doth things with greater weight and grauitie, than the inuentions & deuices of the Poets, bicause it helpeth not it selfe with any other thing than with the plaine truth, whereas Poetry doth commonly inrich things by commending them aboue the starres and their deseruing bicause the chiefe intent thereof is to delight.'[2] To the poet, the historian might often appear as a dry-as-dust; to the historian, the poet might appear as a frivolous purveyor of mere amusement, lacking the *gravitas* which becomes the serious teacher. But these were the differences of specialists. The glory of the Elizabethan age lay in its appetite for both.

[1] See M. Dowling, 'Sir John Hayward's Troubles over his Life of Henry IV', *The Library*, 4th ser. XI (1931), 212–24. N. Scarfe, 'Sir John Hayward, an Elizabethan historian, his life and disappointments', *Proc. Suffolk Inst. of Archaeology & Natural History* XXV (1950), 79–97.

[2] From the Preface to Sir Thomas North's translation of Plutarch's *Lives* (1579).

VI

LOCAL HISTORIANS AND TOPOGRAPHERS

W HEN the eighteenth-century historian of British topography looked back to the age of the Tudors it seemed evident to him that 'The rays that dispelled the gloom of religion illuminated every branch of science. It was not till the monks were turned adrift, and the invention of printing had given circulation to every improvement the mind enlarged could make, that we began to be acquainted with the face of our own country.' The first to open the way was Leland who, in addition to his labours among manuscripts, 'made a particular and regular description of the places he visited'; and Gough rightly regarded Leland's researches as 'the first-fruits of antiquarian science among us.'[1] Among Leland's progeny in the succeeding age, pride of place must be accorded to Camden who tends to overshadow the rest because he alone achieved a general description of Britain. But, as Camden himself was always ready to admit, he owed much to his fellow-workers, to the cartographers, topographers, and local historians who were active throughout much of the land, from Durham to Cornwall, from Pembroke to Kent. Some were stirred, above all, by zest for antiquity; some were eager to preserve their own world for posterity; many shared both these impulses. The common factor uniting them all was love of their native land, that Britain 'So rich in commodities, so beautifull in situation, so resplendent in all glorie, that if the most Omnipotent had fashioned the world round like a ring, as he did like a globe, it might haue bene most worthily the only gemme therein.'[2]

Though we have no evidence of any direct contacts between them, some of the older generation of Elizabethan topographers overlapped with Leland. If William Lambarde and Sampson Erdeswicke were still in their teens when he died in 1552, John Hooker (alias Vowell) and John Stow were men

---

[1] R. Gough, *British Topography* (1780), I. iii–iv.
[2] W. Camden, *Remaines concerning Britaine* (1614), p. 1.

of about twenty-seven, and William Whitlock, the veteran among them, was thirty-two. The youthful memories of these three took them back to the age of the Dissolution. Many of the smaller houses had gone, but the greater still stood unmolested when William Whitlock entered King's College, Cambridge as a young scholar from Eton in 1537, when the orphaned Hooker was at school in Menheniot under Dr. John Moreman, and when John Stow was making himself useful by fetching home milk 'hote from the Kine', from Goodman's Fields, next the Minories.[1] Whitlock's studies of Lichfield, Hooker's of Exeter, and Stow's of London were the work of Elizabethans who could recall a vanished world.

William Whitlock (1520–84) was at home in antiquarian circles. He was a friend of John Twyne to whom, as has been seen, he conveyed information about the fate of Bale's library after his departure from Ireland, and of Francis Thynne who was indebted to him for the excerpts from the Lichfield Chronicle preserved among his collections.[2] One of the very few clergymen to make any significant contribution to local studies in this period, Whitlock, who was a prebendary of Lichfield for over twenty years, devoted himself to its history, more particularly to the history of its bishops. His work (which remained in manuscript for over a century) included eighteen *additamenta* to Thomas Chesterfield's unpublished chronicle of the Bishops of Coventry and Lichfield, which extended to 1347, and a further series of brief biographies from Roger Northburgh (1322–58) to Thomas Bentham (1560–79).[3] His references show him to have been well read in the Canterbury Registers, particularly those of the fifteenth century, but, apart from a few deeds of gift, he seems to have made disappointingly little use of local materials such as the Chapter Act Books, which date from 1384, the 'Magnum Registrum Album', which includes some twelfth-century charters, or the Registers of the Bishops of Lichfield.[4] The only chroniclers referred to, in addition to the Lichfield Chronicle, are Birchington and one of the continuators of Higden. Thus, though Whitlock's collections are useful, they must be judged limited in scope.

---

[1] *Survey of London*, I. 126.   [2] B.M. MS. Cott., Cleopatra C. III, ff. 240–57.
[3] Wharton, *Anglia Sacra* (1691), I. 444–59.
[4] See *Collections for a History of Staffordshire* (1886), VI. 2.

The Exeter historian, John Hooker (1525–1601), uncle of the famous Richard, was a much more assiduous researcher. A native of the city, he went from his Cornish school to Oxford and thence to the continent where he studied law and divinity. He himself has explained how it came about that he abandoned his high intellectual ambitions. Soon after his return from abroad 'he was dryven to take a wyffe, and then all his desyres and zeale to learnynge and knowledge therewith abated. Notwithstandinge he gave himselfe to the readinge of histories and seekinge of antyquities, and somewhat to armorye',[1] clearly a second-best. He settled in Exeter and became its first Chamberlain; some years later he went to Ireland on business for Sir Peter Carew, and he represented Athenry in the Irish parliament of 1568. In 1571, he sat for Exeter in Elizabeth's third parliament.[2] His reputation was evidently considerable, for he was invited to contribute to the new edition of Holinshed which appeared in 1586. He was also the author of an (un-published) 'Synopsis Chorographica, or brief description of the Province of Devon', in which historical and heraldic material and a series of brief accounts of Devon worthies from the fourth to the sixteenth century were conjoined with de-scriptions of the contemporary scene. Yet he devoted much, perhaps most, of his energy to studying the records of his native city; and it was not until late in life that he began to assemble the results of his enquiries. Thus, as he himself wryly explains, *The Description of the Citie of Excester* is an old man's book:

But as the Common proverbe is be the Daye never so longe at lengeth it ringeth at eveninge songe: I after my longe trauells and Drawen in to yeres and bearinge the borden of sondry infirmities wch age bringeth with itselffe and feelinge in my selffe many Defectes aswell in the faculties of the mynde as in the powers of the bodye in both wch I fynde myselffe unweldye and imperfecte to Do the good that I woulde. . . . I thought it most meete to bestowe that parte of my lyffe and weake helthe and olde yeres wch Remayneth in reducinge all my former studyes Contayninge Cheffly the whole state govermt and order of this yor Citie and Commonwelth into one booke or lyeger.[3]

[1] From the 'Synopsis Chorographica'. See *Journal of the British Archaeologica Association*, XVIII (1862), 138–43.

[2] Hooker kept a journal of the proceedings of this parliament. See *Trans. Devon Association* XI (1879), 442–92, and J. E. Neale, *Elizabeth and her Parliaments*, I. 184.

[3] *Trans. Devon and Cornwall Record Soc.* (1919), II. 4. The preface and Index were published in 1947.

The *Description* affords striking testimony to Hooker's unflagging industry, wide-ranging curiosity, and astute appreciation of the nature of historical evidence, but offers its readers little opportunity to judge him as an author. By far the greater part of his enormous folio consists of transcripts of record material, a vast assemblage of *pièces justificatives*, many of them deriving from the sixteenth century. Of the 951 pages of the printed edition,[1] only some 80 embody historical narrative, and 40 of these are devoted to an account of the Rising of 1549 as it affected Exeter. Thus, the ancient and medieval history of the city is condensed into less than 30 pages, and these reveal no very coherent arrangement. We begin, properly enough, with origins, and here Hooker shows commendable caution, admitting that 'no certeyne memoriall' of the foundation of the city remains among its records or in any other source. There can be no doubt, however, that it was founded by the *Britones*, 'the remanente of the blood of Brutus'. The origin of the name is the subject of a lengthy disquisition, leading to the sound conclusion that *Excestria* derives from the river Exe and noting the prevalence of the termination *cestre* among many ancient cities. The situation of Exeter is 'verie pleasaunte and ameouse beinge sett vppon a little hill emonge manye hills.' The reader is told of its ample water-supplies, its springs, fountains and conduits, and then led up the hill to Rougement castle, with its 'goodlie and pleasaunte prospecte towarde the seas: for between that and it is no hyll at all.' Hooker ascribes it not, indeed, to Julius Caesar, but to the 'Romaynes aftr hym' and believes it to have been a palace of the Kings of Wessex before it became the property of the Earls of Cornwall. At the lower end of the city, outside the walls, 'fleetethe a goodlie and a pleasaunte Ryver', well-stocked with fish; the sea is not more than eight miles away and that an arm of it once flowed up to the city-wall 'dothe appeare by certeyne olde and auncyente Records.' Merchandise was unloaded at the Watergate; but the harbour was destroyed in the time of Edward II by Hugh Courtenay, Earl of Devon, who, having quarrelled with the citizens, built a weir through which no vessels could pass. From an account of the destruction of the harbour and the iniquitous conduct of the Earl and his grandson, we pass abruptly to the city churches.

[1] These include the editors' translations of Latin texts.

These were few in number until Innocent III established the doctrine of Transubstantiation[1] '... by wch means the nomber of sacrificienge and massinge preests dyd not onlie increase but Churches also and Chaples beganne in all places and everie where to be builded & erected', the number reaching nineteen in the city and suburbs by the reign of Henry VI. There was also the Benedictine monastery, on the site of which arose the cathedral, 'a verie fayre and a sumptuose buyldinge of free stone and with beautifull pyllers of graye marble'. Athelstan was its founder, and under Edward the Confessor the episcopal see was transferred there from Crediton. By reference to the great charter of the Cathedral which was among his transcripts, Hooker was able to correct Polydore's assertion that the transference took place under William I who, in fact, merely confirmed the Confessor's charter. Further revenues, privileges and buildings were added under his successors. The Close and its water-supplies are briefly described, and we then pass to the populous city, once the abode mainly of clothiers, but now of merchants. In his sketch of the development of civic government, Hooker places the emergence of portreeves and of the mayor and aldermen at dates much earlier than the evidence warrants. A clue to Exeter's history, he suggests, is afforded by the dictum 'The Citie hathe alwayes bene faythfull to the kinge.' Nine examples are cited, ranging from the relief of the city by the British king, Arviragus, when it was besieged by Vespasian, to the Rising of 1549. Recognizing that 'the Recordes & memorialls in those daies for the most parte were lost and consumed', Hooker relies for the details of his early examples on chroniclers such as Geoffrey of Monmouth, Henry of Huntingdon, Howden, and 'Matthew of Westminster', passages from some of these authors being transcribed *verbatim*. For the siege by the Danes in the time of Alfred, he has recourse to Polydore, raising no question as to the relative trustworthiness of his sources. A brief catalogue of the Bishops includes few biographical details, the most startling omission being any reference to the foundations of Walter Stapledon at Oxford and Exeter. All we are told of him is that he 'dyd many good things in his tyme.'

Where Hooker failed as a historian was in his inability to use

[1] Dated by Hooker 1198 instead of 1215.

the valuable record material which he had so laboriously transcribed to reconstruct more than a fraction of the history of the
city. His medieval documents include numerous charters,
valuations and wills, actions of Novel Disseisin and Quo
Warranto, inquests, rentals and petitions; but to criticize these
or to demonstrate their relevance to his theme was a task
beyond his powers. Perhaps he had left it too late.

John Stow was much better equipped for his tremendous
task. His acquaintance with the city of London was lifelong;
he was on friendly terms with most of the leading antiquarians
of his day, with William Camden and William Lambarde, with
Henry Savile and Robert Glover, with John Dee and William
Fleetwood, with Thomas Talbot, Robert Hare and many others.
He was very widely read, not only in public and civic records,
but also in historical literature. He knew all the standard
histories, from Caesar to Polydore Vergil, and some of the less
well known, such as the Bermondsey and Dunstable annals
and the 'Anonimalle Chronicle' of St. Mary's, York, and he
possessed valuable manuscripts of many of them, including one
of the 'Great Chronicle of London', in which he made many
marginal notes.[1] It was an immense advantage to him that
he came to the writing of local history with his reputation as a
general historian of England already established; this enabled
him to set the history of London in a national framework.
In his address to the Mayor, Commonalty, and Citizens which
prefaces the second edition of the *Survey of London* (1603), he
explains that, since the publication of Lambarde's *Perambulation of Kent*, he had heard tell of similar projects for other shires
and, partly on this account, partly to 'giue occasion and courage
to M. *Camden* to increase and beautify his singular work of the
whole', he had 'attempted the discouery of *London,* my natiue
soyle and Countrey.'[2] Lambarde's influence is evident; for the
greater part of the *Survey* also takes the form of a perambulation.[3] From a discussion of the antiquity of London, Stow passes
to descriptions and discussions of the wall, the rivers, bridges,

[1] Thomas and Thornley, *The Great Chronicle of London*, p. xvi.

[2] *Survey of London* I. xcvii. The first edition appeared in 1598.

[3] It has been suggested recently that Stow may have made use of a large map
of London, printed from a set of copper plates, two of which survive. See M.
Holmes 'A Source-book for Stow', *Studies in London History*, ed. A. E. J. Hollaender
and W. Kellaway (1969), pp. 275–85.

and gates; the Tower and other castles; schools and houses of
learning; customs, sports and pastimes; and a list of famous
Londoners. Having explained the division of the city into
wards, he then conducts his reader through all twenty-six of
these, from Portsoken to Bridge Ward Without, noting points
of both antiquarian and contemporary interest. Lists of the
Bishops of London and of the civic officers conclude the book.
Neither his long searches in the records, nor his extensive
knowledge of the chronicles misled Stow into presenting his
readers with a mass of ill-digested and unexplained transcripts.
The material is under control, subordinated to the demands of
the author's plan, and allowing full scope for the exercise of his
skill and the display of his qualities as historian.

These qualities were many and valuable. Whatever the
truth about his own religious opinions, Stow's study of London
shows no trace of the savage Protestant bias that disfigures the
work of so many of his contemporaries. Thus, the facts about
that famous Londoner, Thomas Becket, are presented without
comment, adverse or otherwise; and so, too, is the history of the
Templars. By modern standards he was credulous, of course;
and he has been rightly named as one of the sixteenth-century
popularizers of the British History, of the stories of the Trojans,
Brutus and Arthur.[1] He accepts Simeon of Durham's statement
that London was first walled by the Empress Helen, mother of
Constantine; and his catalogue of the Bishops of London
includes the information that the first Archbishop was Thean, a
contemporary of King Lucius. Yet Stow's credulity is tempered
with a vein of scepticism and common sense. At the opening of
the *Survey*, he refers with approval to Livy's view that 'Antiquitie is pardonable, and hath an especial priuiledge, by inter-
lacing diuine matters with humane, to make the first foundation
of Cities more honourable, more sacred, and as it were of
greater maiestie.'[2] He sees that Caesar's Commentaries
are 'of farre better credit than the relations of *Giffrey Monmouth*'
and he knows that it was not Caesar but William I who built
the Tower. He is not afraid to admit ignorance, as when he
writes of the Standard in the middle of Cheapside, 'of what
antiquitie the first foundation I haue not read';[3] or to refer his

[1] Kendrick, *British Antiquity*, p. 39.   [2] *Survey of London* I. 1.
[3] Ibid. I. 264.

readers, even on such a matter as the etymology of the name London, to 'the more large and learned discourse . . . in that worke of my louing friend M. *Camden*, now *Clarenceaulx*, which is called *Britannia*'.[1] The numerous marginalia in his manuscripts and the many variations and emendations in the printed editions bear witness to the pains he took to verify his facts. The plan of the work entails a certain amount of repetition, as when Londoners who have already appeared in the list of famous citizens recur under their Wards; and the style makes few concessions to the reader. Yet Stow's pride in the grandeur of London, his sense of its past, his desire to preserve its beauty are unmistakable. He writes of the Tower that it is 'a Citadell, to defend or commaund the Citie: a royall place for assemblies and treaties. A Prison of estate, for the most daungerous offenders: the onely place of coynage for all England at this time: the armorie for warlike prouision: the Treasurie of the ornaments and Jewels of the crowne, and generall conseruer of the most Recordes of the kings Courts of iustice at Westminster.'[2] After relating the history of what, in his time, was the Windmill Inn in Old Jewry, he concludes, 'And thus much for this house, sometime the Iewes Synagogue, since a house of Fryers, then a Noble mans house, after that a Marchauntes house, wherein Mayoralties haue beene kept, and now a Wine Tauerne.'[3] He is outraged by the fact that the south side of St. Paul's, 'with the chapter House (a beautifull peece of worke, builded about the raigne of *Edwarde* the third) is now defaced by meanes of Licenses graunted to Cutlers, Budget makers, and other, first to builde low sheddes, but now high Houses, which doe hide that beautifull side of the Church, saue onely the toppe and south Gate';[4] and saddened to observe that, of 'the faire written bookes in Vellem' with which the cathedral library was well furnished, few now remain.[5] Despite numerous errors and the inadequate standards of criticism inevitable in that age, the surveyor of England's greatest city must rank as one of her greatest local historians.

Among those antiquaries who took a county, rather than a city, as their province, pride of place belongs to William Lambarde. The copy of the *Perambulation of Kent* which he presented

---

[1] Ibid. I. 8.   [2] Ibid. I. 59.   [3] Ibid. I. 278.
[4] Ibid. II. 19.   [5] Ibid. I. 328.

to Sir Henry Sydney is prefaced with a letter, written in his own hand from Lincoln's Inn, on 1 June 1576, in which he tells the story of the book's gestation.[1] For some years he had been busy collecting notes for a Topographical Dictionary, and when, on the occasion of his marriage, he removed from London to Kent, he decided to make a pioneer venture with this county, 'to make estimation and tryalle, bothe of the thyng it selfe, of myne owne abilitie, & of other mens lykings.' He showed the first draft to his friend, Thomas Wotton, who urged him to publish it and, after long argument, overcame his objections. He recounts all this so that Sydney may understand 'by what myshap and mydwife this Bearwhelp & untymely byrthe of myne was brought into open lyghte.' Thomas Wotton's preface, in which he expresses the hope that Lambarde will do for other counties what he has done for Kent, is followed by ten lines of Latin verse, composed by William Fleetwood, Recorder of London, in Lambarde's honour—'Ingenio rarus, grauis arte, labore notandus'—and by a key to Old English characters, a list of errata and a coloured map of the Heptarchy.

The *Perambulation* (most of which seems to have been written in 1570) opens with a general description of the county, its situation, climate, products, population and early history. There follow lists of the hundreds and townships, the former religious houses, the nobility and gentry, and Kentish writers, 'drawne (for the most part) out of the Centuries of Maister Iohn Bale.' Lambarde then allows himself a digression, in the form of 'A short counsell, as touching the Bryttishe hystorie', which he is at pains to defend against Polydore Vergil, explaining that his own principle is to try to sift the wheat from the chaff, the true from the false, 'with the fire and fan of iudgement and discretion.' The main study is divided under the two Kentish dioceses, a brief sketch of the origins and early history of the See of Canterbury and a list of the Archbishops, introducing the perambulation of the diocese from Thanet to Leeds (pp. 78–265). After a similar introduction to the diocese of Rochester, we perambulate from Gillingham to Eltham (pp. 266–387). The conclusion, which is followed by a useful discussion of *gavelkind*, affords a good example of the author's self-imposed limitations and cautious handling of his theme.

[1] Bodleian Library, 4to Rawl. 587.

'. . . as for the Feodaries and Tenures of land, Genealogies &
Armes of men, Ebbes, Floudes & Tides of the Sea and Riuers,
Flattes, Barres, Hauens & such other things . . . haue I wittingly,
and without touche, lept ouer them all.' This was partly due to
ignorance, partly for fear of giving offence or disclosing secrets.
As for the description of the rest of the realm, this would be too
big a task for any one man and Lambarde wishes that someone
in each shire would undertake the enterprise, 'to the end that by
ioyning our pennes and conferring our labours (as it were) . . .
wee may at the last by the union of many parts and papers,
compact a whole and perfect bodie and Booke of our English
antiquities.'[1] But when he came to publish the edition of 1596,
the picture had changed. 'Here left I (good Reader) when I first
set foorth this Worke: Since which time I finde my desire not a
little serued by Master Camden's *Britannia*: wherein, as he hath
not onely farre exceeded whatsoeuer hath been formerly
attempted in that kynd, but hath also passed the expectation
of other men & even his own hope: So do I acknowledge it
written to the great Honour of the realme with men abroad &
to the singular delight of us all at home, hauing for mine own
particular found my self thereby to haue learned much euen
in that Shyre wherein I had endeuoured to know most. Never-
thelesse, being assured that the Inwardes of each place may best
be knowen by such as reside therein, I cannot but still encourage
some one able man in each Shyre to undertake his owne,
wherby both many good particularities will come to discouerie
euery where, and Master Camden himselfe may yet haue
greater choice wherewith to amplifie and enlarge the whole.'[2]

The *Perambulation of Kent* is, first and foremost, the work of a
lawyer with an overriding interest in Old English law and the
etymology of place-names. Lambarde's indifference to pre-
Saxon and, above all, to Roman antiquities contrasts sharply
with the attitude of his friend, William Camden.[3] Yet his
extensive searches among records had not blinded him to the
value of chronicles and histories; and the range of his reading
in these sources is impressive. It was natural that a member of
Lincoln's Inn should know Bracton and Littleton; less to be

---

[1] *Perambulation of Kent* (1596), pp. 526-7.   [2] Ibid., p. 386.
[3] See Kendrick, *British Antiquity*, pp. 139-40. Most of what he has to say of
Romano-British towns derives from Leland.

expected that his general reading should include, not only such standard authors as Bede, Henry of Huntingdon, William of Malmesbury, Howden, William of Newburgh, Geoffrey of Monmouth, Gerald of Wales, 'Matthew of Westminster', Higden, and the 'Cronica' ascribed to Thomas Sprott and William Thorne of St. Augustine's (with which a historian of Kent would naturally be familiar), but also Ailred of Rievaulx's life of Edward the Confessor, 'an auncient Chronicler of Couentrie (whose name I have not hytherto learned)',[1] Alfred of Beverley, 'auncient Chronicles of S.Wereburges in Chester',[2] the Chronicle of Battle Abbey, and the 'Chronicon' of Geoffrey le Baker, then commonly ascribed to Thomas de la More.[3] Lambarde read these authors with stout Protestant scepticism, 'reiecting the fonde dreames of doting Monkes and fabling Frears'.[4] His comment on the dissolution of the monasteries reveals his standpoint. He deplores the loss of so many fine buildings: but 'considering the manie Seas of sinne and iniquitie, wherein the worlde (at those dayes) was almost whole drenched, I must needs take cause, highly to prayse God, that hath thus mercifully in our age deliuered us.' To Bede's story of Mellitus and the fire he appends this postscript, 'I wote well, this writer is called, *Venerabilis*: but when I read this, and a number of such, which make the one halfe of his worke, I say with my selfe, as sometime did the Poet, *Quodcunque ostendis mihi sic, incredulus odi*, What euer thing thou shewest me so, I hate it as a lye.'[5] And of the building of Eltham palace by Anthony Bek, Bishop of Durham, he writes:

To say the trueth, this was not to builde up the spirituall house with liuely stones, resting on the chiefe corner to Heauen, and to Godward, but with Mammon and Material stuffe to erect warrelyke Castles for the nourishment of contention: and stately Palaces, for the maintenaunce of worldly pride and pleasure, towardes Hell and the Deuill. Howbeit *this was the whole studie of Bishops in the

---

[1] *Memoriale* of Walter of Coventry.   [2] *Annales Cestrienses*.

[3] '. . . there is hope, that a special hystorie of ye reigne [of Edward II] (penned by S. Thomas Delamore, which liued in ye very time it self) may be hereafter imprinted and made common.' *Perambulation* (1576), p. 263. The chronicle was not in fact, printed until 1603. Lambarde's transcript was the work of Lawrence Nowell (See Nicols, *Bibliotheca Topographica Britannica* I. 510.)

[4] *Perambulation*, p. 13.   [5] Ibid., pp. 235-6.

Popish Kingdome, and therefore* letting that passes, let us see what became of this piece of his building.[1]

'Iudgement and discretion' are not the fruits of such an attitude, and Lambarde lent the authority of his learning to the current legend that the first inhabitants of Britain were descendants of Samothes, son to Japhet and grandson to Noah, and ranged himself with the defenders of the Brutus legend, though not in its most extravagant form.[2] The book reveals no feeling for landscape, and little of the natural beauties or distinctive physical features of Kent emerges from it. Lambarde's usual method, as he conducts his reader to a particular town or village, is to begin with an explanation of the place-name, then to outline its history, with special reference to its manner of government, and the history of its notable buildings, including bridges, making little attempt to describe either towns or villages or to convey any visual image. Archaeology was a closed book to him and he seems almost totally unaware of the potential value to the historian of the ruins which lay thick about the land. Yet the book is packed with learned information, and Lambarde's homely style, his knack of seeming to converse with his reader as together they perambulate the county, makes him eminently readable. Moreover, evidence that his knowledge of local history was not confined to his own county is afforded by his topographical collections which remained in manuscript until the eighteenth century.[3]

The career of the historian of Staffordshire offers an interesting contrast to that of William Lambarde. Sampson Erdeswicke was the son of a Staffordshire gentleman who suffered much, under Elizabeth, for his loyalty to the old order in religion. A commoner at Brasenose from 1553 to 1554 and afterwards a member of the Inner Temple, he chose to spend most of his adult life in retirement: and, although he seems to have been a member of the Society of Antiquaries, there is no record of his having addressed them and it is likely to have been the liberal-minded Camden who gained him admission.[4] His name appears in more than one list of recusants in the

---

[1] Ibid., p. 385. The words between asterisks were omitted in the edition of 1596.
[2] Ibid., p. 13. See Kendrick, op. cit., pp. 70–3.
[3] *Dictionarium Angliae Topographicum et Historicum* (1730). These collections owed much to Lawrence Nowell. See Kendrick, op. cit., p. 116.
[4] A list of those summoned to the meeting of 2 November 1598 concludes with

K

1570s,[1] though his benefactions to the parish church of Sandon, where, in 1603, he was buried in a handsome tomb of his own designing, suggest at least outward conformity with the established Church. But, whatever his private convictions, no trace of Lambarde's Protestant bias appears in Erdeswicke's historical work. When discussing the origin of the alabaster tomb in Burton Abbey, he writes of monks with a tolerance that comes near to approbation. '. . . the monks were very careful to set out gay things for their founders; to the end it might be thought, they were not unmindful of good men, which were their benefactors.'[2] His vivid description of Lichfield Cathedral suggests a certain nostalgia '. . . the west part is, at the end also, exceeding finely cut, and cunningly set forth with a great number of tabernacles; and, in the same, the images or pictures of the prophets, apostles, kings of Judah, and divers other kings of this land, so well embossed and so lively cut, that it is a great pleasure for any man, that takes delight to see rarities, to behold them';[3] and his terse comment on the changes made at Calwich by the 'Lancashire gentleman' who became the new owner of this disused cell carries no hint of approbation: '. . . as I have heard [he] hath made a parlour of the chancel, a hall of the church, and a kitchen of the steeple, which may be true, for I have known a gentleman in Cheshire, who hath done the like.'[4]

It was during the last ten years of his life, between 1593 and 1603, that Erdeswicke compiled his 'View', or 'Survey' of Staffordshire; and the history of the several manuscripts which survive is one of great confusion, for these vary a great deal, not only in orthography, but in language and even in topographical arrangement. At least one seems to have fallen into the hands of Walter Chetwynd of Ingestre; Dugdale said that the original from which he made a transcript and which formed the basis of the first printed edition (1717) belonged to George Digby of Sandon;[5] another, in the library at Wrottesley in Stafford-

---

the words, 'and I left a summons with Mr Carentius for Mr Erswicke.' Hearne, *Curious Discourses* (1775), I. xvii.

[1] W. R. Trimble, *The Catholic Laity in Elizabethan England* (1964), pp. 77–9, 87.
[2] *Survey of Staffordshire*, ed. T. Harwood (1844), p. 475.
[3] Ibid., p. 281.   [4] Ibid., pp. 489–90.
[5] A copy of this edition in the Bodleian Library (Gough Stafford 4) has notes by Hearne.

shire, seems to have been the property of Camden. Erdeswicke had earlier made substantial collections for Cheshire, the most important of which are preserved in the Harleian collection in an octavo volume (MS. 473) to which Sir Simonds D'Ewes prefixed the title, 'Certaine verie rare Obseruations of Chester; some parts of Wales; with diuers Epitaphes, Coats, Armories & other Monuments, verie orderlie & labouriouslie gathered together (. . . All taken by the Author who seems to me to have been Sampson Erdeswicke) A.D. 1574'; and in a quarto volume (MS. 506), entitled 'Mr Erdeswicke's Book of Cheshire'. Some of his observations on Cumberland and Northumberland, mainly heraldic in character, have also been preserved.[1]

The slant of Erdewicke's interests was different from Lambarde's. Though he occasionally indulges in speculation on the origin of a place-name, it is clear that he had no expert etymological knowledge. When he found what he took to be an Old English inscription in Dudley churchyard, he very sensibly told his secretary to make a copy 'and send the same to Mr Camden at Westminster.'[2] He made use of Domesday Book and transcribed a number of charters, but he appears to have been much less well read in the general historical literature of the Middle Ages than many of his fellow antiquaries. His plan was to follow the rivers (as Camden had done) beginning with Trent; he was less interested in the growth and government of urban and rural communities than in the noble and gentle families (his own included) who had inherited estates in the county. Heraldry appealed to him, rather than law, artefacts— houses, castles and monuments—rather than natural features. The result is a book with a charm of its own which owed much to the author's sensitivity, tolerance, and judgement. There is little to cavil at in Camden's view of him as 'venerandae antiquitatis cultor maximus'[3] or in Fuller's verdict: 'Bearing a tender respect to his native County, and desiring the honour thereof: he began a Description. . . . A short, clear, true, impartial work, taken out of ancient Evidences and Records. . . . This is he, who, when I often groped in the dark, yea feared to fall in matters concerning this County, took me by the hand

---

[1] *Newcastle Tracts* VII (1848), ed. M. A. Richardson.
[2] *Survey of Staffordshire*, p. 342.　　　　[3] *Britannia* (1600), p. 518.

(Oh! for the like Conductors in other Counties!) and hath led me safe by his direction.'[1]

Richard Carew (1550–1620), whose *Survey of Cornwall* is probably the best-known and certainly the best-loved of the Tudor county studies, was fortunate in that he combined intimate knowledge of Cornwall with a variety of experience elsewhere. From Christ Church, Oxford, where he became the friend of Philip Sidney and William Camden, he passed to Clement's Inn and the Middle Temple before settling down at Antony to play the part of a leading country gentleman. He served successively as Justice of the Peace, Sheriff, and parliamentary burgess for Saltash and Mitchell; after the opening of the Spanish war he was one of the deputy-lieutenants of Cornwall. Reputed 'the most excellent manager of bees'[2] in the county, he was also an accomplished linguist (though unfortunately ignorant of Cornish) and a prominent member of the Society of Antiquaries. His *Survey* was published in 1602, with a dedication to Raleigh explaining that it had been 'long since begun' and 'a great while discontinued.'[3] It is divided into two books, the first comprising a general description of the county, its climate, products (animal, vegetable, and mineral), land-tenures, roads, bridges, languages, and classes; and the second, a perambulation of the Hundreds, beginning from the East where Carew himself lived. He was not deeply read in history. Howden, 'Matthew of Westminster', and Froissart are the only medieval chroniclers he cites, and the interest of his work is not primarily that of a study of the past. It has been valued as a picture of Tudor Cornwall, rather than as a repository of Cornish antiquities. None the less, the book is infused with a sense of the past and, in some respects, Carew was less credulous than many of his contemporaries.

On the question of the origin of the name of Cornwall, though he is, as he tells his readers, 'not ignorant how sorely the whole story of Brute is shaken by some of our late writers, and how stiffly supported by other some', Carew is inclined to accept the legend that this part of Britain was bestowed by

---

[1] *The Worthies of England*, ed. Nichols (1811), II. 310.
[2] *Survey of Cornwall* (ed. 1811), Introd., p. xv.
[3] Reprinted in 1723, 1769, and 1811. The latest edition is by F. E. Halliday (1953).

Brutus on Corineus after his exploit in wrestling with Gogmagog on Plymouth Hoe.[1] Arthur, 'a Cornishman by birth, a King of Britain by succession, and the second of the three Christian worthies by desert',[2] is allowed the prominence due to him from a historian of the West Country. That he was bred at Tintagel is its chief claim to fame; and Camelford is memorable as the site of the last dismal battle where he met his death '. . . For testimony whereof, the old folk thereabouts will show you a stone bearing Arthur's name, though now depraved to *Atry*.'[3] The history of the county and the creation and subsequent history of the Duchy are severely curtailed, less space being allotted to them than to the history of the family of Carew; yet Carew was wise enough to follow Lambarde's example in refusing to overload his work with heraldry. 'I had also', he writes, 'made a more painful than perfect collection of most of the Cornish gentlemen's names and arms, but because the publishing thereof might perhaps go accompanied with divers wrongs, to my much reverenced friends the heralds by thrusting my sickle into their harvest . . . I rather thought fit altogether to omit it.'[4] He had, however, some appreciation of the importance of numismatic evidence. That the Romans were not ignorant of the tin trade 'may appear by a brass coin of Domitian's, found in one of these works and fallen into my hands':[5] and his transcription of the letters engraved on the Doniert Stone, 'here inserted for abler capacities than mine own to interpret',[6] suggests some inkling of the value of archaeology. Always generous in his tributes to those who have helped him, he refers to John Hooker of Exeter as 'the commendable painful antiquary and my kind friend', to 'the late Master William Carnsew, a gentleman of good quality, discretion and learning,' who was said to have seen a thirteenth-century charter relating to the stannaries, and, of course, to 'my particular kind friend and generally well-deserving countryman, Mr. Camden', 'who as the arch-antiquary Justus Lipsius, testifieth of him, *Britanniae nebulas claro ingenii sole illustravit.*'[7] Carew's sound common sense comes out in his discussion of the origin of the name Liskeard—'I will not join hands with them who term it

---

[1] *Survey of Cornwall* (1953), p. 82.   [2] Ibid., p. 133.
[3] Ibid., pp. 192–3.   [4] Ibid., pp. 136–7.   [5] Ibid., p. 89.
[6] Ibid., p. 202.   [7] Ibid., pp. 130, 99, 129, 125.

Legio, as founded by the Romans, unless they can approve the same by a Roman faith';[1] his feeling for ancient monuments in his description of St. Michael's Mount, which 'looketh so aloft as it brooketh no concurrent for the highest place. . . . Your arrival on the farther side is entertained by an open green of some largeness, which finishing where the hill beginneth, leaves you to the conduction of a winding and craggy path, and that at the top delivereth you into a little plain occupied for the greatest part by a fort of the old making';[2] and his engaging personality in the conclusion of the whole work,

Diogenes, after he had tired his Scolars with a long Lecture, finding at last the voyde paper, Bee glad, my friends (quoth hee) wee are come to harbour. With like comfort, in an vnlike resemblance, I will refresh you, who haue vouchsafed to travaile in the rugged and wearysome path of mine ill-pleasing stile, that now your iourney endeth with the land; to whose Promontory . . . because we are arrived, I will heere sit mee downe and rest.

   Deo gloria: mihi gratia. 1602. April 23.[3]

George Owen (1552–1613), the historian of Pembrokeshire, was born at Henllys, succeeded to the barony of Kemes, and lived all his life in the county, of which he was twice sheriff. 'The First Booke of the description of Penbrookshire in generall' was completed in 1603:[4] only the ground-plan remains of the second book, in which the parishes were to be described. But the so-called 'Vairdre Book', in Owen's autograph at Bronwydd, contains substantial collections for the history and topography of the county;[5] and he was also the author of a treatise on the Marcher Lordships and of a Description of Wales.[6] His map of Pembrokeshire appeared in the sixth (1607) and subsequent editions of Camden's *Britannia*. One of the driving-forces behind his researches was certainly family pride. It was curiosity about the origins of his own Lordship of Kemes that drove him to pursue his enquiries among the records of the Exchequer:[7] and catalogues of earls, the 'discentes and armes' of the nobility, have a prominent place in his narrative. Owen was not well

---

[1] Ibid., p. 202.   [2] Ibid., pp. 231–2.   [3] Ibid., p. 237.
[4] First edited for the *Cambrian Register*, vols. I and II (1795–6), by Richard Fenton: re-edited from the author's autograph (B.M. MS. Harl. 6250) by H. Owen, *Cymmrodorion Record Series*, 1892.
[5] Ibid. 1897.   [6] Ibid. 1906, 1936.   [7] Ibid., pp. 108–9.

read in medieval history. For chronicle material he relied mainly on the works of Powel and Lhuyd, supplemented by Bale, Foxe, Holinshed, Camden, and other sixteenth-century authors. But, like John Hooker, he was ahead of many of his contemporaries in his awareness of the importance of records, and his description of, and collections for, Pembrokeshire include references to Domesday Book, the Red Book of the Exchequer, Inquests *Quo Warranto* and *Post Mortem*, as well as to a number of royal charters. A good geographer and a good geologist, Owen succeeds in conveying a remarkably vivid picture of Pembroke as he knew it, the landscape, fish, flesh, and fowl, the manners of the people, their husbandry and markets, pastimes and recreations. Yet he stands apart from other Welsh antiquaries in his regret that Pembroke should have become assimilated to Wales, his insistence on its origin as a County Palatine and not as part of the Principality.[1] Inevitably, his work invites comparison with Carew's *Cornwall*, for the two were very similar in design. Owen is more pedestrian and consequently less readable; but he was not undeserving of Camden's tribute to him as 'a singular lover of venerable antiquity',[2] and though not a member of the Society of Antiquaries, he was probably the more learned of the two.

The ambitions of John Norden reached beyond the history of a single shire. Born in 1548 into an obscure family, he became a surveyor after leaving Hart Hall, Oxford; and, by 1591, when he was at work in Northamptonshire, he conceived the scheme of a 'Speculum Britanniae', which was to consist of a systematic description, illustrated by maps, of every county in the land. Unlike Lambarde, Norden did not envisage a corporate effort: the whole was to be the work of one man. Burghley showed some interest in the scheme and persuaded the Queen to approve it; and the first-fruits appeared in the *Historicall and Chorographicall Discription of Middlesex*, published in 1593 with a grateful address to the noble patron. Shortly afterwards, Norden obtained a royal commission to make 'more perfect descriptions, charts and maps', and, in 1597, Burghley issued a letter to all Justices of the Peace, 'Requiring them to aid the bearer John Norden, gent., who has very diligently and skilfully, travailed to the more perfect description of the several

---

[1] *Description of Pembrokeshire*, pp. 196 ff.   [2] *Britannia* (1610), p. 654.

shires of the realm . . .'.[1] Yet, though Camden made use of his maps for the later editions of the *Britannia* and James I, in 1609, appointed him Surveyor of some of the Crown Woods at an annual salary of £50, ill-health, poverty and misfortune were his lot and he died, as he had been born, in obscurity. His scheme was too grandiose; and, although five more county surveys were completed after the publication of *Middlesex*, namely *Essex* (1594), *Hertfordshire* (1598), *Cornwall, North-hampton* (*c*. 1610), and *Norfolk* (*c*. 1611), only *Hertfordshire* appeared in the author's lifetime.[2] No doubt, Norden was more than a little distracted by his religious enthusiasm which drove him to compose numerous pious tracts and to 'consecrate' his *Middlesex* to Queen Elizabeth, described as 'powerful protector of the Faith and undoubted Religion of the Messiah, the most comfortable nursing-mother of the Israel of God in the British Isles.'[3]

Norden's work is open to criticism on several counts. It has been said of him, as of others, that it was unfortunate that he chose to deal with history and antiquities as well as with pure topography, for this encouraged the antiquaries among his readers to let loose upon him a flood of criticism which seriously hampered the progress of his scheme. Some of the critics objected that the distances on his maps corresponded to no exact scale of miles.[4] Richard Gough suggests that most of Norden's *Cornwall* was a mere transcript of Carew, that little of moment was to be learned from the rest, and that his drawings were worthless.[5] He was certainly not well read in history; and it may be of some significance that he was never a member of the Society of Antiquaries. His *Hertfordshire*, for example, reveals no knowledge of the St. Albans chroniclers, other than Capgrave; and Camden is the only authority cited in his description of Essex. The text accompanying the maps is often disappoint-ingly thin, sometimes amounting to little more than lists of place-names and gentlemen's seats. Yet there can be no doubt

---

[1] *Hist. MSS. Com., Hatfield House*, VII. 459 (1899).

[2] In 1598. *Cornwall* and *Northampton* were first published in 1728, *Essex* in 1840, *The Chorography of Norfolk*, ed. C. M. Hood, in 1938.

[3] The identity of the antiquary with the religious writer of the same name has been demonstrated by A. W. Pollard in *The Library*, 4th ser. VII (1926–7).

[4] E. G. R. Taylor, *Late Tudor and Early Stuart Geography, 1583–1650* (1934), p. 47.

[5] *British Topography*, I. 266.

that, in modern times, the tendency has been for his stock to rise and that his positive achievement has been recognized more clearly by posterity than by earlier generations. It has been noted, for instance, that his maps were among the first to include roads;[1] that, though ignorant of the chroniclers, he knew Domesday Book and had inspected a number of charters; that he was one of the earliest antiquaries, outside the circle of the heralds, to perceive the importance of recording inscriptions and coats of arms on funeral monuments, especially in Middlesex; and that the 'learning and sense' which he shows in his understanding of English place-names, particularly in his *Northampton*, would in themselves entitle him to rank as an antiquary of note.[2] His faculty for close observation comes out very clearly in his short *Description of Cornwall*, much of it, indeed, a paraphrase of Carew but including items which Carew overlooked, such as Trethevy Quoit, one of the finest neolithic tombs in Cornwall, and remarkably accurate pictures of antiquities like the Doniert stone and Dunheved castle.[3]

Though his approach was very different, Sir John Doddridge is linked with Norden by the fact that his ambitions overreached the bounds of a single shire. John Hooker's 'Synopsis Chorographica' had been entrusted after his death to this fellow-Devonian, who thought highly of it but never achieved its publication.[4] This was hardly surprising; for Doddridge, who crowned a distinguished legal career by tenure of the offices of Solicitor-General and Justice of the King's Bench, had other preoccupations. He was a considerable antiquary in his own right; but his history of the three main estates of the Prince of Wales—the Principality itself, the Duchy of Cornwall and the Earldom of Chester—was not published until two years after his own death in 1628.[5] Yet he had been a leading member of the Society of Antiquaries, one of the three petitioners to the Queen for the formation of a National Library, or Academy, to afford safe custody to manuscripts and rare books.[6] After the Queen's death, however, his interest in the Society seems to have

[1] E. G. R. Taylor, op. cit., p. 50.   [2] Kendrick, op. cit., p. 164.
[3] Ibid., p. 162; *Survey of Cornwall*, ed. Halliday, pp. 50-1.
[4] *Journal of the British Archaeological Association* XVIII (1862), 139-40.
[5] *The history of the Ancient and moderne Estate of the Principality of Wales, Dutchy of Cornewall, and Earldome of Chester* by Sir John Dodridge *Knight* (1630).
[6] Below, pp. 169-70.

waned, as Spelman observed;[1] and it may be of some significance that his history was dedicated to 'King Iames of euer blessed memory', who may have been, in part, responsible for its dissolution.

Even more markedly than Lambarde's, Doddridge's regional studies are the work of a lawyer. Nearly all his material is drawn from legal or official sources, such as statutes, charters, valuations, 'les auncient tenures', close and patent rolls, chancery warrants, ministers' accounts. He shows nothing comparable to Lambarde's wide reading in literary sources: the only authors whom he seems to know are Gerald of Wales, Matthew Paris, Humphrey Lhuyd and David Powel. Yet, if antiquarian studies increasingly became something of a sideshow for him, the learned judge was not lacking in some of the qualities of a true historian. That he hesitated to patronize his ancestors, even when they puzzled him, appears from his observations on the arrangements made by Edward III for the transmission of the Principality. These may seem strange to posterity,

... But when I consider that this age ... was a learned age of Iudges and Lawyers ... much commended for exquisit knowledge of the Laws, by those learned men that liued in the Succeeding times, I cannot but think reuerently of Antiquity, although I cannot yeeld sufficient reason for their doings therein.[2]

Doddridge was sensitive to the tragic element in history and at times his dry prose rises near to eloquence, as when he writes of the deposition of Henry VI,

... he being of the house of *Lancaster*, (such is the mutability, and so vnstable are all humane things) that the said King being a man (as the times then were deuout and religious) the founder of Schooles and Colledges, vertuous, and a louer of peace was ... put from his kingdome ... in a ciuill warre, there is no true victory, in as much as he that preuaileth is also a looser.[3]

—or of the fall of Richard III,

But for that the prosperity of the wicked is but as the florishing of a greene tree, which whiles a man passes by is blasted dead at the roots, and his place knoweth it no more.[4]

[1] *Works* (1727), Pt. II, p. 69.   [2] *The history of the Principality*, p. 9.
[3] Ibid., p. 23.   [4] Ibid., p. 28.

It cannot be claimed, however, that Doddridge made any significant contribution to the history of the regions he studied. Carew was anxious to see the Cornish section of his book when he was contemplating a second edition of his own *Survey of Cornwall* and wrote to Camden, in May 1606, 'I learn that Master Solicitor hath compiled a treatise of our Cornish Duchy, and dedicated it to the Prince; this I much long to see, and heartily pray by your means to obtain a copy thereof . . . I imagine that I may cull out of Master Solicitor's garden many flowers to adorn this other edition.'[1] Yet Carew would have had little to learn from Doddridge, apart from a few points of law and finance. The book takes the form of a treatise on the succession and manner of government of the Principality and of the succession and revenues of the Duchy and the Earldom. It adds little to our knowledge of the local history of any of them.

Those students of local history whose work never achieved literary form are inevitably harder to assess. Thus, James Strangeman (or Strangman), the Essex antiquary, remains a somewhat shadowy figure, although he was the first to make substantial collections of material for the history of the county in which his family had been established since the fourteenth century. The volume in the Cottonian Library, which includes 'Collectanea historica et genealogica Jac. Strangman, ex rotulis parliamentariis aliisque'[2] (though it relates chiefly to monasteries), was badly damaged in the fire of 1731; but manuscripts of his are to be found elsewhere. He was a substantial contributor to the two volumes of heraldic and other collections, preserved among the Lansdowne MSS., where a note at the end of a section of extracts from the records of St. Albans— 'Hiis Collectionibus finem imposuit Jacobus Strangeman, generosus, Julii 7 Anno Dni 1591'—proves that, though not long-lived, he was still alive at this date.[3] The same manuscript includes a letter from Strangman to the Dean of Lichfield, Dr. Boleyn, introducing himself as 'a lover of Antiquities in generall' and asking for leave to inspect some old books in the cathedral library, 'Especially Crouncles or Hystreyes of Ks or

---

[1] *Survey of Cornwall*, ed. F. E. Halliday, p. 63 (from B.M. MS. Cott., Julius C. V).
[2] B.M. MS. Cott., Vit. F. XII, ff. 142–70.
[3] B.M. MS. Lansdowne 860, f. 212v.

nobles'.[1] He was a member of the Society of Antiquaries and seems to have been generous in helping other scholars, not only in questions relating to his own county. In a volume of extracts from Stow's collections made by Robert Glover, a page of details of some manors in Oxfordshire and Buckinghamshire bears the name 'Strangman' on the top left-hand corner;[2] and, as has been seen, it was he who, in May 1589, drew George Owen's attention to a useful reference in the Red Book of the Exchequer.[3] Unfortunately, he did not live to publish, and the fruits of his labours have to be sought in the work of such later historians as Nathaniel Salmon and Philip Morant, who freely acknowledged their debt to him.[4]

Henry Ferrars of Baddesley Clinton in the north-east corner of Warwickshire, was born under Edward VI and died under Charles I. Yet, though his life was more than twice as long as Strangman's, he, too, failed to publish the results of his researches into the history of his county. Like Sampson Erdeswicke, he withdrew from Oxford to his patrimony in order to devote himself to the study of antiquities, heraldry and genealogies in particular. He was a member of the Society of Antiquaries, though we know nothing of his activities there, and his only excursion into public life seems to have been his election as member of parliament for the Cornish borough of Callington in 1597. Erdeswicke regarded him as a great antiquary[5] and Camden acknowledged his indebtedness, particularly for his description of Coventry, to Ferrars, 'a man both for parentage, and for knowledge of antiquity very commendable; and my especiall friend: who both in this place and also else where hath at all times courteously shewed me the right way when I was out, and from his candle, as it were, hath lightned mine.'[6] It seems that Ferrars's intention was to follow Lambarde's example and to publish a Perambulation of War-

---

[1] See *Trans. Essex Arch. Soc.* II (1863), 145.
[2] MS. Ashmole 848, f. 115v.   [3] Above, p. 95.
[4] Salmon, *History of Essex* (1739–42), p. 146: Morant, *Essex* (1768), I. 280.
[5] *Staffordshire*, (ed. Harwood), p. 523.
[6] *Britannia* (1610), p. 568. Among Camden's papers are ten rhymed couplets, written by Ferrars, describing the descent of the manor of Baddesley Clinton. (MS. Cott., Julius F. VI. f. 296). They begin

'This seate and soyle from Saxon Bade, a man of honest fame,
Who held it in the Saxone time, of Badesly took the name.'

wickshire, where only John Rous (1411–91) had anticipated him in the business of making collections. But the material which he bequeathed to posterity is almost exclusively genealogical. Together with Robert Glover, he compiled family trees of members of the Order of the Garter, which were useful to Ashmole;[1] and some of his collections were bound up with those of Strangman.[2] His material was of great service to Dugdale, who noted that his memory was still held in high esteem in the county.[3]

Most obscure of all is William Claxton, descendant of an ancient family sited at Claxton, some miles inland from Hartlepool. What Strangman was attempting for Essex, Claxton was attempting for the Bishopric of Durham: together with the Reverend Christopher Watson,[4] he was one of the first to make any substantial collections relating to its history.[5] His correspondence with Stow, 'his assured ffrynd', extended over a decade. In the spring of 1582, he promised his help in matters concerning Durham; two years later, a bundle of notes was accompanied by a warm letter, '. . . so long as I lyue yow shall not want a friend to the vttermost of his power'. He had a life of Edward the Confessor and a copy of Alfred of Beverley laid up for Stow and, in 1594, was encouraging him to proceed to the publication of further antiquities.[6] Claxton was also on friendly terms with Camden, who described his family as 'of good and ancient note' and himself as 'an affectionate lover of venerable antiquity', and sought his advice on matters touching the Roman Wall.[7] He made himself very useful to the heralds when they visited the north.[8] But there is no evidence that he was ever a member of the Society of Antiquaries; he published nothing; and none of his collections is known to have survived.

Reginald Bainbrigg (c. 1545–1606), headmaster of Appleby Grammar School from 1580, and John Denton of Cardew

---

[1] e.g. MS. Ashmole 1107, ff. 219–309: 'Genealogiolae pertinentes ad antiquissimos ejusdem ordinis Milites, e rotulis inquisitionibus et registris primitus collectae per ROB. GLOVERUM et HICUM FENRERRERS.'

[2] B.M. MS. Lansdowne, 860.

[3] Dugdale, *Warwickshire* (1656), p. 711.

[4] *Durham Wills and Inventories*, ed. W. Greenwell: Surtees Soc. XXXVIII (1860) p. 272.   [5] Above, p. 64.

[6] *Survey of London*, ed. Kingsford, I. lxix, lxx, lxxiii.

[7] *Britannia* (1610), p. 738; *Survey of London* I. lxxxviii. (MS. Harl. 374).

[8] *Durham Wills and Inventories*, p. 272.

have also left little trace. Bainbrigg owed much of his antiquarian enthusiasm to Camden, to whom he wrote in 1600,
'I can not find wordes, to expresse my love towarde you who
take suche paines, that our countrie maie lyve for ever.' He
himself journeyed along the Roman Wall, so far as Redesdale,
making collections of inscribed stones, which were available to
visitors at his house at Appleby. Of Denton, Bainbrigg reported
to Camden that 'he haith wryt the antiquitie of Carelile, holme
cultran and of the most ancient townes in Cumberland, the
petegre and armes of the ancyent gentleman of that countrie,
you will find it a rare and worthie peace of work . . . he goes by
no hearesaies, but by ancient recordes.'[1]

Enough has been said to show how close were the ties which
bound William Camden (1551–1623) to many of his fellow-
antiquaries. Yet, in one sense, he belongs to a different world,
the world of European scholarship rather than of English
antiquarianism. It was the Dutch geographer, Ortelius, who
urged him to undertake the enterprise which resulted in the
Britannia, first published in 1586. No English translation
appeared until 1610, but five editions of the Latin text had been
published before Elizabeth was dead; and it had been reprinted
at Frankfurt in 1590. Camden's correspondents included many
foreign scholars of distinction, such as James Gruter, Jacques de
Thou and Casaubon.[2] Born in London, the son of a *pictor*, he,
like Leland, received his schooling at St. Paul's whence, at the
age of fifteen, he proceeded to Oxford. He spent a short time
at Magdalen, possibly as a chorister, but was later admitted to
Broadgates Hall and, later still, followed his patron, Dr.
Thomas Thornton, to Christ Church, where Philip Sidney
was his fellow-student. His natural bent, from early childhood,
had been towards the study of antiquities and all his spare time
as an undergraduate was devoted to them. When he returned
to London, having failed to win a fellowship at All Souls, or to
complete the requirements for the first degree (probably
because of religious difficulties), Camden seems, at first, to have
had no settled occupation and to have spent much of his time
in travelling about the country and amassing materials, some

---

[1] F. Haverfield, in *Trans. Cumberland Westmorland Antiquarian & Archaeological
Society*, n.s. XI (1911), 343–78.
[2] See *Camdeni Epistolae*, ed. T. Smith (1691).

of which were afterwards incorporated in the *Britannia*. But he was not a rich man and it was necessary for him to earn a living; so, when Dean Goodman of Westminster offered him the post of Second Master of Westminster School, he accepted it, though, no doubt, with some reluctance. 'After he came to be engag'd in the laborious business of teaching School', writes his biographer, Edmund Gibson, 'he would fain have weaned himself from those Enquiries and have confin'd his thoughts entirely to the business he had undertaken. But, whenever a vacation gave him liberty to look abroad, the thirst returned, and he declares it was not in his power to restrain himself from making Excursions into one quarter or another, in quest of Antiquities.'[1] We know that in 1578 he visited 'the country of the Iceni', Norfolk and Suffolk;[2] four years later, he went to Yorkshire, returning to London by way of Lancashire; in 1589 he was in Devon, the next year in Wales, in the company of his friend, Dr. Francis Godwin.[3] Only the long holidays, the schoolmaster's solace, made these excursions possible, for Camden was not one to neglect his profession. He became Head Master of Westminster in 1593, and the Greek grammar which he compiled was in use there for nearly three centuries.

His profession freed Camden from the necessity of seeking an appointment in a great household. 'I never made suit to any man', he wrote to Ussher in 1618, '. . . neither, God be praised, I needed, having gathered a contented sufficiency by my long labours in the School.'[4] The Bishop of Salisbury had granted him the prebend of Ilfracombe in 1589; and retirement became possible when Sir Fulke Greville secured his appointment as Clarenceux King of Arms in the College of Heralds in 1597. This was a post very much to his taste. Unfortunately, it was also to the taste of the York herald, one Ralph Brooke, who gave vent to his chagrin by delivering a ferocious attack on the *Britannia*, in which he had discovered a number of errors, mainly genealogical, and accusing the author of plagiarizing Leland and Robert Glover. In the fifth edition of *Britannia* (1600) Camden met this attack with spirit, and, despite an alarming series of illnesses which troubled him from early

---

[1] *Britannia* (1722).   [2] *Correspondence of Ortelius*, ed. J. H. Hessels, ep. 78.
[3] *Memorabilia de Seipso* (in *Camdeni Epistolae*, p. 85).
[4] *Camdeni Epistolae*, p. 247.

middle age, did not allow himself to be deterred from further publication. He issued a description of the monuments in Westminster Abbey in 1600, a collection of medieval chronicles (printed at Frankfurt) in 1603, and the miscellaneous notes on antiquities, known as his *Remaines*, in 1605. But the great achievement of his latter years was his *Annales Rerum Anglicarum et Hibernicarum Regnante Elizabetha* (1615), a history of the reign which ranks far above all other contemporary accounts. The year before his death, at the age of seventy-four, he made final arrangements for the execution of a scheme which had long been developing in his mind. He founded the Camden Professorship of History in his old university and nominated Degory Wheare as its first holder.[1]

Britannia has long been recognized as the crowning achievement of Tudor and early Stuart antiquarianism. Purporting to be a 'Chorographical Description' of the whole of the British Isles,[2] it necessitated a vast amount of preliminary study, as Camden himself testifies:

I got some insight into the old British and Saxon Tongues for my assistance; I have travell'd almost all over England and have consulted in each County the Persons of best skill and knowledge in these matters. I have diligently perus'd our own Writers; as well as the Greek and Latin who mention the least tittle of Britain. I have examin'd the publick Records of the Kingdom, Ecclesiastical Registers, and Libraries, and the Acts, Monuments and Memorials of Churches and Cities.[3]

He tells his readers that only 'the natural affection I have for my country (by far the strongest affection that is), the glory of the British name and the persuasions of Friends' induced him to undertake and publish a work on this scale. He anticipates and will welcome informed criticism; but he will have little patience with the censures of the philistine:

Some there are, who cry down the whole study of Antiquities, as a fruitless search after what is gone and past; but, as I shall not altogether contemn the Authority of these Men, so shall I not much

---

[1] On the significance of this Chair see Sir M. Powicke, 'William Camden', *Essays and Studies collected for the English Association by F. P. Wilson* I (1948), 68–71.

[2] For the section relating to Ireland, see R. Gottfried in *Journal of English Literary History* X (1943), 117–30.

[3] *Britannia* (1722).

regard their Judgment ... But if there are any, who, desire to be strangers in their own Country, Foreigners in their own Cities, and always Children in Knowledge; let them please themselves, I write not for such humours.

Nor has he any patience with the censures of the fanatic:

There are some, I hear, who take it ill that I have mention'd Monasteries and their Founders. I am sorry to hear it; but (with their leave) they are possibly such who are angry, and would have it forgotten that our Ancestors were, and we are, Christians.

He is aware that his work is only a beginning: 'A new age, a new race of men will daily produce new Discoveries. It is enough for me, that I have broken the Ice; and I have gain'd my end, if I set others to work; whether to write more or to amend what I have written.'[1] The book opens with a geographical note and a historical sketch of early and medieval times. Camden carefully examines the various theories relating to the origin of the Britons, the first preaching of Christianity, the meaning and derivation of place-names and the evidential value of British and Roman coins. He follows Polydore Vergil in rejecting the popular theory of descent from Brutus and the Trojans, suggesting instead that the Britons were akin to the Gauls and derived from the same stock. The bulk of the historical sketch is devoted to the period between the Adventus Saxonum and 1066. There follows a description of the civil and ecclesiastical divisions of England, of the degrees, or ranks, of society, and of the law-courts, all this being by way of introduction to the systematic description of Great Britain, county by county.

In undertaking such a description Camden seemed to be following in the footsteps of Leland, and there was some substance in Brooke's charge of plagiarism, for he did make use of Leland's material without always acknowledging his debt. Yet Bishop Gibson, in his defence of Camden, put his finger on an essential difference between the two, when he protested:

But all impartial men will consider, at what a low ebb Learning was in *Leland's* time, and how little was then understood of the Geographical History of England. To describe the course of a River, and the distance of one Town from another; or to tell whether a Bridge was of wood or of stone, or how many arches it had; was

[1] Ibid.

reckoned an useful instruction at that time when travelling was little in fashion: and the *Counties* of England were possibly greater strangers to the affairs of their neighbours, than the *Nations* of Europe have since been to one another . . . so, everything that inform'd was kindly receiv'd, and a Work look'd upon as a mighty Performance, that at present would be very coldly receiv'd. This was really the case between Mr *Leland* and Mr *Camden*; the different face of things, in the times of these two Writers, had render'd a good part of the *Itinerary* of the one altogether unuseful to the *Britannia* of the other.[1]

Camden was, and could afford to be, much more selective than Leland. Map-making, by this time, had become the preserve of professional or semi-professional cartographers, like Norden; the labours of county historians and topographers had made it possible for an overall survey to concentrate attention on antiquities; and, though Camden's descriptions of towns are admittedly inferior to Leland's, modern antiquaries recognize him as a pioneer in the detailed study of Romano-British inscriptions and numismatics and in his appreciation of the wealth of evidence available in the field and of the importance of going to look at it.[2] Spenser's epitaph has stood the test of time:

> *Cambden* the nourice of antiquitie,
> And lanterne unto late succeeding age.[3]

[1] Ibid., p. xx.

[2] Kendrick, op. cit., pp. 143–55; Stuart Piggott, 'William Camden and the Britannia', *PBA* XXXVII (1951), 199–217.

[3] *The Ruines of Time.*

VII

THE ELIZABETHAN SOCIETY
OF ANTIQUARIES

At this auspicious period, a set of gentlemen of great abilities, many of them students in the inns of court, applied themselves to the study of the antiquities and history of this kingdom, a taste at that time very prevalent, wisely forseeing that without a perfect knowledge of these requisites, a thorough understanding of the laws of their native country could not be attained.

For the better carrying on this their laudable purpose, they about the fourteenth year of the reign of Queen Elizabeth formed themselves into a college or society under the protection of that great patron of letters Matthew Parker. . . .[1]

TRADITIONAL views of the origin of the first Society of Antiquaries have been subject to revision in recent years. The only near-contemporary account of the Society is contained in Sir Henry Spelman's preface (entitled 'The Occasion of this Discourse') to his treatise on the Law Terms, written in 1614; and it has been generally assumed that preface and tract belonged to the same year and, therefore, that the Society was founded in 1572, under the patronage of Archbishop Parker. But 'The Occasion' is undated and, thanks to the researches of Dr. Linda van Norden, it now seems certain that it was completed between February 1626 and July 1628, some dozen years later than the tract, and that the Society was founded about 1586 and continued to meet fairly regularly during the Law Terms, usually on Fridays, until about 1608, except in the years 1594–8, perhaps because London was then stricken with plague.[2] Meetings were normally held in the Heralds' Office in Derby House, near St. Paul's, occasionally in the house of Sir William Dethick in Garter Place, and the members supped together.

Spelman tells us that it was customary for two questions to be

---

[1] *Curious Discourses* (1775), I, Introd., p. iv.
[2] L. van Norden, 'Sir Henry Spelman on the Chronology of the Elizabethan College of Antiquaries', *Huntington Library Quarterly* XIII.2 (1949–50), 69.

propounded at each meeting, for consideration at the next, 'so that every Man then had a Sennight's respite to advise upon them, and to deliver his Opinion.'[1] All members were normally expected to contribute, either verbally, or in writing, even if they had little to say. A form of summons for November 1598 ran as follows:

The place apointed for a conference upon the question followinge, is Mr Garter's howse, upon All Soules day, beinge Thursday the secound of November 1598, at one of the clocke in the after noone, where your opinioun either in writinge or otherwise is expected upon this question.
Of the antiquitie of armes in England.[2]

'Were it not that the order of this learned assembly dothe forbid me to be always silent', declared James Ley, when speaking on Heralds, 'this question having been so judiciously handled by others, and myself unable to say any thing to it, I should, as heretofore, have requested your accustomed favour to have dispensed with me.'[3] 'I have only set down this little you have herd', said an anonymous speaker on 'The Antiquity of Ceremonies used at Funeralls' on 9 February 1599, 'lest I shoulde be condemned for saying nothing'.[4] At least fifteen members gave their views on 'Sterling Money', and eight speeches on 'Epitaphs' have been preserved. But there was little attempt to correlate the arguments put forward, and firm conclusions were hard to reach. Agarde probably spoke for many when, in the course of a debate on 'The Etymology, Dignity, and Antiquity of Dukes in England', he said

... it seemeth to me in that there was not in anye of our former propositions anye judyciall or fynall conclusion sett downe, wherby wee might say this is the judgement or right opynyon that is to be gathered out of everye man's speache. So as leavinge each question undecyded, our assemblye might be rather demed a courte of *Morespeach*, as in old tyme there was such an one at Oxford, than a learned conference. Therefore I wishe this abuse (as I take yt under your better correcsion and reformacyon) might in our nowe meetings be reformed. And that uppon every poynt, men being heard, the soundest judgements might be thereuppon concluded.[5]

---

[1] *Reliquiae Spelmannianae*, ed. E. Gibson (1669), p. 69.
[2] *Curious Discourses* I, Preface, p. xvi.
[3] Ibid. I. 50. [4] Ibid. I. 207. [5] Ibid. I. 184–5.

The Society had a Registrar, or Secretary, among the holders of this office being two lawyers, William Hakewill and Francis Tate; and that members were expected to attend is suggested by Richard Carew's apology to Cotton in 1605 for his absence from meetings of the 'Sweete and respected Antiquarum Society.'[1] Attendance was strictly limited to them, a summons concluding with the injunction 'Yt ys desyred that you bringe none other with you, nor geue anie notive unto anie, but to such as haue the like somouns.'[2]

The forty-three names of members of the Elizabethan Society which survive naturally include many that have already been mentioned—collectors, like Cotton, Holland, Tate, and Thynne; heralds, like Dethick and Camden; archivists, like Agarde, Heneage, and Talbot; local historians, like Stow, Carew, Spelman, and Strangman. A few of the names appear, however, to be dubious or puzzling. Richard Broughton was identified by Hearne with the author of the *Ecclesiasticall Historie of Great Britaine*, printed at Douai in 1633; but it is incredible that a Catholic should have been a member of the Society, and the view that Broughton was the student of the Inner Temple who subsequently became Justice of North Wales is much more convincing.[3] There were two Thomas Doyleys—a lawyer, who acted as steward to Parker and married his niece, and a physician from Magdalen College, Oxford, who lived much abroad, took a degree at Basel and practised in London. The fact that Thomas Doyley's discourse to the Society on Dukes was delivered in French and based on material drawn from French sources suggests the doctor, though an element of doubt remains.[4] Of Walter Cope, later Chamberlain of the Exchequer and Master of the Court of Wards, Hearne knew only that he was a friend of Stow's;[5] and Dr. van Norden rules him out on the grounds that she has found no record of

[1] *Letters of Eminent Literary Men*, ed. H. Ellis, p. 98.
[2] *Curious Discourses* I, Preface, p. xvi.
[3] Ibid. II. 424; R. J. Shoeck, 'The Elizabethan Society of Antiquaries and Men of Law', *Notes and Queries*, n.s. I (1954), 418.
[4] *Curious Discourses* I. 183–4. He is styled 'Mr.' at the head of this discourse and 'Dr.' at the head of an English discourse on the Antiquity of Arms (ibid. I. 75–6). R. J. Shoeck (op. cit., p. 419) favours the lawyer, but Dr. van Norden opts for the doctor: see her unpublished thesis, 'The Elizabethan Society of Antiquaries', p. 286. (Microfilm in the library of the Society of Antiquaries of London.)
[5] *Curious Discourses* II. 427.

scholarship that would entitle him to membership, nor even (though this seems surprising in a friend of Stow) of interest in historical research. It is noteworthy, however, that Lambarde presented a French poem on Edward the Confessor (now in the University Library at Cambridge)[1] 'a M. Cope son tres chur amye', and that the Oseney Register (Vitellius E. XV) was once in his possession.[2]

Another puzzling name is that of William Jones. The *Curious Discourses* include the answers of a 'Mr. Jones' to Tate's questions about the ancient Britons.[3] These reveal considerable learning of a kind that would accord well with Hearne's identification of him as the Sir William Jones whose family had settled in North Wales and who later became Chief Justice of the King's Bench in Ireland and then a Judge in England; but Hearne's view that Sir William 'does not appear to have been a member of the society of antiquaries, although he was extremely well qualified for that honour' has been generally accepted, though for reasons that are not altogether clear.[4] Gough shared Hearne's doubts as to the identity of the Mr. 'Savel or Savile', said to have been a student of the Middle Temple, whence it may be inferred that he 'was not the learned Sir Henry Savile of Over Bradley in Yorkshire, or his young brother Thomas, or the kinsman of Sir Henry Savile, who was usually called Long Henry Savile.'[5] It seems likely that he was Sir Henry's younger brother, John Savile (1545–1607), who was a lawyer and a friend of Camden.[6] Contributions to the debates were also made by 'Mr. Davis' on 'The Antiquity and Office of the Earl Marshall of England', by two men, each entitled 'Mr. Davis' on 'The Antiquity, Use and Ceremony of lawful Combats in England', and by 'Mr. Davys' on 'The Antiquity, Authority and Succession of the High Steward of England.'[7] The lawyer, Sir John Davies, who became Attorney-General of Ireland in 1603, could well have been responsible for the

---

[1] MS. Ee. iii. 59.

[2] *Lives of Edward the Confessor* (R.S.), ed. H. R. Luard, p. ix; Wormald and Wright, *The English Library before 1700*, p. 201.

[3] I. 126–38.

[4] Ibid. II. 448–9. Hearne suggested as a possible alternative one John Jones of Flintshire, 'a great antiquary, and a curious collector of British MSS.'

[5] Ibid. II. 439; *Archaeologia* I. xi.   [6] See article by A. F. Pollard in *D.N.B.*

[7] *Curious Discourses* II. 108–11, 180–8, 187–90, 35–7.

paper on the Earl Marshal which reveals the familiarity with sources characteristic of his weighty *Discoverie of the True Causes why Ireland was never entirely Subdued*;[1] and for the first of the two papers on Lawful Combats, which is clearly the work of a lawyer. The paper on the High Steward, though less well documented, could also have been his. But that there was more than one Davies, or Davis, is evident from the fact that the second paper on Lawful Combats was delivered on the same day—22 May 1601—as the first and represents a different point of view. Another very obscure character, none of whose papers have been published, is 'Mr. Cliffe', who may have been either the Richard Cliffe who was admitted to Gray's Inn in 1548 or, more probably, the John Cliffe admitted to the Middle Temple in 1583.[2] And of Charles Lailand we know nothing beyond the fact that he drafted the list of those summoned to the meeting of 2 November 1598.[3]

Against these obscure or dubious names we have to set those of some well-known public figures. It is unfortunate that none of Robert Beale's addresses to the Society have been preserved, for this fervent Puritan was a prolific writer on contemporary politics, an eminent civilian, who was elected to five of Elizabeth's parliaments, served as secretary to Walsingham, ambassador at the Hague, clerk of the Council, and as one of the negotiators for peace with Spain at the end of the century. Beale made a collection of Spanish chronicles—*Rerum Hispanicarum Scriptores*—published at Frankfurt in 1579, and transcribed from manuscripts in his library.[4] And in a debate in the House in 1593, he cited a precedent from the reign of Henry IV.[5] Other names of political significance are those of Thomas Lake, amanuensis to Walsingham, French and Latin Reader to the Queen, Clerk of the Signet, and destined to rise still higher under James I; and James Ley, of Lincoln's Inn, Member of Parliament for Westbury, 1597–8, and subsequently Chief Justice of the King's Bench and Earl of Marlborough, who was a foundation member of the Society, made numerous contributions to its debates and was one of the three petitioners for a

---

[1] *Ireland under Elizabeth and James the First*, ed. H. Morley (1890), pp. 217–342.
[2] R. J. Shoeck, op. cit., p. 418.
[3] *Curious Discourses* I. xvii.   [4] *Archaeologia* I. vii.
[5] J. E. Neale, *Elizabeth and her Parliaments, 1584–1601* (1957), pp. 304–5.

National Library at the end of the reign.[1] William Lord Compton was a Member of Parliament in 1593 and a Privy Councillor; and Francis Leigh, father of the first Earl of Chichester, was a Knight of the Bath and a close friend of Camden, who remembered him in his will.[2]

Among the numerous lawyers we find William Hakewill of Lincoln's Inn, a relative of Sir Thomas Bodley, Abraham Hartwell and Thomas Wiseman, both of Gray's Inn, the former (who was in orders) secretary to Whitgift, the latter a considerable landowner in Essex. James Whitelock of the Middle Temple and a Fellow of St. John's College, Oxford, was exceptionally well qualified for membership of the Society, since he had combined study of the civil law at Oxford with study of the common law in London and, as he himself has recorded, 'I continued the study of logique and the artes, but above all of historye: in which I toke great delite.'[3] Henry Bourchier, or Bouchier, was probably the Inner Templar of that name who was admitted in 1576 and called to the Bench in 1596. Together with Tate he acted as Moderator at one of the meetings of the Society in 1591, when eleven others were present.[4] And to the list of archivists must be added Robert, son of William Bowyer, who assisted Stow in his record-searching, became Keeper of the Tower records in 1604, and at one time owned the manuscript of the Lindisfarne Gospels which passed from him to Cotton.[5]

It seems probable that the learned Whitgift was a patron of the Society, if not formally its President, but both clergy and academics were chiefly conspicuous by their absence. Despite the fact that many of the lawyers were Oxford or Cambridge graduates, a deep gulf divided most academic studies from those pursued at the Inns of Court; and although, as has been seen, some of the clergy were keen manuscript collectors, most of the topics discussed by the Society tended to be of a secular

[1] Below, pp. 169–70.

[2] 'To these following a peece or memorial rings of the same value. To Sir Francis Leigh of Westminster fower pounds.' *Curious Discourses* II. 391.

[3] *The Liber Famelius of Sir James Whitelocke*, ed. J. Bruce, Camden Society, o.s. LXX (1858), 13.

[4] R. J. Shoeck, op. cit., p. 418; *Archaeologia* I. xiv.

[5] F. S. Fussner, *The Historical Revolution*, pp. 75–6, 86; C. E. Wright in *Camb. Bibl. Soc.* 1951, p. 217.

nature, appealing to the skills of lawyers, heralds, and archivists, rather than of parsons or dons. Some clergy may even have shared the scruples of the Reverend Francis Godwin who clearly felt that his taste for history demanded an apology:

I cannot deny, but my delight in the study of historie and antiquities, hath beene somewhat greater than was needfull for a man that had dedicated himselfe and his labours unto the seruice of Gods church in the Ministery. Which fault acknowledging in my selfe, and being unable wholy to amend . . . I endeuoured long since in some sort to reforme the same by restrayning my selfe within the compasse of such antiquities, as seemed to concerne but ecclesiasticall cause or persons. . . .[1]

Questions of origins proved peculiarly absorbing; for the members' concern was less with the past for its own sake than with the problem of how the nation with which they were familiar came to be as it was. Whence came dukes, marquises and knights, shires, towns, and forests, seals and sterling, castles, heralds, the law terms, funeral ceremonies and epitaphs? To answer these questions adequately demanded understanding of records, chronicles, etymology, and material survivals from the past. In so far as nearly all the topics were concrete, the members showed themselves true antiquaries. Such difficult and dangerous abstractions as natural law, ecclesiastical authority, the functions of monarchy, free of conscience, were not for them. Henry Bourchier was very exceptional in concluding his brief discourse on sterling with a moral:

. . . it is most true, that as the allay or temper of the sterling is perfect and pure, so the love of all men to that metal ought to be tempered with the allay of moderation and contentment, and not corrupted with insatiable desires; lest, as being moderately used it is medicinal and cordial to the heart, yet being taken in over great quantity and to full receipt, it becometh rank poison to the soul.[2]

Arthur Agarde's long experience at the Exchequer had given him unique opportunities to search the records; but there were other members of the Society able to make good use of such records as came to hand. Michael Heneage, who had been joint-keeper of the Tower records and had made collections

[1] From Godwin's Address to the Reader in his *Catalogue of the Bishops of England* (1601).
[2] *Curious Discourses* II. 321.

'out of various charters, registers and instruments relating to many Noble Families in England' which Cotton later purchased from his widow,[1] was well equipped for antiquarian debates. He quotes ordinances of Edward II and Richard II when discussing sterling and, when speaking of the 'Antiquity of Arms in England', he refers to Edward III's grant to Chaucer.[2] Joseph Holland, of the Inner Temple, had the cartulary of Reading Abbey and made many heraldic collections.[3] He told his audience, when 'The Antiquity of Dukes in England' was under discussion, on 24 November 1598, that he possessed 'an auncient Saxon charter made by kinge Eadger', a deed made by the Black Prince, and a letter written by Buckingham to York in the reign of Henry VI—though he did not refrain from using Geoffrey of Monmouth to prove that Dukes were as old as the Romans.[4] In the debate on 'The Antiquity, Etymology and Privilege of Towns' he referred to 'a booke in the Exchequer called Nomina Villarum, made 9 Ed. 2 of all the villages and towns in England'.[5] As the original returns were on rolls, many of which had become badly worn by the fifteenth century, this must have been the transcript made in book form by John Snede, under orders from the Barons of the Exchequer, in the first year of Henry VII, or else the one made early in the reign of Elizabeth.[6] On the question of 'Dimensions of the Land of England', Holland's authorities include charters from Edward the Elder to the Abbot of Hyde and from the Earl of Devon to the Abbot of Quarry, in the time of Henry II, as well as Domesday Book.[7] To illuminate the question of trial by battle (Lawful Combats), he cites a Plea Roll of 19 Henry VI and also an indenture of 42 Henry III between the Abbot of Glastonbury and the Dean and Chapter of Wells, with the explanation, 'The original deed I gaue unto the right honourable the lord cheefe justice of England. But I have a faire copie thereof ready to be showed unto you.' On the 'Antiquity and Office of the Constable of England', he cites an Exchequer book of payments of the time of Henry III: and for the 'Anti-

[1] MS. Claudius C. 1.   [2] *Curious Discourses* II. 322; I. 173.
[3] R. A. Caldwell, 'Joseph Holand, Collector and Antiquary', *Modern Philology* XL (Chicago, 1942–43), 295–301.
[4] *Curious Discourses* I. 179–80.   [5] Ibid. I. 194.
[6] Palgrave, *Parliamentary Writs* II. Div. iii, pp. iii, 301–416.
[7] *Curious Discourses* I. 39–40.

quity, Power, Order, State, Manner, Persons and Proceeding of the High Court of Parliament in England', he uses the writs of summons and the Rolls of Edward III's reign.[1] Richard Broughton, in his only recorded paper—on Sterling—made use of 'an ancient deed dated in the beginning of the reign of King Henry the third.'[2] Another legal expert, James Ley, drew on the Pipe and Statute Rolls for his discussion of Sterling, and on the Issue Rolls for 'The Antiquity, Office and Privilege of Heralds in England.'[3] Sir John Doddridge, a distinguished lawyer, as well as a local historian, summarized part of the Ordinance of Measures of 31 Edward I when discussing land dimensions, and drew also on the civil law:[4] and Francis Thynne, who had been bred at Lincoln's Inn, quotes *verbatim* from the 'Textus Roffensis' and from Exchequer records of the thirteenth and fourteenth centuries, to elucidate the history of the Earl Marshal.[5] Records cited by anonymous speakers include Edgar's charter of 974, and two of Edward the Confessor to Westminster Abbey, as well as various writs enrolled in the Tower from the late thirteenth to the mid-fifteenth century.[6] Camden, when discussing the office of Earl Marshal, quoted from the Red Book of the Exchequer and the Statute of Westminster II, with reasonable accuracy;[7] and Cotton used an impressive range of documents to illuminate the history of trials by battle. These included the Red Book of the Exchequer, the Parliament and Plea Rolls, and the Close and Patent Rolls, as well as a number of French, Spanish, and papal records, though the use of foreign sources seems to have been against the rules of the game.[8]

For chronicle, as distinct from record, sources the antiquaries tended to rely mainly on standard native authors already in print—Bede, Florence of Worcester, William of Malmesbury, Geoffrey of Monmouth, Henry of Huntingdon, Matthew Paris, 'Matthew of Westminster'. One anonymous speaker on the subject of Dukes (27 November 1590) quoted freely from the, as yet unpublished, Anglo-Saxon Chronicle, which he may have seen in Parker's collection;[9] and Agarde

---

[1] Ibid. II. 194–5, 74–7; I. 307–8.   [2] Ibid. II. 318.
[3] Ibid. I. 16; 50–51.   [4] Ibid. I. 41.   [5] Ibid. II. 113–16.
[6] Ibid. I. 182–3; II. 117–25.   [7] Ibid. II. 93–4.   [8] Ibid. II. 160, 172–80.
[9] Ibid. I. 181–3.

quotes not only Jocelyn de Brakelond, but also the Peter-borough monk, Walter Whitlesey, and Knighton. For informa-tion about 'The Antiquity of Ceremonies used at Funerals in England', James Ley consulted the unpublished chronicle ascribed to Simeon of Durham.[1]

Of interest in, or knowledge of, English literature in general the papers afford little evidence. The standard classical authors —Virgil, Ovid, Horace, Seneca, Livy, Caesar, and Tacitus—find a place, most conspicuously in the speeches of the learned Sir William Dethick on Funerals and Epitaphs; and he and a few other speakers, including Agarde, quote the Old Testament. But there are only two brief quotations from Chaucer, one by Thynne, from *The Romaunt of the Rose*, when discussing the Earl Marshal, the other by an anonymous speaker, from the Pro-logue to *The Canterbury Tales*, apropos 'The Antiquity of Motts in England'. 'Of late years', he said, 'our countrymen have applied their witts to effeminate inventions, insomuch that I suppose the mott described by Chaucer in the Prioresse's abbet [i.e. habit] may very well beseeme us; the poet has yt thus,

> Of smale coral about her arme she bare
> A paire of bedes, gawded all with greene.
> And theare on hung a branch of gold full sheene,
> On which theare was wetten a crowned A,
> And after that (amor vincit omnia).'[2]

No awareness of the value of folk-literature to the antiquarian is anywhere suggested. As might be expected from a Society dominated by lawyers, linguistics proved more attractive than literature and much time was devoted to etymology—despite Camden's sound warning that 'such is the uncertainety of etimologyes, that arguments drawne from them are of least force.'[3] A good example is afforded by the discussions on Sterling Money. Speaking in 1590, Sir Thomas Lake stated that there were three common opinions about the origin of the name:

1. Some have said, that it took name of Sterling castle in Scotland, and that K.E.I. after he had entered into Scotland so farr, for a memory of his victories there, caused a coin to be made, which he called *Sterling*.

---

[1] Ibid. I. 211.   [2] Ibid. II. 116; I. 269–70.   [3] Ibid. II. 90.

2. Another opinion is, that it was so called because it had the figure of a starr printed on it, or else of the figure of a bird, called a *Sterling*; and say withall that the birds about the cross in the ancient arms of England were *Sterlings*.

3. A third, that it taketh denomination of *Esterling*, and was a standard used by the *Esterlings* trading in this realm, and received; or of Esterlings that were the workmen of it.

The first is dismissed on the grounds that the penny sterling appears in the reign of John; the second because he had never seen coins stamped with birds or stars; the third convinces him because the word appears as *Esterling* in some ancient writers and because of the tendency to use the plural—*Denarii Sterlingorum*.[1] Francis Thynne took the same view. The coin cannot derive its name either from the town, because we know from the Scottish histories that this was called Striveling in the time of Edward I, or from the Latin words for a starling or a star.[2] James Ley pointed to record evidence of sterling being known in the twelfth century.[3] Francis Tate inclined to favour derivation from *sterling* or *starleng*, meaning a small star impressed upon the coin—but only very tentatively, 'being ready to subscribe to any opinion carrying with it more proabability of reason.'[4] Joseph Holland knew no such diffidence. The word derives from the town where Edward I first caused these coins to be minted—'and this is and hath been the common and received opinion of the people unto this day.'[5] But he commanded little support: the great majority of the antiquaries, including Agarde, Stow, Talbot, and Heneage, preferred the derivation from Esterling. Yet, when 'The Etymology, Antiquity and Privileges of Castles in England' were under discussion, Agarde shied off the first. 'As to the Etymology of the name, I will leave that point to be discoursed of at large by those who have trayvailled in readinge authors of other nations and languages.' So, too, with the office of Constable—'Of the etymology of the name, I leaue it to them that are better skilled with the French than I.'[6]

Tate's doubts about his own aptitude for etymology did not deter him from making an unfortunate venture into the derivation of *hearse*: 'How to render that worde in Latin, or what

[1] Ibid. I. 10–11.   [2] Ibid. I. 13–15.   [3] Ibid. I. 15–18.
[4] Ibid. II. 315–16.   [5] Ibid. II. 319.   [6] Ibid. I. 186; II. 79.

the signification thereof is in English, unless it come of HERE, *Dominus, Princeps*, for in Dutch HERRISH is that which belongeth to a lord, and so the very name of an HERSHE or HERSE should put us in minde, that it is peculiar for lords and great personages.'[1] Thynne, on the etymology of the 'Terms and Times for Administration of Justice in England', was very much better, using many examples to prove his point that *Terminus* signified 'amongst the Romans and us limitation of time'.[2] For the derivation of Parliament, three etymologies were popular— *Parium lamentum*, 'where peers lamented the grievances of the realm'; *Par-lamentum*, 'an equal and just complaint of all members of the nation on sharing of grievances'; or *Parlez-le-ment*, 'because every member of that Court should sincerely and discretely speak his mind.' Agarde did say, however, that he knew the word derived from the French, *parler*.[3]

Interest in concrete memorials of the past is evident in several speeches. Talking of Castles on 15 May 1599, Joseph Holland reminded his audience that

Upon the plains of Salisbury there are to be seen divers great fortifications of earth which are called Castles at this day; and in Dorsetshire, by Dorchester, there remaineth one very strong fortification of earth on top of a hill environed with a double ditch of great depth, and it is called Maiden Castle, for that by report of the countrey it was never won: for the space of ij miles about that Castle do appear divers little hills called Barrows, under the which hath been found the bones of men, and divers ancient coins: the report of the country is, that after the battle that was fought in that place, these Barrows were erected for monuments unto such as were buried there.[4]

Discussing Land Dimensions in the November following, Holland said that he had 'divers antiquities in coin stamped at several towns'; and, a few months later, he again drew on his own observations to illuminate the subject of Epitaphs, recalling one in memory of Oswald, King of Northumbria, which he had seen engraved on the outer wall of Winwick church in Lancashire, and others from Exeter and St. Paul's Cathedrals which 'do comprehend great sence in few lines.'

[1] Ibid. I. 219.   [2] Ibid. I. 35.
[3] Ibid. I. 282, 305. E. Evans, 'Of the Antiquity of Parliaments in England: Some Elizabethan and Early Stuart Opinions', *History*, n.s. XXIII (1938–9), 208.
[4] *Curious Discourses* II. 377–8.

'I will conclude', he adds, 'with an epitaph, wherein there is great sense comprehended in one word, and yet that word is written upon a large marble stone at the foot of the great staires, ascending up unto the quire in St. Paul's, to wit, OBLIVIO. Notwithstanding the brevity of this, the writer's meaning was not that the person there buried should be forgotten, because he hath set his arms at the four corners of the stone, which was significant enough to declare who he was.'[1] Camden's comment on this epitaph is sharper. 'This man yet would not willingly have been forgotten, when he adjoined his arms to continew his memorye. Not unlike to philosophers which prefixed their names before their treatises of contemning glorye.'[2] Participating in the same debate, Francis Thynne declared that '. . . to deliver all such epitaphs as I have registred, either from histories, the books of religious houses, monuments remaining in churches, or such like, would be too tedious to this learned audience.' None the less, he offered them eighteen examples, including that on the tomb of John Caius at Cambridge, 'on which tomb there is nothing sett for an epitaph, but two words, FUI CAIUS',[3] on which Abraham Hartwell commented '. . . in mine opinion it goeth far beyond the *Oblivio* of Poules.'[4] James Ley, in a dicussion of the 'Antiquity of Funeral Ceremonies' on 30 April 1600, referred to ancient burial urns. 'Of these wee have seen some diged upp in the Spittle Feilds with liquors as yett remaining in them.'[5] Two months later, an anonymous speaker said that he had never seen any Roman, British, or Saxon graves or monuments, 'but only that at Lilborne in my own native country, which is a rounde hill of earth, with two toppes, the one a great deal higher than the other.'[6]

It was Cotton, Doddridge, and James Ley who, in the last year of Elizabeth's reign, sponsored a petition, which may be presumed to have had the support of their fellow antiquaries, for the incorporation of an 'Academy for the studye of Antiquity and History', under a President, two Librarians (to be elected annually), and a number of Fellows, with a body of statutes. 'There are', say the petitioners, 'divers gentlemen studious of this knowledge, and which have of a long time

[1] Ibid. I. 39, 258–60.   [2] Ibid. I. 232.   [3] Ibid. I. 251–6.
[4] Ibid. II. 377.   [5] Ibid. I. 211.
[6] Ibid. I. 226. (Northampton is the county referred to.)

assembled and exercised themselves therein, out of which company and others that are desirous, the body of the said corporation may be drawn.'[1] The library was to be called 'The Library of Queen Elizabeth' and was to be well furnished with rare books, original charters, muniments and other manuscripts, 'and that at the costs and charges of divers gentlemen which will be willing thereunto.' The members were to swear the Oath of Supremacy and another to preserve the Library, which was to be visited every five years by the Archbishop of Canterbury ('being of the privy council'), the Lord Keeper of the Great Seal, the Lord Treasurer, the Lord Admiral, the Lord Chamberlain, the Principal Secretary, and the Lord Chief Justice. It was suggested that it might be housed, either in 'some convenient room in the Savoy, which may well be spared', or in the dissolved priory of St. John of Jerusalem, nearby. Five points were urged in support of the scheme. (1) It would afford safe custody to numerous 'monuments worthy of observation', some of which are in the hands of private owners, others as yet untraced, and would render them accessible when required. (2) The Queen's forebears had set a good example by the interest they had shown in the preservation of ancient records, notably Edward I who, in order to justify his claim to the Crown of Scotland, had caused copies to be made of numerous records housed in monasteries and now destroyed or lost, and had purchased the libraries of others. Henry VIII had caused similar searches to be made, in order to support his repudiation of papal authority. (3) The Society would not in any way interfere with the Universities, whose concern is with the liberal arts and philosophy, not with history and antiquities. (4) The more civilized foreign nations, such as Germany, France, and Italy, are at pains to encourage antiquarian studies, by means of libraries, academies and public lectures. (5) If the study of modern languages and of the history and politics of neighbouring countries were to be added to the study of British antiquities, the Academy might serve a useful purpose as a training-ground for public office.

The petition to Elizabeth inevitably invites comparison with that presented to her sister by John Dee, nearly half a century before. Dee was still alive when the second petition was drafted,

---

[1] For details, see *Curious Discourses* II. 324–6 and *Archaeologia* I. iii–iv.

but it contains no allusion to him, possibly because, by this date, his reputation was somewhat unsavoury. Both petitions envisage the creation of a Royal Library, but Dee had no thought of limiting the books and manuscripts to those concerned with history and antiquities; and, whereas the Elizabethan petitioners had in mind 'the better information of all noblemen and gentlemen studious of antiquity', Dee suggested that 'the whole realm may (through your Grace's goodness) use and enjoy the whole incomparable treasure so preserved.' Whether the petition to her ever reached Elizabeth is uncertain. All that is certain is that the request was not granted. Had it been presented earlier, Elizabeth might well have regarded it favourably; but her end was near, and her successor cared little for English antiquities and may even have regarded them as dangerous. As most of the founding fathers disappeared, the Elizabethan Society gradually petered out, some five years after the accession of James I.

M

CONCLUSION

IN this short book an attempt has been made to trace the interests and activities of a number of sixteenth-century Englishmen who were concerned to preserve the memory of their country's past. Almost all of those to whom reference has been made could lay claim to some degree of expertise; to be serious students of history. But interest in England's past reached far outside their ranks; and to gain some idea of what our history looked like to the ordinary man we may conclude by taking a glance at the fantastic work entitled *Albions England*. Its author, William Warner (1558?–1609), was a London attorney, acquainted with Marlowe and Drayton, and a protégé of the two Careys, Barons Hunsdon, each of whom held the office of Lord Chamberlain of the Household under Elizabeth I. Warner had published a collection of tales derived from Greek legends before the appearance, in 1586, of the first edition of his rhymed history of Britain, which extended to 1066. A second edition (1589) carried the story on to 1485, and a third (1592) to 1558. Three further editions of this enormously popular book appeared in Warner's lifetime (1596, 1602, 1606), that of 1602 including a life of Aeneas, grandfather of Brutus the Trojan, and an 'Epitome of the whole Historie of *England*', both in prose. The purpose of the Epitome was to ensure that the ordinary reader 'in one or two howers, may cut thorough, vninterrupted, the whole Legend of the maine State-occurrants hapning howsoeuer, and whensoeuer in England.'[1] Warner here pays warms tribute to Camden's *Britannia*, 'out of which, I confesse my selfe, to haue gleaned not a little apting to this our abridged Historie';[2] and he refers his readers to Powel's *Historie of Cambria*. 'Of the Progresse of that most auncient and valiant Nation . . . hath Doctor *Powell* wel and compendiously written a peculiar Chronicle, whereunto I refer the Reader.'[3] But the main history was written in rhyming fourteeners and it was from this that many Elizabethans must have derived their

---

[1] *Albions England* (1602), p. 350.   [2] p. 351.   [3] p. 359.

image of Britain's past. Warner shared the enthralment of many of his contemporaries with the myths and legends of remote antiquity, their pride in Britain, their deep regard for monarchy, their virulent Protestantism, their loathing of rebellion and civil war.

The first four of the thirteen books into which the later editions are divided take the reader from the Flood to 1066; the fifth from 1066 to 1399; the sixth from 1399 to 1485; the remaining seven (with numerous digressions) cover the reigns of the first four Tudor monarchs. Warner begins by declaring his intention to give priority to the history of his native land:

I tell of things done long agoe, of many things in few:
And chiefly of this Clime of ours, the Accidents pursue.
Thou high Director of the same, assist mine artlesse pen,
To write the gests of *Brutons* stout, and actes of English men.[1]

Book I relates traditional myths, from the Flood to Hercules. Book II continues the story of Hercules and leads us on to Brutus:

Thrise fiue degrees from *Noe* was *Brute*, and fower times sixe was he
From *Adam*: and from *Iaphets* house doth fetch his petigree.[2]

Book III begins

Now, of the Conquerour, this Isle had *Brutaine* vnto name,
And with his *Troians Brute* began manurage of the same.

On the banks of the Thames,

Did *Brute* build vp his *Troy-nouant*, inclosing it with wall:
Which Lud did after beautifie, and *Luds-towne* it did call
That now is *London*:

And since of noble *Brute* his line prodigious things I tell
I skipping to the tenth from him will show what then befell.[3]

So we come to the story of King Lear and his daughters and to the settlement of the Picts and Scots—

Three valiant people thus at once in *Albion* Empire held,
Brutes, Scots and *Pichts*: the latter twine lesse ciuill, but as bold[4]—

[1] p. 1.   [2] p. 62.   [3] pp. 63–5.   [4] p. 69.

through tales of mythical monarchs, to the Roman invasions—

> This Land, the last of Westerne Isles, an Isle vnknowen ere this,
> Which famous now through Caesars fight and our misfortune is.[1]

—to Lucius, 'here the first baptized King', and the Emperor Constantine—

> And was a Prince Religious: yeat (with reuerence be it said)
> If lesse religious, then not he the Empire had decaid.
> By largesse to a pompeous Priest, Apostoloque ere then,
> But now intruding euen on God, insulting ouer men.[2]

—and so, to the coming of the Saxons and to Arthur, about whom Warner shows himself a little sceptical:

> His *Scottish*, *Irish*, *Almaine*, *French*, and *Saxone* Battels got,
> Yeeld fame sufficient; these seeme true, the rest I credit not.[3]

When the Welsh prince, Cadwallader, fled from Britain in tears, to avoid the plague, Warner cannot resist the temptation to use hindsight. He makes Cadwallader say

> 'Yeat (if I shoot not past mine aime) a world of time from me,
> Part of our blood, in highest pompe shall *Englands* glory be,
> And chiefly when vnto a first succeeds a second She.'[4]

After devoting some five pages to a love-affair between a Danish prince and a Saxon princess, Warner deals fairly briefly, in Book IV, with the Saxon settlements and the Danish invasions:

> The *English-Saxon* Kings oppresse the mightier ones the weake:
> Each trifling cause sufficing here their loue and leagues to breake.
>
> .   .   .   .
>
> Meane while the *Danes* with fresh supplies ariue at euery Shoore,
> And warre almost in euery sheire infesting *England* soore:
>
> .   .   .   .
>
> Nothing was done, but all vndone, till King Alured he
> In daunger of his Royall selfe did set his subiects free.[5]

Further troubles followed until, in 1066, the great divide was reached:

> . . . persist, my Muse and tell,
> How, by the *Normane* Conquest, here an other world befell:

---

[1] p. 79.   [2] p. 85.   [3] p. 90.   [4] p. 92.   [5] pp. 98–100.

New lawes (not Labyrinths as now through wrested Quirkes) came in,
New Lords also, at whom, for most, our auncient Crests begin,
The *English* sinke, the *Normans* swimme, all topsie-turuie was,
Vntill the Conqueror had brought his whole command to pas.[1]

One of Warner's main concerns in discussing the significance of 1066 is to stress the ultimate mingling of Norman and English blood in the person of Henry II:

> . . . The Genalogue is thus:
> King *Edmund Irn-side* Issue had *Edward* the Outlaw, he
> Had *Margaret*, *Mawd* by *Malcolme* (then the King of *Scots*) had she,
> *Mawd* to the Conqueror his Sonne, first *Henry*, *Mawd* did beire,
> This second *Mawd*, the *Angeos* wife, had second *Henry* heire.[2]

Warner's handling of the medieval centuries is curiously ill-balanced. Of the Norman kings he has nothing to say, apart from their genealogies. Henry II is described as 'mightie both in Empire and in Armes', but the only aspect of his reign that appears to interest Warner seriously is the quarrel with Becket which affords opportunity for denunciation of the Roman Church:

> Our Popes that seeme (they do but seeme) Saint *Peter* to succeede
> (Who did denie, although deserue, high Styles to him decree'd)
> Are quite vnlike to Peter . . .

After the murder of Becket,

> Which heard, the Pope canonized the stir-strif Priest a Saint,
> In*f*encing Kings against our King, till warres made *Henry* faynt.[3]

Of Henry's military and administrative achievements we hear nothing: and most of the 38 lines dealing with Richard I—'Lyons-hart (his courage got that surname)'—are devoted to a supposed love-affair with the daughter of Duke Leopold of Austria which helped to secure his release from prison. John gets only 16 lines:

> In *Scotland, France, Ireland*, and *Wales* he warred wearied lesse
> Than by the Pope and English Priests wronged without redresse.[4]

Nothing is said of Runnymede; but we are told that John, having accepted the status of a papal vassal, was poisoned by a

[1] p. 113.   [2] p. 110.   [3] pp. 114–16.   [4] p. 118.

monk while spending the night at Swineshead Abbey; and this sparks off a lengthy digression of over three pages on the failings of monks.[1] Henry III, to whose long reign only 19 lines are allotted, prospered until

> A Parliament at *Oxenford* did derogate so much
> From his prerogatiue as that the Quarrell grew to such
> That ciuill warres betwixt the King and Barronage began,
> Not ending, but with tragicke ends of many a worthy man.[2]

To him succeeded the great Edward I,

> Matchles for Cheualrie, and yeat his iustice matcht the same,[3]

but we hear nothing of his legislation; there are only brief allusions to the conquest of Wales and the wars in France and Scotland; of the 53 lines devoted to his reign, 35 are concerned with a death-bed speech to his son and heir. A disproportionate amount of space seems to be given to Edward II; but five of the twelve pages embody a long digression, put into the mouth of Thomas of Lancaster, on the early history of Ireland:

> ... Who knoweth not *Ireland*, our neighbour Ile,
> Where *Noe*, his Neece, ere *Noe* his flood, inhabited a while?[4]

Love-stories and tales of Robin Hood are interspersed; and the chapter ends with a savage denunciation of the Despensers and others

> ... that misled
> The King in Out-rages more great than earst in England bred.
> Prolers, Blood-thirstie, Parasites, Make-shifts & Bawdes did thriue,
> Nor was an ancient English Peere vnbanisht or aliue:
> Yea forraine and domesticke Swords, Plague, Famine and Exile,
> Did more than tythe, yea tythe of men within this Ile.[5]

Though Edward III is allotted only some three pages, the scale of his military reputation is recognized:

> The King became a *Mars* for Armes, a *Iupiter* for Port:
> Th'*Olympids*, the *Pythea* and the prowesse of the Earth,
> Did seeme euen now, and not but now, to haue in him the birth:
> East, South and North, gaue ayme farre off, admiring so the West,
> As if that *Mars*, discarding them, had set our Realme his Rest.[6]

· · · ·

[1] pp. 119–22.　[2] p. 123.　[3] p. 124.　[4] p. 126.　[5] pp. 136–7.　[6] p. 138.

These were the daies when *English* armes had eu'ry where request,
And *Edw.* knights throghout the world had prick & praise for
best.[1]

But towards the end of Edward's reign we move into a period
of decline:

Howbeit, King and Prince at last, misled by counsell ill,
Through Taxes lost a many hearts that bore them earst good will.

.   .   .   .

For little els than ciuill warres our following Penne affords.
French Expeditions badly thriue, whereof we cease to speake,
Not forraine, but Domesticke warres, grew strong to make vs weake.[2]

Richard II gets some forty lines, which include a scathing
comment on the Rising of 1381:

The bace attempts of *Ball*, of *Straw*, of *Lyster*, tag and rag,
Of Villains, Of-skoms, Clownes, and knaues that checkmate durst
to brag
With *Richards* self, & to their deaths his chiefest Princes drag.

Yet Richard himself does not win Warner's approval:

Richard begun that ciuill warre, that till the Seauenth from him
Did last, though often fields with blood of Citizens did swim:
Against the Nobles he vphild innoble, and his Peeres
And Commons went alike to wracke, nor God nor man he feares:
In fewe, Ambition, Auarice, and Counsell lewd had wrought
In him a nature worser than into the world he brought,
Whereby, and thus, himselfe and house at length a down-fall cought.[3]

Henry IV, 'elected to the Crowne', had his troubles

Till lastly Armor ouercame all Enuie and he liues
Of all beloued, and his death a common sorrow giues.

With his son, the glory of the medieval monarchy reached its
height when

The true Idea of a King was not but in this Land:[4]

but he is allotted only 19 lines, whereas 14 pages are devoted to
the courtship of Owen Tudor and Queen Catherine[5] (in the
course of which Owen tells the story of the love-affair of Vulcan
and Venus).

[1] p. 140.   [2] pp. 139–40.   [3] pp. 140–1.   [4] p. 143.   [5] pp. 144–58.

The Queene and this braue Gentleman did marry, and their Seede
Began that royall Race that did, doth, and may still succeed
In happie Empire of our Throne, a famous line in deed.

As for the dynastic conflicts of the fifteenth century, these are
summarized in fourteeners which do little to enhance Warner's
literary reputation:

Fourth *Henry* first *Lancastrian* King put second *Richard* downe:
Fourth *Edward* of the House of *Yorke* re-seazd sixt *Henries* Crowne:
Lad-Princes twaine were stabd in Field, of either Linage one:
Foure Kings did perish: Sundry times, now-Kings anon were none:
Sixe, three of either faction, held successiuely the Throne:
But from the second *Richard* to seuenth *Henry* we pretend
Eight Kings this Faction to begin, continue, and to end.[1]

Albions England is not the work of a poet, and the pleasing lines
with which the best-seller modestly concludes show that the
author himself was well aware of his limitations:

Not perpetuitie my Muse can hope, vnlesse in this,
That the great Name, Elizabeth, herein remembred is.
May Muse, arte-graced more than mine, in Numbers like supply,
What in thine Highnes Praise my Pen, too poore, hath passed-by:
A larger Field, a Subiect more illustrious None can aske,
Then with thy Scepter and thy selfe his Poesie to taske.
Thy Peoples Prolocutor be my Prayer, and I pray,
That vs Thy blessed Life and Raigne long blesse, as at this day.[2]

    [1] p. 163.   [2] p. 328.

INDEX